Universals of Legal Reasoning by Judges

Universals of Legal Reasoning by Judges

A Plea for Candour in Decision-Making

THOMAS LUNDMARK

OXFORD
UNIVERSITY PRESS

OXFORD
UNIVERSITY PRESS

Great Clarendon Street, Oxford, OX2 6DP,
United Kingdom

Oxford University Press is a department of the University of Oxford. It furthers the University's objective of excellence in research, scholarship, and education by publishing worldwide. Oxford is a registered trade mark of Oxford University Press in the UK and in certain other countries

Published in the United States of America by Oxford University Press
198 Madison Avenue, New York, NY 10016, United States of America

British Library Cataloguing in Publication Data

Data available

Library of Congress Control Number: 2023948332

ISBN 978–0–19–878567–5

DOI: 10.1093/oso/9780198785675.001.0001

Printed and bound by
CPI Group (UK) Ltd, Croydon, CR0 4YY

Acknowledgements

This book reflects, and expands upon, topics addressed in the class Legal Theory and Methodology that I regularly taught during my eighteen-year tenure as Professor of Common Law and Legal Theory at the University of Münster.

I am grateful for the help and support provided by numerous people both before and during the writing and preparation of this book.

Those who contributed directly or indirectly to the content of book include my late colleague at Münster Professor Dr Werner Krawietz and Professor Paul Mishkin at Berkeley Law School. More recent contributors include Professor Alan H. Hutchinson, my law school classmate Professor Lewis A. Kornhauser, Professor Gordon Walker, and Professor Tony Ward, all of whom have contributed insights that I have incorporated. I am also grateful to those who reviewed all or parts of the manuscript. This group includes Katharina Brennecke, Mia Mårtensson, OUP project editor Kim Vollrodt, and Wladimir von Samsonow.

Most importantly, I would like to thank my wife, Dr Marie-Louise Poschen, for her love and support.

Contents

1
Introduction and Definitions

A. Introduction

> The remoter and more general aspects of the law are those which give it universal interest. It is through them that you not only become a great master in your calling, but connect your subject with the universe and catch an echo of the infinite, a glimpse of its unfathomable process, a hint of the universal law.[1]

As the title indicates, this book is about universals in the sense of things having general application. This title implies that the things described here can find application throughout the world. And, as this book illustrates, they do find application in the jurisdictions from which the examples are drawn, primarily Germany, California, and the United Kingdom. In short, this book takes the reader on a zigzagging tour of the legal landscapes of Germany, the United Kingdom, and the United States, including Puerto Rico, with whistle stops along the way in Canada, Austria, Australia, Canada, Denmark, France, Sweden, and Switzerland.

At its core, the book is about the arguments used to justify judicial decisions. One main claim of the book is that the stories, justifications, and arguments that can be told about rules are finite in number. Some legal commentators have suggested that there are only three sources or styles of argumentative justification.[2] Other legal commentators identify five constitutional 'approaches to interpretation'.[3] Another commentator has suggested six. This is similar to the claims made by some in the field of literature that there are only three,[4] seven,[5] or thirty-six[6] basic plots. The actual number is less important than the realization that all legal justificatory stories or arguments, as with all cultural phenomena, can be collected into categories. As presented here, there are four such major categories. This number could be reduced if

[1] O.W. Holmes, 'Path of the Law' (1896–1897) 10 Harv L Rev 457, 478. See generally Zenon Bankowski and James MacLean (eds), *The Universal and the Particular in Legal Reasoning* (Ashgate 2006).

[2] See D. Neil MacCormick and Robert S. Summers (eds), *Interpreting Statutes: Statutory Interpretation in the United Kingdom* (Routledge 2016) 512–515.

[3] John Kelly, Gerard Hogan, and Gerry Whyte, *The Irish Constitution*, vol. 3 (3rd edn, Cambridge University Press 1996) identify five different approaches to the interpretation of the Irish Constitution: literal interpretation, the doctrine of 'harmonious' interpretation, the 'broad' approach, the historical approach, and the natural law approach.

[4] William Foster-Harris, *The Basic Patterns of Plot* (University of Oklahoma Press 1959).

[5] Christopher Booker, *The Seven Basic Plots: Why We Tell Stories* (Continuum 2004).

[6] George Polti, *The Thirty-Six Dramatic Situations* (trans. Lucille Ray, The Writer 1944).

Universals of Legal Reasoning by Judges. Thomas Lundmark, Oxford University Press. © Thomas Lundmark 2024.
DOI: 10.1093/oso/9780198785675.003.0001

one were to combine the categories presented here. On the other hand, the number of categories could be increased if one were to break down the categories that are presented here into smaller categories. For example, in a survey of nine countries, MacCormick and Summers identified eleven basic types of argument: ordinary meaning, technical meaning, contextual-harmonization meaning, precedents, statutory analogy, logical-conceptual meaning, meaning in the light of general principles, historical derivation, statutory purpose, arguments from substantive reasons, and legislative intent. But then, after identifying these eleven basic types of argument, MacCormick and Summers went on to combine these basic types of argument into three main categories: linguistic, systemic, and teleological-evaluative.[7]

The four categories described in this book are denominated textual, historical, purposive, and system-contextual. Briefly, textual justifications (Chapter 5: Textual Argument) are those that are fashioned around the terms of a rule. Historical justifications (Chapter 6: Historical Argument) focus on the circumstances surrounding the making or judicial modification of a rule. Purposive justifications (Chapter 7: Purposive Argument) are those that explicitly employ the policies that a rule promotes. These policies are sometimes referred to here, and elsewhere, as values, principles, policies, purposes, or even statutory purposes if the rule is found in a statute.

Contextual arguments are common in judicial decisions and legal publications, particularly arguments around historical context and factual context. However, the category of system-contextual justifications employed in this book (see Chapter 8: System-Contextual Argument) is narrower: this category refers to arguments that employ the terms 'analogical', 'reasonable', 'right', 'legal', 'constitutional', 'legitimate', 'appropriate', 'proportionate', 'fair', 'just', 'equitable', 'merciful', or in accordance with *Treu und Glauben*, good faith, the rule of law, or some other expression of justice.[8] This is, admittedly, a very large collection of legal terms in its own right; but these terms all share in common a claim to some source, insight, revelation, or sentiment[9] that is felt to be superior to the mere words—and often the history and policies—of the rules being employed, what can be thought of as a *senus communis*.[10]

The use of these 'system-contextual' terms as justificatory arguments is seen most obviously in constitutional jurisprudence, where statutes are sometimes construed in a way that comports with a constitutional principle, or, less commonly, even ruled to be incompatible with a constitutional principle. Yet, the constitutional principle is invariably quite broad and therefore readily open to conflicting interpretations. The same broadness characterizes the other justificatory terms

[7] D. Neil MacCormick and Robert S. Summers (eds), *Statutory Interpretation in the United Kingdom, Interpreting Statutes: A Comparative Study* (Routledge 1991) 512–515.

[8] In authoritarian legal systems, this list of system-contextual arguments would include the will of the *Führer* or other exalted leader, which, in any particular case, would be substituted for justice.

[9] For an example of this usage of 'sentiment', see Adam Smith, *The Theory of Moral Sentiments* (printed for A. Millar, in the Strand, London 1759).

[10] Suggested to the author by Professor Tony Ward, Northumbria University.

listed above ('analogical', 'reasonable', 'right', 'legal', etc.), and their use in statutory construction and the use of precedents is widespread.

Because of the breadth of this category of system-contextual argument, this book restricts the coverage to four topics where system-contextual arguments play an observable and readily collectible role: constitutional interpretation, *Drittwirkung*, *Treu und Glauben*, and analogies to principles found in other sources, in particular to those principles found in statutes.

Before describing, demonstrating, and discussing the matrix of arguments extolled here (textual, historical, purposive, and system-contextual), this book begins with three chapters of introductory material to lay the groundwork for the discussions in the chapters that follow. Chapter 2 ('Making, Finding, Applying, and Justifying') explicates and illustrates how judges make law, as that term is used in this book, alongside legislative bodies. This second chapter then elucidates the often-overlooked thinking processes entailed in finding the law before moving on to the topics of applying the law and, critically for the purposes of this book, of justifying one's application of the law.

The next chapter, Chapter 3, summarizes and critiques the literature on the controversial topics of political judging and judicial activism. Chapter 4 addresses rules from statutes and cases. In so doing, it provides the only coherent methodology known to the author for applying case law.

What follow now in this introduction are definitions of, and commentaries on, many of the concepts and terms found in the book.

B. Definition of key terms and concepts

(1) What is reasoning?

The word 'reasoning' in the title of this book can mean at least two things. It can mean the process of using our human ability to draw inferences and conclusions, such as adding and subtracting numbers; employing logic; and even inferring an implicit rule from a story, such as the 'moral of the story'. Confusingly, however, the word 'reasoning' in English can also mean providing reasons in support of our inferences and conclusions. These reasons are often referred to in this book and elsewhere as justifications.

While conceptually different, the two meanings of the word 'reasoning' are intertwined. For example, if a young man puts on a pair of sunglasses from a rack in a store, and then he leaves the store wearing those sunglasses, if the young man is charged with the crime of theft, where conviction requires proof of intent to steal, the judge who hears the case might well conclude that the young man is not guilty of theft. The judge's reasoning? The judge might have concluded that the prosecution had failed to prove beyond reasonable doubt that the young man had possessed the intent to steal the sunglasses when he left the store. This is an example of 'reasoning' in the second sense: providing a (logical) reason for the judge's conclusion.

But how did the judge conclude that there was a reasonable doubt? The judge might have come to this conclusion after hearing the testimony of the young man and his wheelchair-bound mother that the young man had left the store not to steal the sunglasses, but merely to ask his mother if the sunglasses suited him. The judge's conclusion may well have been motivated by the young man's demeanour, his dress, his accent, his social status, his profession, his race, his nationality, his gender identification, and a myriad of other factors that coalesce into a sense or feeling that the young man and his mother should be believed. But the judge does not announce that the motivation—the 'reason' in the first sense—for his or her conclusion was a sense or feeling that the young man and his mother were telling the truth: he or she rules that the testimony of mother and son created a 'reasonable' doubt in her mind about the young man's intent to steal. This is reasoning in the second sense, that is, providing reasons in support of the conclusion. It is this second sense of the word 'reasoning' that is the subject of this book. As Ben Franklin wrote in his autobiography, 'So convenient a thing it is to be a *reasonable creature,* since it enables one to find or make a reason for every thing one has a mind to do.'[11]

Perhaps it would be better to refer to this second sense of the word 'reasoning' as a justification or argument, or even as a story, rather than as a reason. And perhaps the first sense of the word 'reasoning' would be more accurately described as motivation. But the two meanings of the word 'reasoning' are so intertwined, and the usages in legal parlance of both meanings are so widespread, that the distinction would be impossible to maintain.

(2) What is reasoning in a legal setting?

> [L]egal reasoning is ordinary reasoning applied to legal problems.[12]
> [L]egal reasoning is the same everywhere.[13]

[11] Benjamin Franklin, *Autobiography of Benjamin Franklin* (J.B. Lippincott & Co. 1868) 128–129.

[12] Larry Alexander and Emily Sherwin, *Demystifying Legal Reasoning* (Cambridge University Press 2008) 3, citing Kent Greenawalt, *Law and Objectivity* (Oxford University Press 1992) 197–202; Joseph Raz, *Ethics in the Public Domain: Essays in the Morality of Law and Politics* (Clarendon 1994) 310; Frederick Schauer, *Playing by the Rules: A Philosophical Examination of Rule-Based Decision-Making in Life and Law* (Oxford University Press 1991) 187; Melvin Aron Eisenberg, *The Nature of the Common Law* (Harvard University Press 1988) 94; P.J. Evans, 'On Case Law Reasoning' (1985) 30 Jur Rev 85–118; Hanns Hohmann, 'The Nature of the Common Law and the Comparative Study of Legal Reasoning' (1990) 38 Am J Comp L 143. See generally J.F. Bailey III, 'The Civil Law and the Common Law: Some of the Similarities and Differences between the Two Systems' (1978) 6 Int'l J L Libraries 117; Joseph Dainow, 'The Civil Law and the Common Law: Some Points of Comparison' (1966–1967) 15 Am J Comp L 419; Alan Watson, 'Roman Law and English Law: Two Patterns of Legal Development' (1990) 36 Loy L Rev 247; Thomas Lundmark and Helen Waller, 'Using Statutes and Cases in Common and Civil Law' (2016) 7 Transnt'l Legal Theory 429.

[13] Eugene Wambaugh, *The Study of Cases: A Course of Instruction in Reading and Stating Reported Cases, Composing Headnotes and Briefs, Criticising and Comparing Authorities, and Compiling Digests* (Little, Brown, and Company 1892) 32.

Throughout the world, people make, find, and apply rules and principles. People fashion rules regarding all sorts of human behaviour. There are rules of politeness, rules of behaviour in families, religious rules, moral rules, and myriad other rules. Rules are basically about what behaviour 'is right and what behavior is wrong'. And rules are always made by people, even if the people who make them are inspired by something transcendental.

People around the world, for the most part, know where to find rules too. They find them in books on etiquette, in familial practices, in sacred texts, in treatises on ethics, and in countless other places, such as by consulting more knowledgeable people or even by consulting the rule-makers themselves.

Throughout the world, people also apply and enforce rules. Those who enforce rules may be members of the general public or of a family, they may be religious leaders, they may be governmental officials, or they may be any other people one comes in contact with. Very often, if not always, the people enforcing the rules are also interpreting them. Here again, all of the appliers, interpreters, and enforcers are human beings.

The rules and principles discussed in this book have law as their subject. Accordingly, this book elucidates how legal rules are made; how they are found; and, in large part, how they are applied, which involves interpreting the rule or principle in light of a factual situation.

Thus far, we have seen that people make, find, and apply/enforce rules and that, in applying the rules, the appliers/enforcers very often, if not always, need to interpret the rule in light of a particular factual situation. But there is one more step that is also universal: justifying the application of the rule to the particular factual situation.

Justifying the application of the rule at hand entails telling a story about the particular factual situation. Some justifications tell a story about the words of the rule. They tell how these words do, or do not, capture the particular factual situation. Other justifications chronical the circumstances surrounding the origin of the rule. These justifications illuminate how the factual situation can be woven into the historical origin of the rule to reach a result that may well conflict with the present-day meanings of the words of the rule. Still other justifications discern the policies behind the rule at hand. These justifications utilize these policies to tell a story about how the rule should be applied so as to promote the discerned policies. Note that these policy justifications may well conflict with the words of the rule and the rule's historical origin. And sometimes, justifications recruit policies from principles or rules that are not, at first blush, applicable to the factual situation at hand. These justifications recite the policies from 'imported' rules to buttress a particular result.[14]

[14] We will meet a number of principles and rules that are employed in this manner in Chapter 8 (system-contextual argument). These rules and principles are found throughout the confines of what people consider to be the relevant legal system, hence their description as 'system-contextual'.

In all of the situations in the preceding paragraph, the stories that are told will help people to understand why the rules are being applied in a particular way. Said in a more legalistic way, these justificatory stories—or, simply, these justifications—serve to make the results legally plausible.

(3) What are legal rules?

Legal rules are rules of and about law.[15] But what is law? There is a huge amount of literature on this topic.[16] Much of the literature concerns sources of law.[17] Some legal cultures are relatively open to sources of legal inspiration, accepting precepts from holy scriptures, morality, and other sources.[18] Other legal cultures are comparatively closed, insisting upon using a strict hierarchy of more or less closely defined precepts.[19]

There is also a huge amount of literature on whether judicial precedents are a 'proper' source of law. Some authors promote the declaratory theory of law, associated with Blackstone, which asserts that judges find the law that is already there and merely declare what they have found.[20] The declaratory theory has, however, fallen out of fashion for most legal theorists today do not think that there is any law 'there' to find. Other legal theorists promote a view of the law that is termed 'legal positivism'. These theorists tend to underestimate the discretion enjoyed by judges.[21] For example, one leading legal positivist, Joseph Raz, writes that judicial law-making 'is limited and regulated by law. There are no pure law-creating

[15] The prepositions 'of' and 'about' are adopted here to encompass Hart's primary and secondary rules. See H.L.A. Hart, *The Concept of Law* (Oxford University Press 1961) 79.

[16] Introductory publications on this topic include Herbert Lionel Adolphus Hart, *The Concept of Law* (2nd edn, Oxford University Press 1997); Ronald Dworkin, *Law's Empire* (Harvard University Press 1986); S. Prakash Sinha, *What Is Law? The Differing Theories of Jurisprudence* (Paragon House 1989); Raymond Wacks, *Philosophy of Law: A Very Short Introduction* (Oxford University Press 2006); (2008) 1 Am J Jurisprud; Brian Z. Tamanaha, *A Realistic Theory of Law* (Cambridge U Press 2017); Alexander Somek, *Knowing What the Law Is: Legal Theory in a New Key* (Bloomsbury 2021).

On sources of law, see, among countless other sources, Alf Ross, *On Law and Justice* (Oxford University Press 1959); Aleksander Peczenik, Scientia Juris: *Legal Doctrine as Knowledge of Law and as a Source of Law* (Springer 2005) 16–17.

[17] What is meant by 'law' also dovetails with one's understanding of what constitutes a legal system. See generally René Brouwer, 'On the Meaning of "System" in the Common and Civil Law Traditions: Two Approaches to Legal Unity' (2018) 34 Utrecht J Int'l & Eur L 45.

[18] See generally Tamanaha, *A Realistic Theory of Law*.

[19] See generally H. Patrick Glenn, *Legal Traditions of the World: Sustainable Diversity in Law* (5th edn, Oxford University Press 2014).

[20] Allan Beever, 'The Declaratory Theory of Law' (2013) Oxf J Legal Stud 421; Jack Beatson, 'Has the Common Law a Future?' (1997) 56 Cambridge L J 291, 314. This is similar to Dworkin's one-right-answer thesis. See Ronald Dworkin, *Taking Rights Seriously* (Harvard University Press 1977) 14. Because previous judges might have made a mistake, precedents cannot be binding in a strict sense: Peter Wesley-Smith, 'Theories of Adjudication and the Status of Stare Decisis' in L. Goldstein (ed.), *Precedent in Law* (Clarendon Press 1987) 79.

[21] For Germany, see Bernd Rüthers, *Die Heimliche Revolution vom Rechtsstaat zum Richterstaat: Verfassung und Methoden Ein Essay* (Mohr Siebeck 2014).

activities.'[22] Despite their tendency to perceive judicial precedents as subordinate to statutes, many, if not most, legal positivists today, at least in the common-law tradition, view precedents as judge-made law.[23] In this book, it will be seen that, as a practical matter, rules from judicial precedents are employed in the same way as statutory rules no matter whether the former are considered by theorists to be a 'proper' source of law.

Most British and US judges take a broad, realistic, view regarding the discretion that they enjoy. According to Patrick Atiyah, legal realists contend that the judge makes law, '[a]nd for this purpose, he must consider arguments of policy, and arguments of morality and justice, just as he would if he were a legislator'.[24] The topic of judicial discretion has been explored in depth by a great many authors, including by adherents to various schools of legal theory, including legal realism, law and economics, critical legal studies, critical feminism, critical race theory, and legal pragmatism.[25] There are also schools of law and literature,[26] law and language,[27] new legal realism, and legal empiricism.[28] For two recent, and excellent, expositions of broader, realistic, theories of law, the author recommends *A Realistic Theory of Law* by Brian Z. Tamanaha[29] and *Toward an Informal Account of Legal Interpretation* by Allan C. Hutchinson.[30] More immediately, the examples described in the following chapters, particularly in Chapter 8 ('System-Contextual Argument'), give the lie to narrow understandings of judicial discretion.

22 Joseph Raz, *The Authority of Law* (Oxford University Press1979) 195.

23 Having made the law, judges are, of course, free to remake the law by overruling or amending their precedents: Wesley-Smith, 'Theories of Adjudication', 82.

24 P.S. Atiyah, 'Judges and Policy' (1980) 15 Israel L Rev 346, 347. This would also appear to be the view of the positivist H.L.A. Hart in cases beyond the 'plain meaning' of the rule. As will be seen in Chapter 5 (Textual Argument), whether a rule's meaning is plain or not is in the eye of the beholder.

25 Surveyed in Brian Bix, *Jurisprudence: Theory and Context* (6th edn, Carolina Academic Press 1990) and Robert L. Hayman, Nancy Levitt, and Richard Delgado, *Jurisprudence Classical and Contemporary: From Nature Law to Postmodernism* (2nd edn, West Academic Publishing 2002).

26 Good exponents include James Boyd White, *The Legal Imagination: Studies in the Nature of Legal Thought and Expression* (Little, Brown and Co. 1973) and Richard H. Weisberg, *The Failure of the Word: The Protagonist as Lawyer in Modern Fiction* (Yale University Press 2009).

27 See generally Jeremy Bentham, *Of Laws in General* (ed. H.LA. Hart, Athlone Press 1970); Brian Bix, *Law, Language, and Legal Determinacy* (Oxford University Press 1995); Timothy A.O. Endicott, *Law and Language* (Oxford University Press 2002), with an excellent discussion of Bentham and H.L.A. Hart; M. Del Mar, *System Values and Understanding Legal Language* (Cambridge University Press 2008); Mark Greenberg, 'Legislation as Communication? Legal Interpretation and the Study of Linguistic Communication' in Andrei Marmor and Scott Soames (eds), *Philosophical Foundations of Language in the Law* (Oxford University Press 2011) 217–256. See also Thomas Lundmark, *Die Auswirkung der Sprache auf die Vorhersehbarkeit des Rechts in: Positivität, Normativität und Institutionalität des Rechts: Festschrift für Werner Krawietz zum 80. Geburtstag* (Duncker & Humblot 2013).

28 See e.g. Mark C. Suchman and Elizabeth Mertz, 'Toward a New Legal Empiricism: Empirical Legal Studies and New Legal Realism' (2010) 6 Ann Rev L Soc Sci 555; Brian H. Bix, 'Ross and Olivecrona on Rights' (2009) 34 Aust J Legal Phil 103; Stewart Macaulay, 'The New Versus the Old Legal Realism: "Things Ain't What They Used to Be"' (2005) Wisc L Rev 365; Howard Erlanger, Bryant Garth, Jane Larson, and Elizabeth Mertz, 'Is It Time for a New Legal Realism?' (2005) Wisc L Rev 335.

29 Referred to at n. 16 above.

30 Allan C. Hutchinson, *Toward an Informal Account of Legal Interpretation* (Cambridge University Press 2016), reviewed by Thomas Lundmark in (2016) 80 Modern L Rev 1178.

For the purposes of this book, we need not actually define what law is and what it is not. That being said, the examples and discussions in these pages will be limited to rules from the realms of social life traditionally considered to be legal in nature. Thus, the precepts here examined will be legal principles or legal rules, also sometimes called norms. For the purposes of this book, the word 'rule' is used in the sense of 'norm' as defined by Kelsen: a rule that prescribes or permits certain human behaviour.[31]

(4) What are legal principles?

Unless the context suggests otherwise, general references in this book to a legal rule or norm are meant to include legal principles; for legal principles are merely norms which are broad in their scope.[32] To illustrate this equivalence between rules and principles, here is an example.

Most people would agree that the following assertions are principles:

Only do good.
Do no wrong.
Do not harm any living thing.
Do not harm any human being.

And most people would also agree that the following assertions are rules:

Look before crossing a street.
Do not set forests on fire.
Do not intentionally kill another human being.

Yet the only difference between the precepts in the first group and the second group is that those precepts in the first group are broader than those in the second group. In short, people tend to describe relatively broad assertions as principles

[31] See Hans Kelsen, *Principles of International Law* (The Lawbook Exchange Ltd 1952) 6.

[32] This usage is in accord with that of Lloyd L. Weinreb, who writes in his book *Legal Reason: The Use of Analogy in Legal Argument* that he 'frequently refer[s] to "rules" as including rules, principles, and standards': Lloyd L. Weinreb, *Legal Reason: The Use of Analogy in Legal Argument* (Cambridge U Press 2005) 6. Joseph Raz classifies legal principles and legal rules as general legal norms. See Joseph Raz, 'Legal Principles and the Limits of Law' (1972) 81 Yale LJ 823, 824 n. 4. This usage is at odds with Ronald Dworkin, who attempts to distinguish principles from rules. See Dworkin, 'The Model of Rules' (1967) 35 U Cm L Rev 14, 23–24. For a sceptical discussion of this distinction, see Frederick Schauer, 'Prescriptions in Three Dimensions' (1997) 82 Iowa L Rev 911. Posner wrote that Dworkin's principles were Posner's policy consideration: Richard A. Posner, 'Legal Formalism, Legal Realism, and the Interpretation of Statutes and the Constitution' (1986) 37 Case W Res L Rev 179, 181. See generally Jordan Dici, 'Legal Principles, Legal Values and Legal Norms: Are They the Same or Different?' (July 2010) Academicus Int'l Sci J.

and relatively narrow assertions as rules. However, there is no clear demarcation between principles and rules. Consider, for example the precept 'Do not kill.' This precept could readily be assigned to the first group (principles) or to the second (rules).

(5) How does one find legal rules in judicial cases?

The simple—and typically accurate—way to answer this question is that one finds that the rules are articulated by the judges in the decisions that they reach, and these articulations are taken up into the headnotes when the cases are commercially published.[33] The rules articulated by judges are also collected into encyclopaedias, commentaries, practice books, and like publications, including online publications. Of course, these publications will be organized differently depending on the jurisdiction. Typical for the common-law world, *Halsbury's Laws of England* systematizes judge-made law on every topic. This encyclopaedia covers over fifty-six volumes and is also available online. *Halsbury's Statutes* serves the same function for statute law. Lawyers and judges in California in the United States often use the sixty-six-volume Witkin's *Summary of California Law*, but the legal encyclopaedia *California Jurisprudence* is also popular. Both are available online. Another approach in California to find case law is to consult one of the twenty-nine codes of statutes directly. The material in these codes is arranged systematically. The codes are all available in 'annotated' editions, which means that important legal publications and the holdings of leading cases are collected alongside the statutes that they address. These annotated codes in California are quite similar to German commentaries, which also collect references to academic literature as well as quoting the holdings of leading cases.

(6) What is the meaning of *stare decisis*?

Stare decisis ('stand by decisions') is the doctrine of precedent.[34] The doctrine as understood today is quite modern. For centuries, it was thought that the common law was not to be found in individual court decisions; rather, the case decisions in their totality were a reflection of the law.[35] Indeed, it was not until 1765, with

[33] This is also true in Germany, where the headnotes (*Leitsätze*) are sometimes written by the judges themselves. One should, of course, check that the wording of the headnote corresponds to the reported decision, for the headnote is no part of the judgment. Andrew Goodman, *How Judges Decide Cases: Reading, Writing and Analysing Judgments* (Tarquin 2005) 200.

[34] For an excellent description in English of what is meant by legal doctrine and dogma, and their importance, see Fritz Jost, 'The Adjudication of Law and the Doctrine of Private Law' in Mark van Hoecke and Francois Ost (eds), *The Harmonisation of European Private Law* (Hart Publishing 2000) 167.

[35] This is described as the declaratory theory of law, described at n 20.

Plowden's Reports, that court judgments themselves, rather than summaries of arguments and decisions, were even recorded regularly and reliably in England. The year 1865 saw the publication of the *Law Reports* by the Incorporated Council of Law Reporting for England and Wales, a commission that had been set up specifically for this purpose and that still exists today. The availability and reliability of these law reports were crucial in the development of the doctrine of *stare decisis* as we know it today.[36]

In fact, it was only from the beginning of the nineteenth century that some appellate judges began to speak about the binding power of single legal decisions or, in other words, of determining the law from individual precedents.[37] This view quickly spread throughout the common-law world, with the result that the birth of the modern doctrine of *stare decisis*—that the applicable law is to be found in the rules (usually called *ratios* or holdings) announced in individual cases—can be dated to the middle of the nineteenth century.[38]

One of the most significant drivers behind this modern view of the doctrine of *stare decisis* was the work of John Austin (1790–1859), a pioneer of legal positivism in the common-law world. Austin contradicted the then widely held view that the common law was transcendent, customary, and capable of being found, but not created. The distribution of Austin's book *The Province of Jurisprudence Determined* disseminated the notion that law 'properly so called' consisted only of the rules that originate from the deliberate pen of the legislator or other 'law giver' or the 'tacit commands' of the sovereign.[39] The logical consequence of this realization was that, to the extent that Parliament was not making law, then the judges must be doing so.[40] Without meaning to minimize the influence of Thomas Hobbes (1588–1679) and Jeremy Bentham (1748–1832), after Austin, judicial pronouncements of the common law were understood, pretty much for the first time on a worldwide basis, as intrusions upon the legislative prerogative.[41] By following precedents, and consequently reducing the instances of law-making, judges were not only protecting the equal application and predictability of the law but also showing respect for separation of powers and for democracy.[42]

[36] John H. Baker, *The Common Law Tradition: Lawyers, Books and the Law* (Hambledon Press 2000) ch 14. Duxbury, *The Nature and Authority of Precedent* (Cambridge University Press 2008) 17–18.

[37] Max Radin, *Handbook of Anglo-American Legal Theory* (West Publishing Company 1936) 356.

[38] Gerald I. Postema, 'Some Roots of Our Notion of Precedent', in Goldstein, *Precedent in Law*, 9; Jim Evans, 'Change in the Doctrine of Precedent During the Nineteenth Century' in Goldstein, *Precedent in Law*, 35. See also Sir Carleton Kemp Allen, *Law in the Making* (7th edn, Clarendon Press 1964).

[39] John Austin, *The Province of Jurisprudence Determined* (John Murray 1832).

[40] Austin did accept that the judges made law, but unlike law and language, he found this acceptable, though not ideal, and he developed quite a sophisticated account of precedential reasoning that also took account of informal pressures on judges. Communication to the author from Professor Tony Ward, Northumbria University.

[41] See E.C. Clark, *Practical Jurisprudence: A Comment on Austin* (Cambridge University Press 1883) 4 *et seq.*

[42] Perhaps it should be mentioned that the word 'democracy' has different connotations in Germany. See Thomas Lundmark, 'East Germans' Conversion to Democracy' (1996) 20 Fordham Int'l LJ 384.

In order to apply a previous decision, the first task is to find a decided case with basically similar operative facts (a process of equivalence). This process involves the same mental process as looking for relevant statutes for all statutes contain operative facts. In fact, even in the common-law world, and most definitely in the civilian world, many, if not most, precedents are concerned with the interpretation of statutory law. Such case decisions, referred to here as 'glosses', contain judicial concretizations of what the statute means in various circumstances.[43] Once a case decision with similar facts has been found, whether or not the case decision is one concerning 'pure' common law or a judicial gloss on a statute, it is necessary to identify the rule—the *ratio decidendi*—of that case. The *ratio*, which is sometimes referred to as the holding or the rule of the case, represents that aspect of the case that may constitute a binding precedent, that is, may possess the authority of law in some form. In almost all cases, the *ratio* has been stated as a rule by one or more of the judges who decided the precedential case. Ordinarily, as stated above, the *ratios* can be found as headnotes at the beginning of the published report of a case.

Once identified, the *ratio decidendi* is used like a statutory rule. The most common approach in the common-law world is to apply the *ratio* according to its wording, just as one would apply a statute in a textual manner. Another approach is to read the case decision itself to learn the factual background in which the *ratio* is announced and then to ask oneself how the judges in the precedential case would likely decide the case that one is confronted with. This is the same mental exercise that is involved in using the legislative history and historical setting when construing a statute.

Furthermore, just as with statutory rules, case-based rules can be expanded and restricted. As described by Kornhauser in his discussion of the doctrine of *stare decisis* in *The New Palgrave Dictionary of Economics*,[44] one might look behind the *ratio* for a broad legal principle. This corresponds to looking behind a statutory rule for a function or purpose. On the other hand, one might narrow the *ratio* to the fact-based result of the case. This corresponds to a teleological reduction of a statute. There is, therefore, flexibility in how a judge may choose to use the *ratio* from a precedential case, in the same way as there is flexibility in how statutes are applied.[45]

[43] Glosses on statutes are defined at n. 70. On statutory interpretation in general, see e.g. Ruth Sullivan, *Statutory Interpretation* (2nd edn, Irwin Law 2007) 53 *et seq*; Francis A.R. Bennion, *Statutory Interpretation* (1984); Antonin Scalia, *A Matter of Interpretation: Federal Courts and the Law* (Princeton University Press 1997); Kent Greenawalt, *Legislation: Statutory Interpretation: 20 Questions* (Foundation Press 1999); Eisenberg, *The Nature of the Common Law*; William N. Eskridge, *Legislation and Statutory Interpretation* (Foundation Press 2000).

[44] Lewis A. Kornhauser, 'Stare Decisis' in Peter Newman (ed.), *New Palgrave Dictionary of Economics and the Law*, vol. 3 (Palgrave Macmillan 1998) 509.

[45] On identifying the *ratio* or *ratios*, see e.g. Arthur Goodhart, 'Determining the Ratio Decidendi of a Case' (1930) 40 Yale LJ 161; Arthur Lehman Goodhart, *Precedent in English and Continental Law: An Inaugural Lecture Delivered before the University of Oxford* (Stevens and Sons 1934); Rupert Cross and J.W. Harris, *Precedent in English Law* (4th edn, Clarendon Press 1977) 78. Edward Levi, for example,

The doctrine of precedent (i.e. the practice of employing *ratios* as statutes) is respected both in the common-law world and in civilian jurisdictions like Germany, where there are numerous statutes that command judges to adhere to judicial precedents.[46]

(7) What is meant by the word 'argument'?

It would be beneficial at this point to define what is meant in these pages by 'argument'. Merriam-Webster.com defines 'argument', in this context, as 'a coherent series of statements leading from a premise to a conclusion' or, more simply, 'discourse intended to persuade'.[47] Cristina Redondo defines arguments as reasons in support of actions.[48] A simpler definition for purposes of this book might be: argument means justification.[49]

Du Plessis prefers the nomenclature 'reading strategies' instead of arguments or justifications. He writes, 'A "better answer" is ... more likely to result from a "fuller

writes that 'the rules change as the rules are applied': Edward Levi, *An Introduction to Legal Reasoning* (Clarendon Press 1949) 2 ('the rules change from case to case and are remade with each case'). For critical summary of these and other definitions from a number of common-law jurisdictions, see Arthur Peltomaa, 'Obiter Dictum of the Supreme Court of Canada: Does It Bind Lower Courts?' (1982) 60 Canadian Bar Rev 823. Peltomaa also critiques Eugene Wambaugh's 'inversion test' for identifying the *ratio*:

> In order to make the test, let him first frame carefully the supposed proposition of law. Let him then insert in the proposition a word reversing its meaning. Let him then inquire whether, if the court had conceived this new proposition to be good, and had had it in mind, the decision could have been the same. If the answer be affirmative, then, however excellent the original proposition may be, the case is not a precedent for that proposition, but if the answer be negative the case is a precedent for the original proposition and possibly for other propositions also.

Wambaugh, *The Study of Cases* (footnote omitted).

[46] Thomas Lundmark, *Charting the Divide between Common and Civil Law* (Oxford University Press 2012) 354–362, also discussing Swedish statute law. On the role of judicial precedents in Germany, see e.g. D. Neil MacCormick and Robert S. Summers (eds), *Interpreting Precedents: A Comparative Study* (1997) ch. 2; Lundmark, *Charting the Divide*, ch. 9; Peter Stainer and Dominik König, 'The Concept of Stare Decisis in the German Legal System—A Systematically Inconsistent Concept with High Factual Importance' (2018) XXVII Studia Iuridica Lublinensia 1,; Martin Brenncke, *Judicial Law-Making in English and German Courts: Techniques and Limits of Statutory Interpretation* (Mohr Siebeck 2018). See also Svein Eng, 'The Doctrine of Precedent in English and Norwegian Law—Some Common and Specific Features' (January 2000) Scand Stud L. See generally Bojan Spaić, 'The Authority of Precedents in Civil Law Systems' (2018) XXVII(1) Studia Iuridica Lublinensia 10.

[47] *Merriam-Webster's Collegiate Dictionary* (11th edn, Merriam-Webster 2004) 'argument', 66.

[48] See M.C. Redondo, *Reasons for Action and the Law* (Oxford University Press 1999) 1. Redondo distinguishes three 'lines' of thinking about the word 'reason': reason as a human faculty, reasons for action, and reasons as premises of arguments.

[49] The analysis in this book of these arguments and justifications might, in earlier times, have been described as a rhetorical study for the term 'rhetoric' formerly meant the study of all forms of public speech. Today, however, '[t]he most common modern acceptations of the term are pejorative or poetic and bear little trace of the discipline which was originally to have charted the interrelations of language and power': Peter Goodrich, *Legal Discourse Studies in Linguistics, Rhetoric and Legal Analysis* (Palgrave Macmillan 1987) 85.

reading" of a provision—and this is where a consciousness of and reliance on the four methods of Von Savigny . . . are helpful.'[50] In using the nomenclature 'reading strategies', du Plessis is echoing the distinction made in German academic literature between the interpretation (understanding) of the law, on the one hand, and the application of the law on the other.

Understanding and applying are, in fact, two separate mental processes of the interpreter. But there are more mental processes involved. Consider the following: the interpreter (let us assume that she is a lawyer), having investigated the facts (first mental process); having pinpointed the relevant, operative facts (second mental process); and having tracked down the applicable rule (third mental process) must then reconcile those pinpointed facts with the rule (fourth mental process).[51] This fourth process of reconciliation is termed 'applying the law to the facts' in the common-law world. In other traditions, it is often called 'subsumption', that is, subsuming the facts under the rule.[52] This fourth process is the subject of the next discussion: what is meant by applying the law to the facts?

(8) What is meant by applying the law to the facts?

Let us examine this fourth mental process: applying the law to the facts. This is the step at which the lawyer must fashion a story—a justification—to explain how the rule dictates, suggests, or might suggest a particular result. Having read the rule, or learned of it in some other way, the lawyer may well decide (consciously or unconsciously) to content herself with a superficial examination of the legally relevant words of the rule, that is, the legal terms. Accordingly, she will justify her conclusion using the legal terms contained in the rule. This type of justification is generally known as literal or textual interpretation.

However, the lawyer may not be content with a superficial examination of the legal terms. For some reason or another (e.g. she might not like the result that she has tentatively reached), the lawyer may want to know how the terms have been understood by others. At this point, she may well choose to examine sources such as practice manuals, encyclopaedias, commentaries, or articles to help find another interpretation that will help her reach the result she desires. This is also a mental

[50] Lourens du Plessis, 'The (Re-) Systematization of the Canons of and Aids to Statutory Interpretation' (2005) 122 S African LJ 591, 612. Savigny's methods are discussed in Chapter 2.

[51] Whether 'applying' or 'subsuming', the lawyer will need to have read the rule, been told the rule, have inferred the rule, or have learned the rule in some other way.

[52] For instance, in the leading German legal dictionary, *Subsumtion* is defined as subordination of relevant facts to the legal rule ('*Unterordnung eines Sachverhalts unter einen Rechtssatz*'): Creifelds (ed.), 'Subsumtion' in *Rechtswörterbuch* (22nd edn, C.H. Beck 2017). See Stanley L. Paulson, 'Subsumption, Derogation, and Noncontradiction in "Legal Science"' (1981) 48 Univ Chic Law Rev 802. The term was also used by Austin.

process (sixth mental process). Furthermore, the lawyer may consider the history of the rule, the policies behind the rule, or even policies from other rules. The point being made here is that there are myriad mental processes that may potentially be involved in legal reasoning in general, and in applying the law to the facts in particular. These processes will be discussed further in Chapter 2 when describing judicial 'hunches'.

(9) What do 'norm' and 'normative' mean in this book?

Occasionally in this book, legal rules will be referred to as norms. Consequently, this book can be said to be normative in the sense that it describes and discusses norms. However, this book is not normative in the sense of being subjective, judgemental, or prescriptive.[53] This may well cause confusion among people from different legal language backgrounds, such as German, where the German *normativ* in law is often employed in conjunction with efforts to change the law. Just to make it clear: no claim is made in this book that any source of inspiration for making or identifying norms is superior to any other source, nor that any story, justification, argument, or reason for making or interpreting a legal norm is intrinsically superior to any other.

The discussion so far has mentioned the making, the finding, and the applying/enforcing of rules. For the remainder of this book, the making and the finding of legal rules will be treated separately, although it will be seen that finding legal rules often involves modifying or making legal rules for the domains of making and finding law are interwoven. The domains of finding and applying/enforcing the rules are also interwoven, so they will also be treated separately in this book.

While this last point—that making, finding, and applying the rules are interwoven—may be obvious to most readers, it is a point well worth emphasizing at this juncture and a point worth illustrating by way of an example.

One classic example of where making, finding, and applying rules are interwoven is the technique of so-called *contra legem* interpretation of statutes. This technique of interpreting statutes, if one can call it interpretation, results in concluding that the statute means exactly the opposite of what it says, or at least what it seems to say.[54] Another example of where making, finding, and applying rules

[53] Here is an example of a judgmental usage of the word of the word 'normative'. 'The usual idea of the "value judgment" exponents, however, is that a normative judgment is nothing but an act of preference for some attitude or mode of action. If so, this amounts to an assertion that so-called normative judgments, in which acts are compared to norms, are based solely on personal preference': Stephen C. Pepper, 'Values and Value Judgments' (1949) 46 J Philos 429, 434. On the various usages of the word 'normative' see Judith Jarvis Thompson, *Normativity* (2008).

[54] Examples of cases discussed in this book are *Herrenreiter* ('*Dressage rider*') from Germany, discussed in Chapters 5 and 8, *American Motorcycle Association v. Superior Court* from California, discussed in Chapter 8, and *A v. Hoare* from the United Kingdom, discussed in Chapter 8. Examples from

intertwine is when statutes are simply ignored by the legal establishment. One might say that such rules are being interpreted, if one can call it interpretation, out of existence. Still other rules are held to violate some superior law, such as a constitution: they are interpreted, if one may call it that, to be invalid.

(10) How is the term 'analogy' used in this book?

A word should be said at this juncture about the usage of the term 'analogy' in this book. The reader may notice that the term is used very sparingly in these pages. There are two reasons for this deliberate infrequency of usage. One reason is that the term is used very often in the English-language legal literature, and often imprecisely, which causes confusion. Thus, by using other terminology, it is hoped that confusion can be reduced, if not totally avoided. The second reason, perhaps the more important one for the purposes of this book, is the prevalence of a canard that civilian jurists reason by deduction whereas common-law jurists reason by analogy.[55] By providing examples from both civilian and common-law jurisdictions, this book will prove the falsity of this contention.[56]

One phrase that may contribute to confusion on this topic is the expression that a certain precedential case 'is on all fours'[57] with a case before the court, leading some people to believe that one merely has to compare similarities and differences between cases in order to apply case law. Professor Melvin A. Eisenberg debunks this belief in his book *The Nature of the Common Law*:

> Assume that (1) on January 1, 1987, (2) a manufacturer (3) of grouting machines (4) in Cleveland (5) sells a grouting machine (6) to a machine-shop operator (7) in Cleveland (8) who on March 1 (9) injures his hand while using the machine (10) as a result of a defect in the machine. The court holds that the manufacturer is liable under the principle of strict product liability. Now a second case arises, which differs from the first only in that the injury does not result from a defect in the machine. Here there are nine similarities between the cases and only

France can be found in *Dog: A Comparative Study* (2016) 135, reviewed by Thomas Lundmark, (1998) 46 Am J Comp L 211. See generally J. Neuner, *Rechtsfindung contra legem* (Munich 1992).

55 See Lundmark, *Charting the Divide* 287 *et seq.* and Frederick Schauer, *Why Precedent in Law (And Elsewhere) Is Not Totally (Or Even Substantially) about Analogy, 3 Perspectives on Psychological Science* (Blackwell 2008) 454; Dan Hunter, 'Reason Is Too Large: Analogy and Precedent in Law' (2001) 50 Emory LJ 1197.

56 See generally Bartosz Brozek, 'Is Analogy a Form of Legal Reasoning?' in Hendrik Kapein and Bastiaan van der Velden (ed.), *Analogy and Exemplary Reasoning in Legal Discourse* (Amsterdam University Press 2018) 49.

57 Katja Langenbucher, 'Argument by Analogy in European Law' (1998) 57 Cambridge LJ 481.

> one difference, but obviously the difference is decisive, and it would be decisive if ninety more similarities were added.[58]

Judges can also be frustrated by lawyers who place too much emphasis on the facts of previous cases. Here is just one frustrated statement by the UK House of Lords, this one taken from the case of *Jolley v. Sutton London Borough Council*:

> Both counsel nevertheless at times invited your Lordships to compare the facts of the present case with the facts of other decided cases. That is a sterile exercise. Precedent is a valuable stabilising influence in our legal system. But, comparing the facts of and outcomes of cases in this branch of the law is a misuse of the only proper use of precedent, viz to identify the relevant rule to apply to the facts as found.[59]

While there are passing references to analogies in other chapters of this book, the primary discussion of analogies will be found in Chapter 8.[60] That chapter will elaborate and illustrate the civilian technique of 'statutory analogy'. This technique entails an explicit reference to a statute, other than the one being applied, as an argument to bolster the plausibility and acceptance of a judicial interpretation of the statute being applied in a way that would otherwise not be possible and which often creates a new cause of action. Stated another way, a statutory analogy is a technique of legal argument in which judges borrow policies—usually called principles—from other statutes to justify a decision, including the creation of a new cause of action, that cannot readily be justified by textual, historical, or purposeful arguments emanating from the statute that they are applying.

(11) What is meant by 'methods' of statutory interpretation?

In most publications, including those in many different languages, and including some publications by the author, the justifications regarding statutory interpretation are referred to as 'methods'. The word 'method' often denotes—or, at least, suggests—a systematic, perhaps even scientific, technique or procedure. In one sense, this is a correct description of legal interpretative techniques: they are systematic because they can be arranged into a system, and they are scientific in the same sense that political science is scientific.

[58] Eisenberg, *The Nature of the Common Law*, 84.

[59] *Jolley v. Sutton London Borough Council* [2000] 1 WLR 1082.

[60] Compare Alexander and Sherwin, *Demystifying Legal Reasoning*; Schauer, *Playing by the Rules*; Larry Alexander, 'Constrained by Precedent' (1989) 63 S Cal L Rev 1; Julian S. Weitzenfeld, 'Valid Reasoning by Analogy' (1984) 51 Phil Sci 137.

There are, however, dangers—or, at least, disadvantages—to the use of the term 'method' when referring to the justifications employed when applying rules. For one thing, one finds innumerable interpretative methods in the legal literature, and there are divergent definitions of these methods.[61] For example, while one finds general agreement on what is meant by textual interpretation, and to a lesser extent by historical and purposive interpretation, there are vast differences in how legal commentators treat contextual interpretation and also analogical reasoning and interpretation. This diversity and numerosity reveal more than a lack of consistency in terminology: they also reveal a failure to comprehend commonalities and a failure to systematize accordingly.

In addition, and more importantly, speaking of method puts the cart before the horse for it strongly implies that the method dictates the decision. Indeed, one commentator writes that legal methodology consists of 'methods of thinking, leading to the "correct" resolution of cases'.[62] This is true neither in theory nor in practice. In truth, the method is the result of—not the cause of—the decision. Put another way, the method is just an aspect of the justification for a decision already reached.

This truism is discussed in Chapter 2 of this book and also briefly in section B(12). Consequently, a more accurate word for 'method' in this context is 'argument'.

(12) Do people use methods when applying legal rules?

For judges, lawyers, officials, and others to be able apply a rule, they must first have selected (found) a rule to apply. Accordingly, these judges, lawyers, officials, and others must be concerned about whether some particular facts conform to a rule. To state the obvious: the people who are looking to apply a rule must already have a factual scenario in mind for without a factual scenario, they could not find the rule that they think might apply to the factual scenario; and, obviously, they can only apply the rule after they have found it. Thus, even at the beginning of the process of legal reasoning, it is the rule-finder horse that precedes the rule-applier cart and not the other way around.

As will be explained in more detail in Chapter 2, this activity of searching for the rule—the *Normsuche* ('norm search') in German—presupposes that the seeker has gained considerable knowledge of the legal system for finding the rule involves a

[61] See generally Daniel A. Farber and Philip P. Frickey, 'Legislative Intent and Public Choice' (1988) 74 Va L Rev 423, 456: 'statutory interpretation involves a myriad of interpretive sources in potential tension'.

[62] Peter Raisch, *Vom Nutzen der überkommenen Auslegungskanones für die praktische Rechtsanwendung* (Müller, C.F. 1988) 1. According to Raisch, legal methodology consists of 'methods of thinking, leading to the "correct" resolution of cases', ibid n. 12.

process of ascertaining equivalence between the relevant facts of a factual scenario and the operative facts of the potentially employable legal rules in the legal system.

Having found the rule, the rule-applier will proceed to examine whether or not the particular facts conform to the rule. Let us assume that the rule-applier believes that the application of the rule to the factual situation is clear. If so, how should one describe the decision-making process—the legal reasoning—in the above scenario to this point? Since the rule-applier believes that the application of the rule to the factual situation is clear, this must mean that something in the rule or about the rule (perhaps a previous interpretation of the rule) must have readily convinced the interpreter that the factual situation is either in conformity with the rule or that it is not in conformity with the rule.

Rather than considering all possible permutations, let us consider two: one with a legally unsophisticated interpreter called Simon and one with a legally sophisticated interpreter named Solomon.

Simon is a layman. He knows very little about the law. He types his factual situation into an internet search engine and finds a rule that seems to apply. He applies the rule to his situation and comes to a conclusion. Without knowing more, if the legally unsophisticated Simon finds a rule, it is likely that Simon has been convinced by the wording of the rule, that is, its text. Solomon is not a layman. He is a judge with years of experience. He knows the rule well, and he knows that his colleagues on his court, and on the appellate court, all interpret the rule to mean something other than what it says, perhaps even the exact opposite to what it says.[63] If Solomon were to let himself be convinced by the text of the rule, he would be going against the considered opinion of his colleagues; and he would risk not only the disapproval of his colleagues but also almost certain reversal on appeal. These are the considerations that influence Solomon's decision-making in this instance, not the wording of the rule. So, whereas Simon probably chose textual interpretation unconsciously to reach his decision, Solomon had no reason to consider any of the methods of interpretation: his considerable knowledge on the topic dictated his decision. To summarize, it was not the methods that were dictating the result, it was the interpreter. This is another reason why it is more accurate to speak of arguments rather than methods.

The discussion in this section will be developed in more detail in Chapter 2.

(13) What about legal issues of first impression?

When faced with a factual scenario that has not been interpreted previously, the applier/interpreter, usually a judge, does have discretion on how to construe the

[63] See *contra legem* the interpretation discussed at n. 55.

rule. If a judge, let us call her Judith, is faced with a novel factual scenario, she may or may not find a rule that she believes should apply. Let us assume that she does find such a rule. If so, she will, of course, read the rule. Perhaps she will, like legally unsophisticated Simon, simply apply the rule's text to the novel factual scenario to reach a result.

But what if Judith believes that the result reached by a textual application could not have been intended by the drafters of the rule or that the result is unduly harsh and unjust? In such a situation, Judith may well look for a way to construe the rule so as to avoid having to reach the result that the text seems to mandate.

Judith might, for example, consult the historical record for evidence that the drafters did not intend such a result. This might enable her to make a historical argument. Or Judith could look beyond the text of the statute to the policies that the statute seeks to effectuate. This might enable her to make a purposive argument. Or Judith might be able to use other statutes, or the constitution, to construe the statute in a way that comports with her sense of justice. This might enable her to make a system-contextual argument even if the result does not comport with the text, history, or purposes of the rule: for all legal systems, however defined and wherever constituted, share the conviction that laws must, in their application, be reasonable, right, legal, constitutional, legitimate, appropriate, proportionate, fair, just, equitable, merciful, or in accordance with *Treu und Glauben*, good faith, the rule of law, or some other expression of justice. Judith might be able to use one or more of these expressions of justice to support a result that she considers to be just even though her result does not comport with the result that the text seems to mandate.

Moreover, Judge Judith might be able to use a related statute or other source of law to create a right on behalf of the party she believes would otherwise be treated unjustly (analogical use of a statute). Here, again, it is the applier/interpreter of the rule—Judge Judith—who is choosing and making the arguments.

(14) What is meant by construction of a statute?

Before continuing, a word or two should be said about the legal word 'construction'. This word is employed almost exclusively for arguments based on statutes, not on the *ratios* from case decisions: hence the nomenclature 'statutory construction'. This nomenclature confuses some students because the term 'statutory construction' suggests to them that the statute is being constructed in the sense of being made. In actuality, the noun 'construction' shares a common heritage with the word 'construe', which means to understand, explain, or interpret a text. In this book, the words 'interpretation' and 'construction' are used interchangeably. One reason for the author's decision to continue using the term 'construction' is that the students are right: construing a statute very often means remaking the statute (i.e. constructing it) in some sense. This phenomenon of remaking the statute is referred to in this book as putting a 'gloss' on a statute, which, in effect, amounts to an amendment to the statute, the adding of a subsection to the statute, as it were.

(15) What is (also) unique about this book?

The similarity between reasoning from cases and reasoning from statutes has been noted by previous scholars.[64] Benjamin N. Cardozo remarked that 'the work of deciding cases in accordance with precedents that plainly fit them is a process similar in its nature to that of deciding cases in accordance with a statute'.[65] And Richard A. Posner insightfully writes that 'it is unhelpful and misleading to distinguish [common-law reasoning and statutory reasoning] by calling the first inductive and the second deductive'.[66]

In his book *Rhetoric and the Rule of Law: A Theory of Legal Reasoning*, Neil MacCormick explicitly states that reasoning from statutes and reasoning from cases are identical apart from the difficulty of ascertaining the major premise (i.e. the rule) from case law:

> In the nature of the case, the premises of any syllogism we start from in common law adjudication are weaker and more tentative or defeasible than in reasoning with statutes. But it is no less true that we aim towards a concluding syllogism whose premises have the full solidity that a good legal argument can secure. The elements of such interpretative arguments are not essentially different as between common law cases and statute-based cases within common law systems. It would be quite extraordinary if anything else were the case.[67]

One major contribution of this book to jurisprudence and legal practice is the insight—and the proof—that legal reasoning with rules involves the same intellectual processes regardless of the source of the rule. As illustrated by abundant examples, reasoning with statutes and reasoning with cases are fundamentally the same. Further, contrary to popular belief, the ascertainment of the rule of a case is generally a straightforward endeavour. This book is unique in that it treats

[64] Levi notes that there is 'striking similarity' in the interpretation of case law, statutes, and constitutions: Edward H. Levi, 'An Introduction to Legal Reasoning' (1948) 15 Univ Chic Law Rev 501, 505.

[65] Benjamin N. Cardozo, *The Nature of the Judicial Process* (Yale University Press 1921) 20.

[66] Posner, 'Legal Formalism', 179, 190. But see Carlton Kemp Allen, *Law in the Making* (Oxford University Press 1930) 249: 'It is customary to think of case-law reasoning as inductive and the application of statutes as deductive. The thought seems erroneous but the emphasis has some meaning.'

[67] Neil MacCormick, *Rhetoric and the Rule of Law: A Theory of Legal Reasoning* (Oxford University Press 2005) 47, excellently reviewed in Torben Spaak, 'Deduction, Legal Reasoning, and the Rule of Law' (2006) 23 Constitutional Commentary 121.

reasoning from cases on a par with reasoning from statutes.[68] This illustrates the universality of reasoning from and with rules.

As stated above, the present book is not intended to be subjective, judgemental, or prescriptive. This intention also extends to the various categories of argument mentioned above. Accordingly, and in conscious disagreement with any number of prominent legal scholars, the author does not hold that textual arguments are intrinsically superior to historical, purposive, and system-contextual (including analogical) arguments. Furthermore, the author is not of the opinion that historical arguments are in any way superior to purposive or system-contextual arguments. Nor does the author rank the sundry categories of argument on a scale of legality, constitutionality (specifically separation of powers), integrity, mercifulness, coherence, logic, or any other abstract or concrete criterion or concept. Rather, all of these arguments are at least potentially available for use by judges and others. These arguments constitute instruments that judges, whether appointed or elected, can, and often do, use to fulfil their obligation to cooperate with legislative bodies in the governing of societies that respect rules.

That being said, this book exposes dozens of examples of sanctimonious statements by judges and academics that seek to obscure the central truth about the choice between the so-called methods of statutory and other legal interpretation: it is value-laden and goal-orientated.

If legal argumentation is a search for truth, it is a subjective truth, presumably one that is shared by a large segment of the population or, at least, of the population that matters from a juridical standpoint. For legal reasoning cannot, as some academics insist,[69] provide objectively 'correct' solutions.

To enhance the persuasiveness and efficacy of judicial precedents, to foster democratic legitimacy, and to permit political accountability, the author will argue in the final chapter (Chapter 9: A Plea for Transparency and Candour) for judicial transparency, which requires that judges and others reveal their thoughts and motivations—their ultimate reasons—rather than hide behind the façade of disinterest and impartiality. Consequently, this book is a plea for candour.

[68] A few other titles among dozens that similarly disappoint, if only in this regard, but which are found on the author's home bookshelves: Stig Strömholm, *Rätt, Rättskällor och Rättstillämpning: En lärbok i allmän rättslära* (2nd edn, 1984); Robert Alexy, *A Theory of Legal Argumentation: The Theory of Rational Discourse as Theory of Legal Justification* (transl. Ruth Adler and Neil MacCormick 1989); Mitchel de S.-O.-L'E. Lasser, *Judicial Deliberations: A Comparative Analysis of Judicial Transparency and Legitimacy* (Oxford University Press 2004); Goodman, *How Judges Decide Cases*; W. Hamilton Bryson and Serge Dauchy (eds), Ratio decidendi: *Guiding Principles of Judicial Decisions* (2006); Christian Bumke (ed.), *Richterrecht zwischen Gesetzesrecht und Rechtsgestaltung* (Mohr Siebeck 2012); Karsten Naundrup Olesen and Troels Michael Lilja, *Domsanalyse* (2nd edn, Samfundlitteratur 2016); Peter L. Strauss, *Legal Methods: Understanding and Using Cases and Statutes* (Foundation PR 2005), except for the reprinted article by R. Kent Greenawalt, 'Reflections on Holding and Dictum' (1981) 39 J Leg Ed 431.

[69] See e.g. Raisch, *Vom Nutzen der überkommenen Auslegungskanones*, 1: legal methodology consists of 'methods of thinking, leading to the "correct" resolution of cases'.

C. Summary

This chapter primarily provides succinct definitions of what the author of this book means when he employs various important terms (some would say 'concepts'). 'Reasoning' in this book generally means providing reasons in support of conclusions. 'Principles', as that term is used here, is synonymous with rules that are broad in their scope, that is, rules that can be said to be abstract or open-textured. 'Rule' and 'norm' are used synonymously to mean a rule that prescribes or permits certain human behaviour. 'Construction' of a statute means 'interpretation'. Statutory construction or interpretation often involves putting a 'gloss' on a statute, which, in effect, amounts to a judicial amendment to the statute.

'Law' is not defined in this book. That being said, all of the examples given and discussed here involve what is considered to constitute law in the respective jurisdictions that are discussed. 'Applying the law to the facts' is equivalent to subsuming facts under the rule.

Stare decisis is the doctrine of precedent. In practice, but not necessarily in academic theory, the practice of employing *ratios* as statutes is respected both in the common-law world and in civilian jurisdictions like Germany, as the examples in this book will prove.[70]

A very important, frequently appearing, word is 'argument'. In these pages, arguments are merely justifications—that is, articulated reasons—for decisions reached by judges and lawyers who are interpreting rules. This introductory chapter also sketches the matrix of the four categories of arguments or justifications that are covered in this book. These are the textual, historical, purposive, and system-contextual. The actual number is less important than the realization that all legal justificatory stories or arguments can be collected into categories. Two short examples of these methods are provided, one involving an interpreter who is not legally sophisticated (Simon) and the other involving a judge with years of experience (Solomon).

Finally, this chapter makes clear that, while the author chronicles criticisms levelled at these arguments, he deliberately avoids making any claims as to the superiority of any particular argument over another. That being said, he will argue, in his final chapter, for candour and transparency in judicial construction of statutes and of 'pure' common law, that is, law-making in the absence of statutes.

[70] See also the discussion in Lundmark, *Charting the Divide*, ch. 9.

2

Making, Finding, Applying, and Justifying

A. Introduction

This chapter presents a synopsis of a great number of interconnected, and sometimes subtle, processes that are the subject of extensive, and sometimes heated, disagreements among legal theorists and legal philosophers throughout the world.

Very often, the disagreements are about terminology. For example, many commentators contend that judges in a democracy cannot, by definition, make law.[1] Thus, these commentators insist, for example, that judicial pronouncements, informal administrative practices, and other non-parliamentary official acts be relegated to separate, subordinate categories. The disagreements about terminology often take on an ideological flavour, reminiscent of prescriptive grammarians, by insisting that no other terminology can be tolerated by educated jurists.

At the risk of offending prescriptive jurisprudes, the synopsis in this chapter deconstructs the processes of law-making and law-applying into four steps in sections B. 'Making law', C. 'Finding the law', D. 'Applying the law', and E. 'Justifying the result'.[2]

Breaking the processes down into steps in this manner is risky because it tends to obfuscate the ultimate interdependence of the steps; for the processes often influence each other, or even overlap, to such an extent that they disguise each other. Despite these risks, breaking the processes down in this manner demonstrates that the realm of legal reasoning is not confined to the judiciary: it starts, in many cases, in the legislature. Further, breaking the processes down into steps illustrates how judges necessarily make law in the sense of the term employed in this book.[3]

[1] David Pugsley, 'When in Rome . . .' (1988) 20 BLJ 15, 18, discussing Italian legal terminology; John Henry Merryman, 'The French Deviation' (1996) 44 Am J Comp L 109, 112, discussing French legal terminology; Yong Wan, 'China's Regulations on the Right of Communication through the Information Network' (2007) 54(2–3) J Copyright Soc USA 525, 526, discussing Chinese legal terminology; Woraboon Luanratana and Alessandro Romano, 'Stare Decisis in the WTO: Myth, Dream, or a Siren's Song' (2014) 48 J World Trade 773, 794, discussing Thai terminology.

[2] On the distinction between arriving at a conclusion and justifying the conclusion, see Richard A. Wasserstrom, *The Judicial Decision: Toward a Theory of Legal Justification* (Stanford University Press 1961) 25–30.

[3] Larry Alexander and Emily Sherwin, *Judges as Rule Makers, Common Law Theory* (ed. Douglas E. Edlin, Cambridge University Press 2010) 51–80. For a defence of this phenomenon, see Jack G. Day, 'Why Judges Must Make Law' (1976) 26 Case W Res L Rev 563.

Universals of Legal Reasoning by Judges. Thomas Lundmark, Oxford University Press. © Thomas Lundmark 2024.
DOI: 10.1093/oso/9780198785675.003.0002

B. Making law

The discussion in this section divides the topic of making law into three, admittedly overlapping, categories: (1) Making statutory law, (2) making law (by judges) that is based on a statute, and (3) making law (by judges) in the apparent absence of a statute, so-called 'pure' common law.

(1) Making statutory law

Democracies entrust the legislative branch with the primary, if not exclusive, role of making law. This is the first sense in which making law is used in this book: the act of legislating, which implies the setting up of rules of general application.[4]

Merriam-Webster.com defines 'legislation' as 'the act of legislating, specifically: the exercise of the power and function of making rules (such as laws) that have the force of authority by virtue of their promulgation by an official organ of a state or other organization'. While this definition does not define what is meant by an 'official organ', in common legal and everyday parlance, the 'official organ' is understood to be the legislature.

Legislatures are known by various names, such as parliaments, congresses, and assemblies, to name only English-language examples. The members of these legislatures are also known by various names, such as members of parliament, senators, assemblymen and -women, council members, and any similar descriptive words in languages other than English. In this discussion, and in this book, these members will commonly be referred to as legislators.

It should also be borne in mind that legislators need not be democratically elected. According to the democracy index maintained by *The Economist*, 51 of the 167 countries on this index are ruled by authoritarian regimes, which are often absolute monarchies or dictatorships. Approximately 34 per cent of the world's population live under authoritarian rule. Another 18 per cent (in thirty-seven countries) live in so-called hybrid regimes, where elections are often not fair and where the governments put pressure on opposition parties and candidates. While authoritarian and hybrid regimes do have systems of courts, there is little or no judicial independence from the governing regime.

Whether they be dictators or members of a democratic parliament, legislators are tasked with identifying which activities in society should be regulated in some way, and they are tasked with recommending or deciding what shape the new regulation should take. In democracies, these decisional processes generally

[4] See Edward Hirsch Levi, 'An Introduction to Legal Reasoning' (1948) 15 Univ Chic Law Rev 501, 505.

involve various steps: consultation with various groups, consideration by committees, preparation of reports, consideration of input from the public, and discussion both within and beyond the walls for the legislative chambers. Dictatorships and other authoritarian or hybrid regimes will possess their own decisional processes to identify activities that those in power think should be regulated and to decide what shape the regulation should take.

While we do not often think that the processes involved in legislating constitute legal reasoning, at least in the narrow sense of the term 'reasoning', these processes do necessarily involve the consideration of numerous legal questions. Among the legal questions that are involved in the process of legislating are, 'Which activities are to be regulated?', 'Which purposes ought to be served by the proposed legislation?', 'Which measures should be adopted to reach these purposes?', 'Is there jurisdiction (power or competence) to enact the proposed legislation?', and 'Does the proposed legislation conflict with other laws, including constitutional or other supreme law?' One would expect that the legislative counsel, if not the legislators themselves, would pay attention to these and other legal questions during the legislative process and would ask questions about how the proposed statute would apply in various hypothetical factual scenarios.

What about subsidiary legislation? Subsidiary legislation includes rules and regulations promulgated by regulatory agencies, public authorities, ministries, bureaus, councils, municipalities, counties, and many other public entities and authorities. The purposes (the jurisdiction, power, or competence) of these entities are limited, as are the choices of measures available to reach these purposes. Accordingly, these entitles must, just like legislatures, also consider the extent of their authority, the appropriateness of their measures, and potential legal conflicts. The legal questions just mentioned—legislative and regulatory purposes, choice and appropriateness of measures, jurisdiction (competence) to enact, and potential legal conflicts—all involve what might be called legal reasoning in the broad sense of the term. After all, they are all matters that judges have to deal with on occasion.

But what of the other processes mentioned above, specifically, deciding whether some activities in society should be regulated in some way? Do these processes also belong to legal reasoning? Whether they do or not, we will see below that judges also have to deal with these matters on occasion.

(2) Making law (by judges) that is based on a statute

If the act of legislating implies the setting up of rules of general application, then, in this sense at least, appellate judges 'legislate' when they construe statutes. This can be seen most obviously when the statute is drafted broadly, which is also referred to as the statutory language being 'abstract' or 'open-textured'. Section 1714 of the California Civil Code, as enacted in 1872, is one such broadly drafted statute:

> Every one is responsible, not only for the result of his willful acts, but also for an injury occasioned to another by his want of ordinary care or skill in the management of his property or person, except so far as the latter has, willfully or by want of ordinary care, brought the injury upon himself.[5]

The statutory language 'want of ordinary care or skill' means acting negligently. Does a licensed tavern owner show a 'want of ordinary care and skill' when he serves a patron very large quantities of alcoholic beverages, knowing that the patron is becoming excessively intoxicated, and also knowing that the patron, upon leaving the tavern, intends to drive his car down a very steep, winding, and narrow mountain road? The California Supreme Court in *Vesely v. Sager* held that a tavern owner in just this situation did show a want of ordinary care and skill, and, consequently, that he was liable for the injuries that the patron caused when the patron drove his car into oncoming traffic.[6] This is an example of a case where judges, not legislators, decide that some activities in society—here, the serving of alcoholic beverages by the owner of a licensed tavern—should be regulated. The judges do so by making the tavern owner potentially liable. This, then, is an example of what we have identified as a legislative process.

Further proof that this decision of the California Court should be seen as a legislative process is supplied by the reaction of the California Legislature to this judicial decision. As a reaction to *Vesely v. Sager* and similar cases, the California Legislature added subsection (b) to §1714 of the California Civil Code:

> It is the intent of the Legislature to abrogate the holdings in cases such as Vesely v. Sager (1971) 5 Cal.3d 153, Bernhard v. Harrah's Club (1976) 16 Cal.3d 313, and Coulter v. Superior Court (1978) 21 Cal. 3d 144 and to reinstate the prior judicial interpretation of this section as it relates to proximate cause for injuries incurred as a result of furnishing alcoholic beverages to an intoxicated person, namely that the furnishing of alcoholic beverages is not the proximate cause of injuries resulting from intoxication, but rather the consumption of alcoholic beverages is the proximate cause of injuries inflicted upon another by an intoxicated person.

[5] This statute has been amended. The sentence cited in the text can now be found in subsection (a), which now reads in part:

> Everyone is responsible, not only for the result of his or her willful acts, but also for an injury occasioned to another by his or her want of ordinary care or skill in the management of his or her property or person, except so far as the latter has, willfully or by want of ordinary care, brought the injury upon himself or herself.

[6] *Vesley v. Sager* (1971) 5 Cal.3d 153. The holding in this case has been abrogated by an amendment to §1714 of the Civil Code, discussed below.

We would all agree that, in enacting the above provision, the California Legislature was legislating, that is, making law. By the same token, it must be the case that in applying §1714 of the California Civil Code to tavern owners, the California courts were also legislating, that is, making law.

Here is an example from Germany, where the legislative response does not cite case decisions but still demonstrates that the German *Bundestag* is cognizant of the fact that the German courts are, in effect, legislating when construing §823 of the German Civil Code, which reads in translation as follows:

> (1) A person who, intentionally or negligently, unlawfully injures the life, body, health, freedom, property, or some other right of another person is liable to compensate the other person for the injury arising therefrom.
> (2) The same duty is held by a person who commits a breach of a statute that is intended to protect another person. If, according to the contents of the statute, it may also be breached without fault, then liability to compensation only exists in the case of fault.[7]

The express language of §823 limits liability to intentional and negligent injuries, what is referred to as 'fault' in subsection (2). There is no room for no-fault or so-called absolute liability. Yet, the German courts have held that negligence in some cases is to be presumed, such as when a bottle of sparkling water explodes in the hand of a girl who has been asked by her parents to fetch a bottle of water from the basement of their house.[8]

In practice, this presumption of negligence, in this case of an exploding water bottle, amounts to an irrebuttable presumption, in other words, to no-fault or absolute liability; for the manufacturer of a bottle of sparkling water, and the company that fills the bottle with water, cannot possibly prove that they acted without negligence in manufacturing and filling the particular bottle that exploded. The German courts have therefore gone beyond the language of §823. In the act of construing the law, they have stretched the reach of the statute to cover presumed manufacturing defects. They have decided on their own that the manufacturing of products should be further regulated by making manufacturers presumptively negligent for injuries resulting from defects in their products. This is an example of judicial legislating.

Some years later, the German legislature, the *Bundestag*, enacted the Product Liability Act[9] to cover cases of defective products. Section 1(1) of the Product Liability Act reads in translation:

[7] Section 823 of the German Civil Code.
[8] Bundesgerichtshof (Sixth Civil Senate) (9 May 1995) NJW 2162.
[9] Produkthaftungsgesetz (Gesetz über die Haftung für fehlerhafte Produkte—ProdHaftG) vom 15. Dezember 1989 (BGBl. I S. 2198).

> In such case as a defect in a product causes a person's death, injury to his body or damage to his health, or damage to an item of property, the producer of the product has an obligation to compensate the injured person for the resulting damage.

We would all agree that, in enacting the Product Liability Act, the German *Bundestag* was legislating, that is, making law. By the same token, it must be the case that, in presuming negligence under §823 of the German Civil Code for injuries caused by products, the German courts were also legislating, that is, making law.

The process that has been described above—making law (by judges) that is based on statute—produces a holding or *ratio* of a case that elaborates or concretizes the statute. In *Vesely v. Sager*, the California Supreme Court concretized 'want of ordinary care or skill' in §1714 of the California Civil Code to include the negligent serving of alcoholic beverages to obviously intoxicated patrons. Similarly, the German courts concretized 'negligently, unlawfully injures' in §823 of the German Civil Code to include a reversal of the burden of proof for injuries caused by products.[10]

As just seen, this process of judicial concretization or elaboration of a statute amounts to a judicial rearticulation of the statute in a way that looks like subsidiary legislation. This process is referred to here, and elsewhere, as 'putting a gloss' on a statute.[11]

Let one last example illustrate what is meant by putting a gloss on a statute. Section 30(1)(g) of the Landlord and Tenant Act 1954[12] in the United Kingdom provides that the landlord may refuse an application for a new lease by the tenant if the landlord 'intends to occupy the holding for the purposes of a business carried on by him' upon termination of the current tenancy. Does this provision mean that a mere intention on the part of the landlord to occupy the holding for the purposes of a business is a sufficient ground for refusing to enter into a new lease, or must the landlord possess (1) a bona fide intention to occupy the holding for the purposes of the business (a subjective element) coupled with (2) a real possibility of starting the particular business (an objective element)? The British courts have accepted the second construction of the statute.[13] In other words, a 'mere intention on the part of the landlord' is insufficient. Accordingly, one could say that §30(1)(g) of the Landlord and Tenant Act 1954 has been judicially extended, or subsidiarily amended, to require that the landlord show both (1) a bona fide intention to

[10] When developing the common law (i.e. law in the absence of statute), judges in the common-law world also employ a reversal of the burden of proof in certain cases, such as when they employ the doctrine of *res ipsa loquitur*. See e.g. the English judicial decision *Byrne v. Boadle*, 159 Eng. Rep. 299 (1863).

[11] See e.g. László Péter, *Hungary's Long Nineteenth Century: Constitutional and Democratic Traditions in a European Perspective* (Brill 2012) 278.

[12] Section 30(1)(g) of the Landlord and Tenant Act 1954.

[13] *Zarvos v. Pradhan* [2003] EWCA (Civ.) 208 (England).

occupy the holding for purposes of a business plus (2) a real possibility of starting the business.

One can rightly say, in an objective sense, that the British courts in the preceding example have concretized the statute in the process of interpreting it. But some would say that, in doing so, they have gone too far and have substituted their subjective will for that of Parliament. The question of the extent to which judges should be able to concretize statutes by extending their reach will be dealt with at length in Chapter 3 on political judging. For the purposes of this chapter, it is sufficient to note that such judicial glosses, concretizations, or amendments look very much like statutory norms and that they are frequently employed in practice alongside the bare provisions of the statute. This will be illustrated in later chapters on judicial uses of textual, historical, purposive, and system-contextual arguments.

(3) Making law (by judges) in the apparent absence of a statute

As described in more detail in later chapters, it does sometimes happen that judges are forced to decide cases in which there is no obvious applicable legislative rule to rely on. This situation is sometimes referred to in international law and in the civil-law tradition[14] as judicial decision-making *praeter legem*, meaning 'outside of the law' or 'beyond the law', where 'law' is understood to mean statute law.[15] Realizing that this situation does occasionally arise, the legislatures in some countries have even enacted legislation for this eventuality. Article 1 of the Swiss Civil Code[16] is a prime example of such legislation:

> 1 The law applies according to its wording or interpretation to all legal questions for which it contains a provision.

[14] This term is also employed in conjunction with the United Nations Convention on Contracts for the International Sales of Goods (CISG). Article 7(2) of CISG provides:

> Questions concerning matters governed by this Convention which are not expressly settled in it are to be settled in conformity with the general principles on which it is based or, in the absence of such principles, in conformity with the law applicable by virtue of the rules of private international law. On the term's use in international law, see Catharine Titi, *The Function of Equity in International Law* (Oxford University Press 2021) 87. See generally James Gerard Devaney, 'The Role of Precedent in the Jurisprudence of the International Court of Justice: A Constructive Interpretation' (2022) 35 LJIL 641.

[15] For a good summary in English of *praeter legem* and *extra legem* as understood and applied in Germany, see Martin Brenncke, *Judicial Law-Making in English and German Courts: Techniques and Limits of Statutory Interpretation* (Intersentia 2018) 72–86.

[16] See generally René David (ed.), *The Legal Systems of the World: Their Comparison and Unification*, vol. II (J.C.B. Mohr (Paul Siebeck)–Martinus Nijhoff 1975) 140. Article 6 of the Spanish Civil Code contains a similar provision. Giacinto della Cananea, *Due Process of Law beyond the State: Requirements of Administrative Procedure* (Oxford University Press 2016) 156.

2 In the absence of a provision, the court shall decide in accordance with customary law and, in the absence of customary law, in accordance with the rule that it would make as legislator.
3 In doing so, the court shall follow established doctrine and case law.

This article of the Swiss Civil Code constitutes an explicit delegation of legislative authority to the judiciary. Another example is provided by Article 7 of the Austrian Civil Code: 'If the case still remains in doubt, it shall be decided according to the principles of natural law, taking into careful consideration all the circumstances of the case.' And Article 4 of the French Civil Code provides: 'judges who refuse to decide a case on the pretext of silence, obscurity or insufficiency of the law are liable to be prosecuted for a denial of justice'.

A statute in California, which, unlike most common-law jurisdictions, has a civil code, also addresses the eventuality that judges will be forced to decide cases in which there is no applicable legislative rule to rely on. This statute, §22.2 of the Civil Code, provides: 'The common law of England, so far as it is not repugnant to or inconsistent with the Constitution of the United States, or the Constitution or laws of this State, is the rule of decision in all the courts of this State.'[17]

But even in the absence of statutes such as those just mentioned from Switzerland, Austria, France, and California, one finds major areas of law that consist entirely of rules announced by judges rather than set down by legislatures. The law in Germany regarding industrial disputes (*Arbeitskampfrecht*), such as the right to strike, is made up of myriad judicial case decisions of the Federal Labor Court, the Federal Supreme Court, and the Federal Constitutional Court.[18] No statute in Germany stipulates that one may demand compensation for slander, libel, or other non-pecuniary injury to one's reputation (*Ehrverletzung*), yet the German Federal

[17] The California courts construe 'common law' in §22.2 to include not only case decisions but also statutes enacted by Parliament prior to the time of separation of the American colonies from Great Britain: *Moore v. Purse Seine Net*, 18 Cal. 2d 835 (1941).

[18] See generally Wolfgang Däubler (ed.), *Arbeitskampfrecht: Handbuch für die Praxis* (3rd edn, Nomos 2011); Moti (Mordehai) Mironi, Moti (Mordehai) Mironi and Monika Schlachter (eds), *Regulating Strikes in Essential Services: A Comparative 'Law in Action' Perspective* (Wolters Kluwer 2018). Article 9, §3 of the Basic Law protects freedom of association, which the Federal Labor Court has held to protect collective bargain and the right to strike. Initially, the Court held that strikes were only protected as a last resort (*ultima ratio*) when negotiations between the union and the employer had broken down. But in 1976, the Federal Labor Court ruled that a strike of a few hours' duration during negotiation was legal:

> The principle [of *ultima ratio*] is only meant for a stake of longer duration or an indefinite period . . . If the only intention of a strike is to promote the negotiations by showing the opposing party the readiness of the employees to go on strike then this mild pressure, by way of a short warning strike, may be exerted before the means of negotiations are exhausted. Federal Labor Court decision of 17 December 1976.

Supreme Court has allowed recovery in such cases since 1958.[19] The annual report of the Federal Constitutional Court in 1966 states the matter succinctly:

> Jurists at least must agree that the applicable law is a mixture of statutory law and case law and the law applied by the court has never correlated with the law issued by the legislator. What is debatable is not the existence but the degree of case law.[20]

In democratic countries with independent judiciaries, the decisions of the highest courts are usually available in written form, although they may not always be collected, published, and made generally available. Furthermore, these decisions will ordinarily contain not only the rulings of the judges but also the explanations for why the judges ruled as they did. These explanations are usually referred to as reasons, and the judges' explanations are consequently referred to as reasoning. A less confusing way to refer to these explanations is that they constitute the judges' justifications for their rulings.[21] In any event, when judges are faced with a case in which there is no legislative rule to rely on, they will resolve the dispute in favour of one party or the other. Put another way, judges who find themselves in this situation will have two alternatives: they will either decide to grant relief or to deny relief for the fact that there is no legislative rule to rely on does not necessarily mean that the petitioner will not be entitled to relief.

Let us first look at the second alternative: denying relief. When deciding to deny relief in this situation, are the judges performing a legislative process or function? Like legislators, even like dictators, the judges in this judicial process will have been presented with a set of circumstances in society. As in the legislative process, the judges will have been told by at least one person, the petitioner, that this particular set of circumstances needs to be regulated in some way favourable to the petitioner. Somewhat similar to the legislative process, the judges will have consulted with at least one party who sees no need for regulation: the respondent. If the judges are sitting on the highest court in the jurisdiction, they may have heard from various groups, such as by means of *amicus curia* ('friend of the court') submissions or briefs. However, in contrast to the legislative process, there will have been no direct input from the public. And the only discussions beyond the walls of the courtroom are likely to be those found in academic and other legal publications.

Consider the case of *Merrifield v. Canada (Attorney General)*,[22] in which Peter Merrifield, a junior constable in the Royal Canadian Mounted Police, claimed that

[19] Entscheidungen des Bundesgerichtshofes in Zivilsachen [BGHZ] (14 February 1958) Neue Juristische Wochenschrift (NJW) 827 (Germany).

[20] Jahresbericht des Bundesverfassungsgerichts 1966.

[21] For more on the distinction between the judge's motives and the judge's justifications, see Wasserstrom, *The Judicial Decision*, 25–30.

[22] *Merrifield v. Canada (Attorney General)*, 432 DLR (4th) 433 (2019).

he was the subject of harassment and bullying by his superior officers over a period of more than seven years. After forty days of trial, the trial judge found in Merrifield's favour and awarded him almost 1 million Canadian dollars in damages and costs of the action. On appeal, the Court of Appeal for Ontario reversed, holding that no common-law tort (i.e. no non-statutory tort) of harassment exits in Canada, and concluding that no such tort should be recognized. Here is the justification of the Court of Appeal refusing to recognize (i.e. create) a tort of harassment:

> Merrifield submits that the new tort must be created because there is an increased societal recognition that harassment is wrongful conduct. He notes that moral damages for mental distress can be awarded only at termination of employment, leaving a gap that the tort of harassment should fill. He asserts that the decision of the Supreme Court in *Saadati v. Moorhead*, 2017 SCC 28, [2017] 1 S.C.R. 543, supports the creation of the tort of harassment, and that the test the trial judge recognized for the tort is sufficiently stringent to limit the reach of the tort.
>
> We disagree.
>
> *Saadati* is concerned with proof of mental injury in the context of a known cause of action. Although it may make damages for mental injury more readily available in negligence actions, it does not require the recognition of a new tort. Moreover, this court has not allowed negligence to ground a claim for mental suffering in the employment context: *Piresferreira v. Ayotte*, 2010 ONCA 384, 319 D.L.R. (4th) 665.
>
> In summary, while we do not foreclose the development of a properly conceived tort of harassment that might apply in appropriate contexts, we conclude that Merrifield has presented no compelling reason to recognize a new tort of harassment in this case.

Most people would agree that the judges in this situation, both at the trial court and on appeal, are at a disadvantage when compared with members of the Canadian Parliament because the judges have less access to information, including access to the general opinion of the public. Another difference might be that the judges in this situation—unlike members of the members of the Canadian Parliament—would likely consider the doctrine of separation of powers: the judges might have thought, for various reasons including separation of powers, that it would be better to leave the question to Parliament for Parliament would not be hindered by the doctrine of separation of powers.

Putting these two differences—access to information and concern for separation of powers—aside, are the judges in this situation doing something that the members of Parliament would not or could not do? Are the judges in this situation somehow thinking differently? Are the judges perhaps reasoning legally, whereas members of Parliament would be thinking politically? The answer should be obvious: they are thinking in the same way.

One obvious difference between the activity, but not the thinking, of judges and the activity of members of the legislature is that the members of the legislature, with more information available to them, are likely to be more in touch as an institution with the needs and desires of the electorate. From a democratic, institutional standpoint, members of the legislature are in a better position than the judges to assess the need for legislation. Accordingly, from a democratic, institutional standpoint, referring the aggrieved petitioner to the legislature makes sense.

However, it can also be argued that, in refusing to grant relief, the judges in our hypothetical situation are also acting very much like members of the legislature for they are refusing to grant relief in a situation where they have the jurisdiction (power) to do so. This situation is reminiscent of the predicament described in Article 1 of the Swiss Civil Code: 'In the absence of a [statutory] provision, the court shall decide in accordance . . . with the rule that it would make as legislator.'

We turn now to examples of when judges decide to grant relief in the absence of statutory authority, where we will ask how the judges' decision-making should be characterized. Without rehearsing the arguments above, the answer should be clear: the judges are acting very much like members of the legislature. The point being made here is that neither the process of denying relief in the absence of a statute nor granting relief in this situation should be thought of as legal reasoning in a narrow sense: both denying and granting relief in this situation are legislative in the sense of making law.

The first example of a case in which judges decide to grant relief in the absence of statutory authority is, like the last example, from Canada. In the case of *Bhasin v. Hrynew*,[23] the plaintiff, Harish Bhasin, worked as an independent contractor (not as an employee) for a company that sold registered educational savings plans. Bhasin's contract with the company was for a period of three years, with automatic renewal unless six months' written notice was given before the expiration of the three-year period. The contract contained an 'entire agreement clause' that stated that there were no 'agreements, express, implied or statutory, other than expressly set out' in the contract. The defendant, Larry Hrynew, worked for the same company. Hrynew also worked on the same contractual basis and in the same geographical area, the province of Alberta. This put Hrynew in direct competition with Bhasin.

The company was required by the Alberta Securities Commission to appoint a compliance officer. Over Bhasin's strenuous objection, the company appointed Hrynew as the company's compliance officer. In his position as compliance officer, Hrynew was given access to confidential information about Bhasin's business. This access enabled Hrynew to take over much of Bhasin's business.

[23] *Bhasin v. Hrynew*, 2014 SCC 71 (2014). See generally Angela Swan, 'The Obligation to Perform in Good Faith: Comment on Bhasin v. Hrynew' (2014–2015) 56 Can Bus LJ 395.

Faced with the loss of a substantial part of his business, Bhasin filed suit, alleging that there was an implied term in the contract that the company act in good faith. The trial court agreed and ruled that the company had breached this implicit contractual term by appointing Bhasin's competitor as the company's compliance order.[24] The Alberta Court of Appeal reversed the trial court's judgment, ruling that the courts cannot imply a term of good faith in this situation for the contract was unambiguous, and it also contained an entire agreement clause.

Bhasin appealed to the Supreme Court of Canada, which allowed his appeal:

> Anglo-Canadian common law has resisted acknowledging any generalized and independent doctrine of good faith performance of contracts. The result is an 'unsettled and incoherent body of law' that has developed 'piecemeal' and which is 'difficult to analyze' [citation]. This approach is out of step with the civil law of Quebec and most jurisdictions in the United States and produces results that are not consistent with the reasonable expectations of commercial parties.
>
> In my view, it is time to take two incremental steps in order to make the common law less unsettled and piecemeal, more coherent and more just. The first step is to acknowledge that good faith contractual performance is a general organizing principle of the common law of contract which underpins and informs the various rules in which the common law, in various situations and types of relationships, recognizes obligations of good faith contractual performance. The second is to recognize, as a further manifestation of this organizing principle of good faith, that there is a common law duty which applies to all contracts to act honestly in the performance of contractual obligations.
>
> In my view, taking these two steps is perfectly consistent with the Court's responsibility to make incremental changes in the common law when appropriate. Doing so will put in place a duty that is just, that accords with the reasonable expectations of commercial parties and that is sufficiently precise that it will enhance rather than detract from commercial certainty.

By recognizing a duty 'to act honestly in the performance of contractual obligations', the Canadian Supreme Court in *Bhasin v. Hrynew* is engaged in legislating or law-making as those terms are employed in this book. Should the Canadian Supreme Court have waited for the Canadian Parliament to enact such an obligation? As the Supreme Court notes in the passage above, the Civil Code of Québec (which is not applicable in Alberta) already contains a requirement of good faith in the performance of contracts.[25] Article 1375 provides: 'The parties shall conduct

[24] *Bhasin v. Hrynew et al.*, 2011 ABQB 637.

[25] See generally Rosalie Jukier, 'Good Faith in Contract: A Judicial Dialogue between Common Law Canada and Québec' (2019) 1 Commonw Law J 83.

themselves in good faith both at the time the obligation arises and at the time it is performed or extinguished.'

Notice, too, that not all of the judges who heard the case of *Bhasin v. Hrynew* agreed that judges should recognize a duty of good faith in the performance of contracts. While the decision of the Supreme Court of Canada was unanimous, so was the decision of the judges of the Alberta Court of Appeal, who would have reversed the trial court. Does this suggest that it might have been better, from a legislative and separation-of-powers standpoint, to wait for the Canadian Parliament to act? Consider the following case from England, which also involves contract law.

In legal actions for breach of contract in England and Wales, the non-breaching party is ordinarily entitled to the 'benefit of the bargain'. This means that he or she will be awarded an amount of money (called expectation damages) to place him or her in the same situation as if the contract had been performed.[26] However, the courts long ago carved out an exception to this rule when it comes to contracts for the sale of land or sale of an interest in land. This exception can be traced back at least to the case of *Flureau v. Thornhill*, which was decided in 1776.[27] Since then, the courts have limited a land-buyer's damages to the recovery of expenses as long as the only reason for the vendor's breach was that, through no fault of his or her own, the vendor was not able to provide good title. This exception from the benefit-of-the-bargain rule was reaffirmed in 1874 by the Judicial Committee of the House of Lords in *Bain v. Fothergill*.[28] Thereafter, this exception became known as the rule in *Bain v. Fothergill*. Notice that the benefit-of-the-bargain rule and the rule in *Bain v. Fothergill* are both products of the English common law in the absence of a statute: they are judge-made law in the sense of making law. However, the latter case, *Bain v. Fothergill*, can also be described as applying the law as it had been announced in *Flureau v. Thornhill*.

In any event, the British Parliament has, in the meantime, expressly rejected the rule in *Bain v. Fothergill*. Section 3 of the Law of Property (Miscellaneous Provisions) Act 1989 (chapter 34)[29] simply reads: 'The rule of law known as the rule in Bain v. Fothergill is abolished in relation to contracts made after this section comes into force.'

The reader will agree that both the rule in *Bain v. Fothergill* and the abolishment of the rule by Parliament are examples of law-making as the term is employed in this book.

26 *Robinson v. Harman* (1848) 1 Exch. 850 at 855; 154 ER 363 at 365.

27 *Flureau v. Thornhill* (1776) 2 W Bl 1078 at 1078; 96 ER 635 at 635, discussed in New South Wales Law Reform Commission, 'Community Law Reform Program: Damages for Vendor's Inability to Convey Good Title: The Rule in Bain v Fothergill', Report 64 (1990) at n. 10 and p. 7 *et seq*. This was a judgment of the Court of Exchequer Chamber, which no longer exists.

28 *Bain v. Fothergill* (1874) LR 7 HL 158.

29 Law of Property (Miscellaneous Provisions) Act 1989.

C. Finding the law

Finding the law is used in this book in two senses. First, finding the law is used to describe the process that lawyers and judges employ to select a pre-existing statutory or case-law rule that they will use to judge the legal consequences of a factual situation before them, whether the factual situation is real (such as a case before a court) or imagined, such as judging the legality of proposed action. This usage of the expression 'finding the law' is referred to as *Normsuche* ('search for the rule') in German. For the sake of clarity, the term *Normsuche* will be used for the activity of searching for the applicable rule, and the term *Normsucher* ('norm seeker') will be used to describe the person involved in this activity, whether he or she be student, practitioner, scholar, or judge. Second, finding the law is often used in justifying one's choice of the appropriate norm. This sense of the term is discussed above under 'putting a judicial gloss on a statute' in (2) 'Making law (by judges) that is based on a statute' in section B.

In most real or imagined cases, it will be obvious to the *Normsucher* which statutory norm, which judicial gloss on a statute, or which case-law *ratio* or other rule applies. Criminal cases serve as a good example. In criminal prosecutions, it is the charging prosecutor or police officer who is the *Normsucher*. And in these criminal cases, the choice of the crime (i.e. the norm) to be charged is usually clear to all those involved, having been established by custom and practice. Once the accused has been charged with having violated the chosen criminal norm, the question becomes whether the prosecutor can prove the charge in court. The process of the *Normsuche* in such routine cases will, in all probability, go without mention by the judge who hears the case; for in routine cases, custom and practice produce a generally accepted understanding of the parameters of criminal and other norms. If, however, a question about the appropriateness of the choice of the norm should arise, the judge will consult his or her personal experience, and perhaps the experience of other judges, to decide whether the behaviour of the accused is properly to be judged by the norm which has been charged.

Notice that the thought processes involved in the *Normsuche* are identical, regardless of the source of the rule and the kind or number of sources of law that are recognized in the particular jurisdiction: the *Normsucher* has a particular factual situation in mind, and he or she hunts for a rule whose text might conceivably find application to that particular factual situation. The point just made (i.e. that the thought processes involved in the *Normsuche* are identical regardless of the source of the rule) is worth emphasizing because some people wrongly contend that searching for a rule among thousands of statutes—the European continental *Normsuche*, if you will—constitutes a different mental process than searching for a rule in thousands of case decisions in what might be termed the common-law *Normsuche*.

Can the *Normsuche* be described as legal reasoning? Legal reasoning was defined in the introduction to this book as the process of using our human ability to draw inferences and conclusions, such as inferring an implicit rule from a story, adding and subtracting numbers, and employing logic. To answer this question, we should look more closely at the process of the *Normsuche*.

Before embarking on a hypothetical search for an appropriate rule to apply, the reader should remember that the common law and continental European *Normsucher*, like any *Normsucher* from any other jurisdiction, must have a specific factual situation in mind before the search can begin. In addition, the *Normsucher* must be able to identify one or more factual features that have potential relevance to the law. This is where legal education and experience prove indispensable.

On the European continent, as in most of Central and South America, would-be lawyers learn by rote where to find the rules that one should employ to a great number of factual situations. The way they learn this is by studying not only the text of the statutes but also by learning to recognize the classic factual patterns to which these statutes are ordinarily applied. German law students, for example, write scores of examinations, at university and at the *Repetitor*, in which they must identify and apply the rules that are used to resolve various hypothetical fact patterns. At least by the time of their first state examination, generally after three years of university study, German students will have memorized and practiced where to find hundreds of statutory rules. Usually, they will highlight the statutes or mark them in some other way in the statutory collections. This is good preparation for an all-round lawyer and for judges with heavy case loads. Following their university studies, German students must complete a two-year traineeship (*Referendariat*) in which they learn more about legal practice.

During their three years at university, British law students spend relatively more time learning about general legal topics and learning how to apply rules. This is relatively good preparation for a more specialized lawyer and advocate. Following their university studies, British students will complete the one-year legal practice course or bar professional training course, in which they learn more about legal practice.

At the end of these periods of study, these new lawyers will probably know which statutory rule, or common-law rule, to apply to the most general factual situations that present themselves in legal practice. If, for example, the specific factual features suggest that criminal liability might attach, the knowledgeable German *Normsucher* will limit his or her search to the Criminal Code (*Strafgesetzbuch*) and the ninety or so other statutes that contain criminal provisions. Or, more likely, lawyers in this situation will consult the books that were used during their education. The British *Normsucher* will also fall back on educational materials. As continental European and British lawyers gain more practical experience, they will consult practice books and publications or perhaps simply ask colleagues. If the answer is not readily available from memory or from these sources, the *Normsucher* on the European continent will likely consult a commentary, while the British *Normsucher* will consult *Halsbury's*, the legal encyclopaedia.

With this background in mind, we should be able to answer the question whether the process of finding the law involves using our human ability to draw inferences and conclusions, such as inferring an implicit rule from a story, adding and subtracting numbers, and employing logic. It should be clear that the process of finding the law outlined above does not employ logic, at least not logic in the classical sense. It cannot be deductive reasoning because there is no major premise. And it cannot be described as simply adding and subtracting numbers. But the process of finding law does entail the recognition of rules and inferences drawn from the stories to which the rules will apply for all rules contain stories in abstract form. In this way, at least, finding the law is a legal reasoning process.

D. Applying the law

Applying the law, and justifying the result, are the subjects that will be addressed in the remainder of this chapter. At this juncture, it would be prudent to consider the logical syllogism because many academics consider it to be the mainstay of legal reasoning.

The syllogism is not a separate logical method. Rather, it is at the heart of traditional deductive reasoning. It can be thought of as a kind of argument containing three categorical propositions: a major premise, a minor premise, and a conclusion. Most readers will recognize the syllogism 'All men are mortal (major premise), Socrates is a man (minor premise), therefore Socrates is mortal (conclusion).' The great attraction of the syllogism for someone seeking truth is that, assuming the premises are true, then the conclusion must also be true.[30]

(1) The legal syllogism

Unfortunately for lawyers, use of the syllogism is subject to pitfalls, often referred to as fallacies. Logicians have identified over 100 distinct fallacies.[31] Of particular relevance to the law are fallacies of ambiguity. These occur when the meaning of a key word or phrase shifts and changes so that the terms do not really match up within the argument. For example, Jonathan Swift quipped, 'No man will take counsel, but every man will take money; therefore, money is better than counsel.'[32]

[30] The technical term is 'valid', not 'true'. See generally Mark Sainsbury, *Logical Forms: An Introduction to Philosophical Logic* (2nd edn, Wiley Blackwell 2001) ch. 1.

[31] Irving M. Copi and Carl Cohen, *Introduction to Logic* (11th edn, Pearson 2001) 115.

[32] Quoted in ibid 153.

The lawyer who wishes to employ the powerful logic of the syllogism has an a priori problem as well: how does he or she find the major premise? Here, the syllogism is of no assistance. In other words, the lawyer who wishes to come to the one logical conclusion, assuming there is one, must first possess knowledge of all of the potentially applicable premises. Second, use of the syllogism will be compromised if there is more than one possible major premise. Third, there is no syllogistic process for determining whether the minor premise corresponds in all details with the major premise. These and other problems will be explored briefly in this section.

Subsumption in law refers simply to the process of subsuming the facts of the case to be decided under a legal rule as one would subsume the minor premise under the major premise in a syllogism. The terms 'legal syllogism' or simply 'syllogism' are used more widely in English than subsumption, which is the preferred term in German.[33] However, even more common in English is the expression 'applying the law to the facts', which is the same process as subsumption or syllogistic reasoning.

Perhaps a word should be said about the centrality of subsumption (*Subsumtion* in German) to German legal education for its centrality to German legal education is likely to be similar to legal education in other continental European countries and in Central and South America. An important component of learning to think like a lawyer in Germany is mastering the task of *Subsumtion*, that is, applying the law to the facts. The word and the activity of subsuming are borrowed from logic, but in the place of a statement of a proposition as the major premise, the lawyer inserts a legal rule. The minor premise consists of the operative facts, which might be either brought into conformity with the rule or not, depending upon how the lawyer or judge decides to interpret the law and the facts.

A simple hypothetical example will illustrate that subsumption is nothing more than applying the law to the facts. The crime of theft is made punishable in Germany by German Penal Code §242(1):

> Whoever takes personal property not his own from another with the intent of unlawfully appropriating the property for himself or for a third person shall be punished with imprisonment for not more than five years or with a fine.[34]

In order to be found guilty of theft under this statute, the court must be satisfied that (1) personal property that (2) did not belong to the accused was (3) appropriated by the accused for him- or herself or for another person (4) unlawfully. If Anja takes a pair of sunglasses that do not belong to her from a store rack, drops

[33] See Neil MacCormick, *Rhetoric and the Rule of Law: A Theory of Legal Reasoning* (Oxford University Press 2005) 32–33, 43–47 (the legal syllogism is 'central to legal reasoning'); Wolfgang Fikentscher, 'The Evolutionary and Cultural Origins of Heuristics that Influence Law-Making' in Gerd Gigerenzer and Christoph Engel (eds), *Heuristics and the Law* (The MIT Press 2006) 207, 220.

[34] Section 242 (1) of the German Penal Code.

them into her purse, leaves the store, and then puts them on so that she can go to the beach, she will, in all likelihood, be found guilty of theft. In other words, the activity of subsuming, for legal purposes, means testing in a logical way whether all the elements of the crime have been met.

Of course, the operative facts found in real life, or in law school examinations, are often much more difficult to subsume under the applicable rule than the hypothetical example just given. Consider the application of §212 of the German Penal Code to the two hypothetical factual situations.[35]

Section 212(1) (manslaughter) provides:

> Whoever kills a human being without being guilty of murder [which requires proof of base motives, etc.] shall be punished for manslaughter with imprisonment for not less than five years.[36]

The elements of the crime of manslaughter in Germany are consequently (1) killing of a (2) human being without (3) possessing the requisites for the crime of murder (acting for base motives).

Hypothetical factual situation 1: Tanja performs an abortion on Anja. Is an abortion a (1) killing? Does it matter if the foetus is old enough to survive outside the womb? Is the foetus (2) a human being? Does it matter if the abortion is performed after Anja goes into labour at the end of the term of the pregnancy? Do Tanja's motives for the abortion matter? If Tanja is not a physician, can she be said to be acting for (3) base motives?

Hypothetical factual situation 2: Tanja's mother lies in a coma. A brain scan confirms that her mother is brain dead, but her heart is still beating, and she is breathing on her own. Tanja removes the feeding tube and the intravenous apparatus for administering liquids. Eventually, her mother stops breathing and her heart stops beating. Does removal of the tubes constitute (1) killing? Is Tanja's brain-dead mother (2) a human being? Does it matter whether Tanja removed the tubes for (3) base motives?

In the legal world, these questions must not only be asked but also answered. The question for our purposes therefore becomes: what mental process is used in trying to subsume the operative facts of these two hypothetical cases under (what we assume to be) the relevant statute? Many academics in the common-law world describe the process as one of analogy.[37] Thinking analogically, one imagines scenarios that are similar to the one at hand and tries to draw conclusions from

[35] This hypothetical factual situation is only for purposes of illustration. Abortion is actually covered in §218 of the German Penal Code.

[36] Ibid §212(1).

[37] See Douglas Walton, Fabrizio Macagno, and Giovanni Sartor, *Statutory Interpretation: Pragmatics and Argumentation* (Cambridge University Press 2021) 218; Eileen Braman, *Law, Politics, and Perception: How Policy Preferences Influence Legal Reasoning* (University of Virginia Press 2009) 84.

them. In the first hypothetical situation, it might make a difference, to some people at least, how the abortion is performed and, even more importantly, how early it occurred in the pregnancy. In the second hypothetical factual situation, it might make a difference, to some people at least, to know whether Tanja's mother had provided for this eventuality in a living will or other instrument.

Notice that the mental process involved in applying §212 of the German Penal Code to the hypothetical fact situation involves imagining other hypothetical cases; for example, does it matter if the abortion is performed after Anja goes into labour at the end of the term of her pregnancy?

Notice, too, that we did not, at least explicitly, employ (analogical) examples to decide the sunglasses case under §242(1) of the German Penal Code because the facts, as stated, so clearly fell within the template of the statute. Even the requisite mental state was stated: Anja put on the sunglasses 'so that she can go to the beach'. But imagine that the facts of the case had been silent on this point. Imagine that Anja had merely left the store with the sunglasses in her purse. In that case, the student, lawyer, or judge would be forced to construct various hypothetical scenarios about Anja's mental state at the time she left the store: Was she distracted by something in the store or elsewhere which prompted her to drop the sunglasses into her purse as a matter of habit? Did she simply forget that she had the sunglasses in her purse? Had she merely gone outside the store to get a better view of an item in the store window?

There are legal scholars, including the author of this book, who refer to the process just described as one of deduction. These scholars might even constitute a majority.[38] Their main reason for preserving this terminology is apparently because the device of the syllogism is borrowed from classical logic, and in classical logic, the process of employing the syllogism is described as one of deduction.

Other scholars disagree, or at least seem to disagree, with this usage of the term 'deduction'.[39] These scholars argue that one should not compare the legal syllogism to the schoolbook syllogism because the crucial activity of the legal syllogism is the process of trying to massage the facts of the case to look like a minor premise that can be fitted under the template of the major premise. That process, we can all agree, is not deductive in nature. Rather, it constitutes thinking by analogy, induction, abduction, or something else, maybe even intuitive, emotional thinking, depending on the rules and the facts under scrutiny. These scholars rightly point out that use of legal skills to select the major premise (*Normsuche*) and, often more poignantly,

[38] See e.g. MacCormick, *Rhetoric and the Rule of Law*, 43–47; Richard A. Posner, 'Legal Formalism, Legal Realism, and the Interpretation of Statutes and the Constitution' (1986) 37 Case W Res L Rev 179; Levi, 'An Introduction to Legal Reasoning', 501.

[39] See e.g. Cass R. Sunstein, 'On Analogical Reasoning' (1993) 106 Harv L Rev 741, 781: '[Reasoning by analogy] may even be said to be the central feature of the common law method'; Scott Brewer, 'Exemplary Reasoning: Semantics, Pragmatics, and the Rational Force of Legal Argument by Analogy' (1995–1996) 109 Harv L Rev 923; Lloyd L. Weinreb, *Legal Reason: The Use of Analogy in Legal Argument* (Cambridge University Press 2005).

to apply the norm to the facts, constitute the heavy lifting of legal reasoning; and it is the command of these skills that explains why one cannot merely pick up a code or other law book and call oneself a lawyer. These scholars also argue that the legal syllogism differs in another very important respect from the logical syllogism: in deductive reasoning, if the major and minor premises are both true, then there can be only one conclusion, and it must be true. With subsumption, on the other hand, there can be more than one conclusion, and none of them need necessarily be true. Consequently, as incisively stated by John Dewey 100 years ago, 'The trouble is that while the syllogism sets forth the *results* of thinking, it has nothing to do with the *operation* of thinking.'[40]

Those scholars who belong to what might be called the contra-deduction school of legal analysis (i.e. those scholars who describe the application of the law to the facts as inductive, analogical, abductive, or something else) are to be found, with few exceptions, in common-law jurisdictions. German and other continental scholars, while recognizing the differences from deductive logic, consistently describe the use of the legal syllogism (*Subsumtion*) as deductive.

(2) Discretion in applying the law

Later in this chapter, and in later chapters, we will see how interpreters, particularly judges, utilize arguments to justify the decisions they have reached. The reader will recall that the four clusters of arguments discussed in this book are the textual, historical, purposive, and system-contextual. The reader will also recall that, in this chapter, we have already discussed (1) making the law and (2) finding the law; and that the present topic of discussion is (3) applying the law. In this section, we consider to what extent, if any, the activity of applying the law to the facts should be described as discretionary.

The terminology 'applying the law' implies that the law will, at least some of the time, have an effect on behaviour. Is there really any doubt about this? We all experience this phenomenon in our daily lives. When we get up in the morning, we experience that our accommodation is properly heated, which means that the company that supplies our energy, whether gas or electricity, is honouring their contract with us. When we leave the house, we are not surprised when cars stop for us at zebra crossings and at red traffic signals. After all, there are traffic laws that prescribe that car drivers must stop their cars in these situations. When the post office employee affixes stamps that we have paid for onto our properly addressed envelope, we expect that the envelope will be delivered. Or consider criminal prosecutions. If a suspect is arrested because she walked out of a shop after secreting

[40] John Dewey, 'Logical Method and Law' (1924) 10 Cornell L Rev 17, 22.

a pair of expensive sunglasses, belonging to the shop, in her bag, we expect her to be charged with shoplifting, or theft, or larceny, or something similar, but not murder. The same holds true in court. If a prosecutor has charged a suspect with murder, and the judge is convinced of the suspect's guilt, the judge will not find the suspect guilty of drug smuggling or some other unrelated crime. In conclusion, the law will—at least some of the time, if not most of the time—have an effect on behaviour.

The question then becomes: how much effect does law actually have on the interpreters of the law?[41] It is important to recognize that the interpreters of the law are not a homogeneous group. Rather, they are individuals and groups of individuals who have more discretion or less discretion to interpret the law depending upon many factors.

One can think of these law interpreters as being on a spectrum of discretion. At one end of the spectrum are people working in governmental offices such as post offices, public recycling facilities, and local councils. These workers, as a group, are involved in following the law but also in the application and interpretation of the law. These interpretations are sometimes formalized into written rules and policies. At other times, these interpretations are shared with others throughout the governmental office by informal means and eventually ripen into administrative practices. For the most part, frontline interpreters like these will approach their work in a straightforward, ministerial way. They do not see themselves as interpreters. They generally do not see themselves as exercising discretion: they are merely applying the law as written and as understood in light of the administrative practice. If a new or tough question arises, they are likely to ask their colleagues or even a supervisor, who, in turn, might send the question out to a legal advisor for an opinion.

Police officers, and even parking attendants, probably see themselves individually as having somewhat more discretion than the administrative personnel described in the preceding paragraph. Is the car parked too far from the curb? Was an overtaking manoeuvre in a car dangerous enough to merit punishment? Has a verbally belligerent pub-goer who clenches her fists while talking with a policewoman committed an offence? The answers to all of these questions involve a degree of discretion.

If the belligerent woman in the last scenario were arrested, or perhaps only issued with a citation to appear in court, a person or persons in the position of a judge, perhaps in a magistrates' court, may have to decide whether the woman has committed an offence and, if so, what the penalty should be. Judges in these situations consider themselves to be constrained by the law, and properly so. But they also generally see themselves as having more discretion than the police.

[41] For an excellent overview of this topic, see Lewis A. Kornhauser, 'Three Roles for a Theory of Behavior in a Theory of Law' (2000) 31 Rechtstheorie 197.

But how much discretion do they have when applying the law to the facts? For the most part, the black-letter criminal law itself that is being applied by judges in the first instance (i.e. in the trial courts) will seem clear to experienced judges. Judges sitting in criminal courts are likely to know the law, as written and as applied according to custom and practice, very well; and if they encounter difficulties, the lawyers involved in the case (including the lawyer advising the lay 'justices of the peace' sitting in magistrates' courts) will assist the judges in determining the applicable law. Accordingly, the discretion enjoyed by the judges in trial courts, while considerable, is, in most cases, the inherent discretion in finding the facts, not in finding the law.

Much, if not most, of criminal legal practice is concerned with evaluating forensic evidence, with considering the testimony of witnesses, and with judging the motives and state of mind of the accused. This, too, involves legal reasoning for the judge must consider what is meant by the term 'intent', for example, and must scrutinize the evidence to find whether or not the accused person acted with intent or not: metaphorically, whether the factual 'shoe' story fits the 'rule' foot. This mental process of considering and scrutinizing draws on the judge's human ability to draw inferences and conclusions in order to weave these sources of information into a coherent story of what transpired, a story that is in sync with the law.

It is remarkable that many, if not most, jurisdictions include lay people (i.e. non-lawyers) in the process of finding the facts. The common-law tradition makes use of the jury in more serious criminal cases.[42] In the civil-law tradition, lay judges sit alongside professional judges in more serious criminal cases. The inference can therefore be drawn that a legal education is not considered to be necessary, perhaps even not always desirable, for the fact-finding aspect of legal reasoning.

On rare occasions, disputes such as the ones addressed in the previous paragraphs will work their way up through the appellate courts to the highest courts in the land. By the time the case arrives at this level, the facts will have long since been ascertained by the trier of fact, be it a jury, judge, or a panel of judges with or without lay judges. The intermediate appellate judges will have satisfied themselves that the finding of facts at the trial court level—the story, so to speak—is supported by the evidence adduced and considered. At the level of the highest courts (let us call them the supreme courts), the facts as found at the trial court level will no longer be open to dispute. However, the interpretation of the facts will, indeed, still be open to dispute. This is where the facts and the norm collide most visibly.

This predicament—where the facts are stated and are not in dispute—describes a great number of civil cases, perhaps most of them. In the common-law world, where over 90 per cent of civil cases settle before trial, those cases that do go to trial,

[42] On the issue of how often, if at all, professional judges disagree with juries, see e.g. Thomas Lundmark, 'Split Verdicts' in Scotland: A Judicial Survey' (2010) 14 Edin L Rev 225.

in the author's experience, involve either a troublesome client who does not want to settle or a troublesome set of facts that do not allow themselves to be neatly subsumed under a rule.

This predicament—where the facts are not in dispute—is where we find the judges with the most legal (as opposed to fact-finding) discretion. And this is where we find the judges who have enjoyed the most public and academic scrutiny. With few exceptions, it is only these appellate judges, not the trial court judges, who are revered in some quarters and ridiculed in others. These are the judges whose decisions are criticized by some for being too political and by others for not paying heed to current affairs. These are the judges who write the longest judgments, also called opinions. With few exceptions, these are the judges whose judgments are parsed and systematized in this book.

The reader will recall that, in this chapter, we are still discussing the topic (C) Applying the law. We concluded above that law must, to some extent, influence the decisions of judges. Indeed, for the vast majority of judges, those who grind away at the lowest levels of the judiciary, the influence of the law, as enacted by the legislatures and as interpreted by the appellate courts, is observably powerful. These judges are not ordinarily called upon to interpret rules in a new way in order to resolve the controversy before them. After having determined the facts, they are, for the most part, content with applying the law as they and their colleagues have been doing for years. This is done in a textual, deductive manner that employs rules consisting of statements of law from statutes and from the appellate judicial pronouncements construing statutory law and common law, that is, judge-made law. If confronted with an unusual set of facts or a novel legal argument, the judges will, of course, resolve the case to the best of their ability; but they will seldom have the time or resources to research and expound upon statutory and case law, not to mention the various permutations and nuances that accompany authoritative resolution. With few exceptions, such matters can only be considered in a rigorous manner at the appellate level.

How, then, do appellate judges in particular resolve such matters? This question will be addressed in the next section.

(3) Intuition ('hunches' and 'lurches') in applying the law

In 1967, the English rock band Procol Harum recorded 'A Whiter Shade of Pale', a chart-topping song that is still widely played. People remember the song by its mystifying lyrics and its prolonged baroque organ improvisation inspired by J.S. Bach. The organist, Matthew Fisher, who was not credited at the time for his co-authorship, filed suit, in 2005 in England, against his former band mates, claiming co-authorship and royalties from the song, which had already sold 10 million copies.

The High Court judge ruled that Fisher had co-written the song and that he was consequently entitled to royalties. The Court of Appeal upheld the ruling on co-authorship but held that Fisher's claim for royalties was time-barred.[43]

On appeal to the House of Lords, the five law lords who heard the case struck a compromise. They held that, while Fischer was, indeed, entitled to royalties, he could only recover for royalties that have accrued after he filed his claim.[44]

In joining the unanimous ruling, Baroness Hale wrote: 'As one of those people who do remember the '60s, I am glad that the author of that memorable organ part has at last achieved the recognition he deserves.' In this sentence, Baroness Hale is candidly laying bare the process by which judges decide cases: upon reading the facts, they get a sense of how they think the case should be decided; then they proceed to examine whether the law, including the court's precedents, would allow them to decide in that manner.[45]

Bennion writes that there are 'a thousand and one interpretative criteria ... that the interpreter must figuratively weigh and balance' before reaching a decision.[46] Lord Wilberforce would agree: 'I still think that the interpretation of legislation is ... a multi-faceted thing, calling for many varied talents; not a subject which can be confined in rules.'[47] What Bennion and Wilberforce are talking about is the process of applying the rule (here, a statute) to various factual situations. And both Bennion and Wilberforce are objecting to the dogmatic rules or canons of interpretation taught at law school, at least insofar as these rules and cannons are sometimes understood to straightjacket the judge's scrutiny, empathy, imagination, and sense of justice; in short, to reduce judging to a mechanical, computer-like exercise, which it is not.[48]

How, then, do judges reach decisions on disputed matters of law? At a conference at the University of Münster, a retired president of the Supreme Court of Justice of Austria discussed how she and the other appellate judges went about reaching their decisions. She explained that, upon reading the facts, she would get a sense of how she thought the case should be decided, and then she would proceed to examine whether the law, including the court's precedents, would allow her to decide in that manner. In a nutshell, her approach is identical to that of Baroness Hale and other judges. Justice Holmes of the United States Supreme Court wrote

[43] *Fisher v. Brooker et al.* [2008] EWCA (Civ.) 287.

[44] *Fisher v. Brooker et al.* [2009] UKHL 41.

[45] On the role played by oral argument in this process, see Brian Sheppard and Andrew Moshirnia, 'For the Sake of Argument: A Behavioral Analysis of Whether and How Legal Argument Matters in Decision-Making' (2013) 40 Fla St U L Rev 537.

[46] Francis A.R. Bennion, *Statutory Interpretation* (Butterworths 1984) xxviii, cited and reviewed in John Bell, 'Bennion's Statutory Interpretation' (1986) 6 OJLS 288, 292.

[47] Lord Wilberforce, HL Debates, vol. 418, col. 73 (9 March 1981), cited in William Twining and David Miers, *How to Do Things With Rules* (4th edn, Butterworths 1999) 261. Lord Wilberforce, HL Deb 09 March 1981, vol. 418, cols 73, cited in Twining and Miers, *How to Do Things with Rules*.

[48] See Robert A. Samek, 'Language, Communication, Computers and the Law' (1985) 9 Dalhousie LJ 196.

something similar over 100 years ago: 'General propositions do not decide concrete cases. The decision will depend on a judgment or intuition more subtle than any articulate major premise.'[49] Lord Denning and his successor as Master of the Rolls, Lord Donaldson, decided 'intuitively what should be the outcome of a case, and then [went] on to analyse the law in such a way as to justify [their] intuitive decision'.[50] Judge Joseph C. Hutcheson, Jr described the same judicial intuition as 'hunches'.[51]

Maurer[52] utilizes psychological terminology[53] to describe legal reasoning in much the same way as the judges above just described. In doing so, he distinguishes Type 1 (intuitive) thought processes from Type 2 (logical) thought processes. Intuitive thinking (Type 1), which is unconscious, is necessary to recognize patterns and to exercise judgement. Maurer perceives intuitive thinking in the drafting of legal documents (legislation, contracts, and judicial opinions), which reduces 'massive amounts of life experience to Type 1 insights'. Having searched for, and found, the appropriate pattern (referred to in this book as the *Normsuche*), the judge can use the pattern in a logical (Type 2) process of applying the pattern (the rule) to the facts.

While it is true that a judge's political leanings do not necessarily colour his or her hunches in every case that the judge hears, it is no less true that political leanings might, and sometimes do, colour judges' hunches. This is a topic explored in Chapter 3 on political judging. It will be seen, most obviously in the chapter on system-contextual arguments (Chapter 8), that judges sometimes announce major changes to the existing legal order, a phenomenon referred to in this book as 'lurches'.

Many judges and academics defend judicial law-making, whether it be in the course of statutory interpretation or of pronouncements of the common law, by praising and encouraging what they refer to as an incremental approach. And this is undoubtedly how most appellate judges around the world would describe their attitude, an attitude that reflects respect for separation of powers. A good example

[49] *Lochner v. New York*, 198 U.S. 45, 76 (1905) (Holmes J. dissenting).

[50] John Donaldson, *Judicial Techniques in Arbitration and Litigation* (International Arbitration Centre 1987), quoted in Garry Williams, 'How Judges Decide Cases—Reading, Writing and Analysing Judgments, 2nd Edition' (31 August 2018) 921 Law Talk NZ Law Society. See generally Chris Guthrie, Jeffrey J. Rachlinski, and Andrew J. Wistrich, 'Blinking on the Bench: How Judges Decide Cases' (2007) Cornell Law Faculty Publications. Paper 917 <http://scholarship.law.cornell.edu/facpub/917> accessed 22 November 2023 and Andrew Goodman, *How Judges Decide Cases: Reading and Writing Judgments* (Universal Law Publishing Company Pvt Limited 2005).

[51] Joseph C. Hutcheson, Jr, 'The Judgment Intuitive: The Function of the "Hunch" in Judicial Decision', 14 Cornell L Q 274 (1929). See generally Chad M. Oldfather, 'Aesthetic Judging' (2018) 52 UCD L Rev 981, 1066; Guthrie *et al.*, 'Blinking on the Bench', 1–44.

[52] Stephen M. Maurer, 'Beauty Is Truth and Truth Beauty: How Intuitive Insights Shape Legal Reasoning and the Rule of Law' (2018) 42 Seattle U L Rev 129. See also Max Radin, *Law as Logic and Experience* (Yale University Press 1940).

[53] See Daniel Kahneman, *Thinking, Fast and Slow* (Farrar, Straus and Giroux 2011).

of this attitude can be seen in the following quotation from Beverly McLachlin, former Chief Justice of Canada:

> Over time, the law in any given area may change; but the process of change is a slow and incremental one based on the mechanism of extending an existing principle to new circumstances. [and] major revisions of the law are best left to the legislature.[54]

While there are many other books and articles on the subject of how judges reach their decisions generally, and on intuition specifically, the few examples just supplied serve to show that judicial decision-making is a complex, personal, and poorly understood subject. However, that is not the primary focus of this book, which is on how judges and others justify their decisions once they have been made. This topic is briefly introduced in the following section of this chapter.

E. Justifying the result

As discussed in section D on applying the law, the vast majority of judges in the vast majority of cases apply rules according to their text and their accepted interpretation. Notice that we are talking here about 'rules', a term that includes statutory and common-law rules. And the term also includes judicial 'glosses' on statutes, which are discussed above.[55]

According to Maurer, discussed in section D,

> [S]cientific intuitions converge because there is only one physical world. We cannot know whether there is some similarly uniquely best way to write legal documents. But if there is, there cannot be many, and we should expect practitioners to converge on similar lessons in any society where 'lawyering' is a discernible activity. In the modem world this arguably includes every nation on earth.[56]

[54] *Watkins v. Olafson*, 2 S.C.R. at 760–761 (1989), discussed in Allan C. Hutchinson, *Toward an Informal Account of Legal Interpretation* (Cambridge University Press 2016) 76 *et seq*. On the feasibility and advisability of judicial incrementalism and the role of constitutional courts, particularly of the United States Supreme Court, see e.g. Cass R. Sunstein, *Constitutional Personae: Heroes, Soldiers, Minimalists, and Mutes (Inalienable Rights)* (Oxford University Press 2015) discussing 'minimalists'; Mila Sohoni, 'The Major Questions Quartet: Comment on Alabama Ass'n of Realtors, National Federation of Independent Business, Biden v. Missouri, and West Virginia v. EPA' (2022) 136 Harv L Rev 26; Kristine E. Hickman, 'The Roberts Court's Structural Incrementalism' (2022) 136 Harv L Rev F 75. For an interesting comparison, see Ermek B. Abdrasulov and Aizhan E. Abdrasulova, 'Application of Methods for Interpretation and Analogy of Law in Court's Activities and the Constitutional Control Body in the Republic of Kazakhstan' (2020) 11 Vestnik Saint Petersburg U L 447.

[55] Glosses on statutes are discussed at n 11.

[56] Maurer, 'Beauty Is Truth and Truth Beauty', 147.

Scholars have always been interested in how to improve their understanding of important texts. Interpretative or hermeneutic writings have been found from Roman, Ancient Greek, and even from Mesopotamian times, where there are texts interpreting the Code of Hammurabi. Scholars in more recent centuries have written enumerable commentaries on sacred texts, such as the Hebrew *Bible*, the *Quran*, and the Christian *Bible*, to name only a few. These secular and religious commentaries employ, consciously or unconsciously, various methods of interpretation, for example, to try to understand as closely as possible what the authors of the texts meant, to use the texts as a window through which to view society in earlier times, to search for symbolism (allegories), to seek moral guidance, to divine the will of a higher power, or to divine hidden knowledge such as might enable one to predict the future.

While the interpretive goals of religious commentators are not all readily transferable to modern legal realms, legal commentators have also identified and classified in various ways the various types of arguments and materials that are used to justify judgments that are based on statutory or constitutional law. Some of these classifications or types of arguments are discussed in the next section.

(1) Sources and types of legal argument

Some legal commentators examine the sources of the arguments that judges rely on to support their decisions, that is, to make their decisions more plausible. One academic breaks down these arguments into four source types: interpretive authorities; founding documents; respected jurists; and respected non-jurists, such as philosophers, scholars, and Constitutional Founders.[57] Another academic identifies six sources of authority employed by the United States Supreme Court when construing statutes: legislative, executive, judicial, constitutional, canons of interpretations, and other.[58] Still another academic classifies the arguments used to justify judgments into five types: the proverbial, prescriptive, principal, pragmatic, and pronormless.[59] The classifications just mentioned seem to be geared towards countries with constitutional courts or else appear to be idiosyncratic. If one is looking for universals (Maurer's convergence on similar lessons), one is not likely to find them here.

Rather than classifying arguments according to their source, as seen in the preceding paragraph, the vast majority of authors in the common-law world

57 Robert J. Hume, 'The Use of Rhetorical Sources by the U.S. Supreme Court' (2006) 40 Law & Soc'y Rev 817.

58 Nicholas S. Zeppos, 'Use of Authority in Statutory Interpretation: An Empirical Analysis' (1992) 70 Tex L Rev 1073, 1089.

59 Anthony R. Blackshield, 'Five Types of Judicial Decision' (1974) 12 Osgoode Hall L J 539. According to Blackshield, 'pronormless' means 'shaped by an *aspiration* to total normlessness': ibid 556.

traditionally recognize three, four, or five basic categories of legal argument employed in the interpretation of statutes. These categories are based on the type of argument employed, not on the source of the argument. One academic employs the categories textualism, originalism (comprising intentionalism and purposivism), and dynamism.[60] Still another divides arguments into textualism, intentionalism, and purposivism.[61] Yet another employs the categories text, intent, precedent, tradition, and policy.[62] And still another identifies textualism, legislative intent, interpretative canons, and pragmatism as what he calls the leading methods and theories of statutory interpretation.[63] James Holland and Julian Webb, in their best-selling *Learning Legal Rules: A Students' Guide to Legal Method and Reasoning*, identify four 'so-called rules of interpretation' that are traditionally taught and employed in England and Wales: the literal, golden, purposive, and mischief rules.[64] There are also many more or less minor variations and articulations of these categories.

The examples in the preceding paragraph are from common-law jurisdictions. What can we learn from Continental Europe, specifically from Germany?

(2) The Savigny canons

The discussion to this point brings us to Savigny's quadripartite theory (*Viererkanonlehre*) of interpretation, which is found in his seminal work *System of the Modern Roman Law* (*System des heutigen römischen Rechts*), published between 1840 and 1848. Savigny's theory of interpretation and its four categories form the basis of the approach employed in this book as well as constitute the starting point of virtually all of the methodological discussions in Germany and in much of the rest of the civil-law world today.

Savigny views statutory interpretation as reconstruction of the 'thought' that dwells within the statute. He sees the interpreter as the agent of the legislature. He writes that, in interpreting the law, one must 'imagine that one changes places with the legislator and artificially repeats the legislator's activity, in other words, allow the statute to arise anew in thought'.[65] This sounds very much like 'channelling' the spirits of departed parliamentarians, but it should not be understood in this sense.

[60] Karen Gebbia-Pinetti, 'Statutory Interpretation, Democratic Legitimacy and Legal-System Values' (1997) 21 Seton Hall Legis J 233, 267.

[61] Paul Brest, 'The Misconceived Quest for Original Understanding' (1980) 60 B U L Rev 204.

[62] Wilson R. Huhn, *The Five Types of Legal Argument* (2nd edn, Carolina Academic Press 2008). Notice that the category 'precedent' relies on the source of the argument, not its type.

[63] Frank B. Cross, *The Theory and Practice of Statutory Interpretation* (Stanford University Press 2008) ix.

[64] James Holland and Julian Webb, *Learning Legal Rules: A Students' Guide to Legal Method and Reasoning* (Oxford University Press 2022) 270.

[65] Carl Friedrich von Savigny, *System des heutigen Römischen Rechts*, vol. I (Veit 1840) 213. Savigny adds a footnote to the word 'thought':

Rather, the process described by Savigny means that the interpreter should ask, 'What would the legislator do if confronted with this question?'

Savigny describes legal interpretation as having four categories, which he terms 'elements'.[66] These elements correspond roughly to the textual, historical, purposive, and system-contextual categories of argument presented in this book and are discussed in that order in this book for sake of consistency and ease of understanding, even though Savigny presents them in a different order.

(i) The grammatical element (textual arguments)

Textual arguments are termed the 'grammatical' element by Savigny. This technique of argumentation is also known in Germany as philological interpretation. Blackstone called it simply construing statutes 'by the words'. Grammatical interpretation focuses on the text of the statutory norms and analyses the linguistic usages employed by the legislator. Savigny writes that grammatical interpretation must consider 'the word that transfers the thought of the legislator into our thought. [It] consists of an exposition of the phraseology employed by the legislator.'

(ii) The historical element (historical arguments)

Historical interpretation, according to Savigny, looks to the historical circumstances in existence when the statute was enacted, in particular, what the members of the legislature had in mind. This mode of interpretation might entail consideration of legislative materials. A number of German academics refer to this approach as the 'subjective method' because the interpreter is attempting to ascertain what the legislators at the time of enactment subjectively meant to accomplish.[67]

(iii) The logical element (purposive arguments)

Savigny calls this category the logical element. Unfortunately, he does not provide a comprehensive definition of this element, forcing readers to 'connect the dots'. As a consequence, academics disagree about what Savigny actually meant.[68] We can be sure, however, of one thing: Savigny's logical element must denote a process of

I use the word THOUGHT because I find it express [*sic.*] in the most definite manner the intellectual import of the law. Others use, not less properly, the expression SENSE. On the other hand, OBJECT is to be avoided, because it is ambiguous since it may also have reference to the aim of the law lying outside its contents upon which the law will have an influence. The Romans use interchangeably the expressions *mens* and *sententia*. *System of the Modern Roman Law*, vol. I (transl. William Holloway, Veit 1867) 172–173.

[66] Savigny, *System des heutigen Römischen Rechts*, vol. 1, §33 at 213 *et seq*.

[67] Philipp Heck, *Interessenjurisprudenz* (Mohr 1933) 19 *et seq.*; Philipp Heck, *Die Interessenjurisprudenz und ihre neuen Gegner* (Mohr 1936); Johann Braun, *Einführung in die Rechtsphilosophie: Der Gedanke des Rechts* (Mohr Siebeck 2006) 199.

[68] Some claim, for example, that Savigny employs the teleological method as we know it today, which also integrates the objective purposes of the regulation into the overall interpretation. See Karl Larenz and Claus-Wilhelm Canaris, *Methodenlehre der Rechtswissenschaft* (3rd edn, Springer 1995) 153 *et seq*.

reasoning that is not textual, historical, or systematic, the last of which is discussed in section E(2)(iv). Indeed, Savigny even writes that textual and logical interpretation are 'opposed to and exclusive of one another'.[69] According to Savigny, logical interpretation is so dissimilar and antithetical to textual interpretation that he exhorts interpreters that the logical element should be 'kept under control' and permitted only in 'exceptional' cases. Why? Because this mode of interpretation 'takes no small liberties'.[70] What are these liberties that Savigny is talking about? He is talking about taking liberties with the text. And taking liberties with the text was seen by Savigny as intruding upon the prerogative of the prince.

During the European Enlightenment (1715–1789), there was widespread agreement among monarchs and other persons in power that the discretion of judges should be reduced. One way of holding judges in check was to require that they apply statutes strictly, according to the text. In the oft cited words of Montesquieu (1689–1755), judges should be the 'mouth that pronounces the words of the law'.[71] Extensive statutory interpretation was seen as legislative, not judicial, activity. A number of German states, including Prussia, even enacted statutes requiring that judges either adhere to the wording of statutes or, if they declined to do so, refer the case to the government for resolution. This is the world Savigny (1779–1861) inherited.

Against this background, Savigny's reticence in embracing interpretation that does violence to the text, either by extending or reducing it, is understandable. Nevertheless, Savigny does refer to using both the 'grounds' and *ratio juris* (i.e. policies or purposes) behind the text to extend and restrict the scope of the text. And he also mentions the possibility of using these grounds to draw analogies. Contrary to Savigny's canons, the author of this book includes analogies within the category of what is here termed system-contextual argument.

(iv) The systematic element (system-contextual arguments)

Savigny's 'systematic element', which is encompassed by the category of system-contextual argument as discussed in this book, 'is concerned with the innate connexion in which all the institutions and rules of law are bound up into a great unity'.[72] Savigny posits that this 'great unity' was in the 'eye of the legislator' and, consequently, that systematic interpretation, when joined by grammatical and

[69] Savigny, *System of the Modern Roman Law*, vol. I, 259.

[70] Ibid 259–260.

> The grammatical is to proceed merely according to the meaning of the words, the logical merely according to the intention or ground of the law: the grammatical is as a rule to prevail, the logical only to be exceptionally permitted. In this contrast the only thing clearly conceived and generally admitted, is that logical interpretation is such as takes no small liberties, and such as must therefore be kept under control: moreover the most heterogeneous matters are collected under this expression.

[71] Baron de Montesquieu, *The Spirit of the Laws* (transl. Thomas Nugent, D. Appleton 1900 [1748]).

[72] Savigny, *System of the Modern Roman Law*, vol. I, 172–173.

historical interpretation, will enable the interpreter to 'completely understand' the legislator's thought.

This technique of argument means more than that the interpreter should try to define words consistently; it means that the interpretation chosen should be the one that is most consistent with the entire legal system. Interpreters today, with digital databases at their disposal, will find it easier than lawyers in Savigny's time to take into account how their interpretation of a particular term, rule, or institution relates to other terms, rules, and institutions.

But is this all that Savigny means by his 'systematical element', that interpreters should seek consistency? If so, then this element deserves the epithet 'rather questionable' conferred on it by Edwin Charles Clark.[73] Or perhaps it suffices to describe Savigny's systematic element as 'vague and ambiguous', as another commentator has suggested.[74]

It might be argued that, because interpretations and arguments seeking consistency or coherence[75] in interpretation can readily be characterized as textual in the sense that they can all be reduced to text, the category of systematic interpretation is unnecessary. However, the mechanisms to ensure consistency and coherence were much weaker in Savigny's day. Not only were there no databases, but also previous decisions were hard to find, and publications by academics, judges, and practitioners were few and far between.

It might shed light on Savigny's thinking to remember that he considered law, in its essence, to be a living organism—a 'body of law'—and that the organism of the law must be allowed to develop naturally. This is why he argued that if and when civil law should be codified in Germany, the norms should not be drafted too narrowly lest they stunt the growth of the law. Following this line of thinking, Savigny could not have been concerned with a merely mechanical consistency of the law for machines are not living organisms. He must have been concerned with what we would today call the context of the law within not only the legal system but also within society at large as the legal system matures along with society.

Before leaving Savigny, we should note that Savigny counsels against using his four elements 'according to taste and pleasure'. These four elements 'must be united if the interpretation is to succeed'. He continues,

[73] Edwin Charles Clark, *Practical Jurisprudence, a Comment on Austin* (Bibliolife 2009) 233. For further exposition of systematization, see Lourens du Plessis, 'The (Re-) Systematization of the Canons of and Aids to Statutory Interpretation' (2005) 122 S African LJ 591, 603 et seq.

[74] See Erhard F. Oeser, *Evolution and Constitution: The Evolutionary Selfconstruction of* Law (Springer 2003) 187. According to Adomeit and Hähnchen, even if von Savigny designated this method systematic, he was nevertheless thinking of the teleological method: Klaus Adomeit and Susanne Hähnchen, *Rechtstheorie für Studenten* (5th edn, C.F. Müller in Hüthig Jehle Rehm 2008) mn. 66.

[75] See e.g. Aleksander Peczenik, *A Coherence Theory of Juristic Knowledge, On Coherence Theory* (Aulis Aarnio ed., Juristförlaget 1998) 7; Amalia Amaya, 'Legal Justification by Optimal Coherence' (2011) 24(3) Ratio Juris 304; Leonor Moral Soriano, 'A Modest Notion of Coherence in Legal Reasoning: A Model for the European Court of Justice' (2003) 16(3) Ratio Juris 296.

> The success of every interpretation is dependent upon two conditions in which the four elements may be shortly summed up: first that we have present to us in a life-like manner, the intellectual activity from which the expression lying before us has sprung. Secondly that we have in adequate readiness the intuition of the historio-dogmatic whole, from which this individual can alone receive light, so as immediately to perceive the relations of that whole, to the text lying before us.[76]

This quotation from Savigny foretells the opinions of scholars, discussed elsewhere, who, for various reasons, advocate one style of interpretation ('elements' in Savigny's parlance) over another. That is not the opinion of the author of this book.

F. Summary

This chapter began with defining three categories of law for purposes of this book: statute law (including subsidiary legislation, such as regulations); law called 'glosses' that are announced by judges when concretizing (amending) statutes; and judge-made law in the absence of a statute.

When discussing statute law, it was seen that the process of enacting statutes involves legal reasoning in a broader sense in that the process requires the consideration of legal issues, such as the purpose of the proposed legislation, the appropriateness of the means chosen to serve those purposes, the authority to enact the chosen means, and consideration of conflicts with other laws, including constitutional law or other supreme law.

When discussing law made by judges on the basis of statutes, and judge-made law in the absence of a statute, we saw that judges, who have less access to relevant information and enjoy less democratic legitimacy that legislators, must consider not only the same legal issues as legislatures but also one additional issue: separation of powers.

The discussion on finding the law called attention to the fact that the process of finding both statute law and case law entails the recognition of rules and of insights drawn from the factual scenarios (i.e. the stories) enshrined in the rules that might conceivably be applied. In this way, at least, finding the law also involves legal reasoning.

The discussion of applying the law begins with the legal syllogism, which might mislead people into believing that applying the law is a more or less mechanical, deductive process. As the examples in the text illustrate, even if rules are, indeed, applied using a deductive format, reaching a result often involves a great deal of discretion. Judges admit that they employ intuition or 'hunches' to arrive at the

[76] Savigny, *System of the Modern Roman Law*, vol. I, 173–174.

result that they consider to be correct and just. What follows these hunches are more or less convincing attempts by judges to shoehorn the results of their hunches into the rule. This sometimes requires art or sometimes artifice and a great deal of effort. This process is described here as the heavy lifting of legal reasoning.

What then follows is the justification of the result that the judge has reached. Justifying the result is an act of practiced artistic expression. It calls upon the judge's training, experience, and ingenuity to tell a story—or spin a yarn—that convinces others that the result is rooted in law and not in whim, caprice, or some other unsightly or prohibited motive. According to Savigny, these stories—he referred to them as 'elements'—fit into four groups. Savigny did not develop his elements in any detail, and he described them somewhat differently from how they are employed in this book. That being said, the categories into which justificatory arguments are organized in this book substantially correspond to Savigny's elements.

3
Political Judging

A. Introduction

Political judging, also sometimes conflated with judicial activism, has many critics. It is a topic that prompts innumerable newspaper, television, and online editorials and pontifications. The topic has also spawned a great deal of academic debate, some of which is discussed in this chapter.

The purposes of the chapter are twofold: first, to understand what critics mean by the term 'political judging' and why they disapprove of it; second, to explore what role political judging plays in legal reasoning. The discussions in this chapter on various definitions or themes of what is meant by political judging are brief: they are not examined exhaustively. Further, there are numerous other definitions that are not reviewed at all because they are, in essence, variations on the themes here presented.

Up to this point in the book, the word 'political' has been mentioned only occasionally. One such occasion was a reference to political science. Political science is a field of knowledge that concerns itself with the state, with governance, and with power relations.[1] All judicial activity occurs within a system of governance, and it all involves power relations broadly defined. Consequently, if the word 'political' in the term 'political judging' were employed in this sense, the word 'political' would be redundant for all judging would be political. Let us therefore consider other potential definitions of the term 'political judging'.

The sections below summarize and critique various criticisms of political judging gathered under five themes: B. 'Judicial law-making as political judging', C. 'Fact-finding and "hunches" as political judging', D. 'Judicial "lurches" as political judging', E. 'Judicial overruling as political judging', and F. \Ideological bias as political judging'.

It may be prudent, at this point, to remind the reader that no claim is made in this book that any source of inspiration for making or identifying norms is superior to any other source or that any reason for making, or interpreting, a legal norm (including political or other bias) is intrinsically superior to any other.

[1] It also analyses decision-making processes, the working of institutions, the allocation of resources, and the inter-relations and intra-relations between institutions and countries: Raphael Cohen-Almagor email to the author, 29 December 2020.

Universals of Legal Reasoning by Judges. Thomas Lundmark, Oxford University Press.
DOI: 10.1093/oso/9780198785675.003.0003

B. Judicial law-making as political judging

In Chapter 2, the word 'political' was employed in juxtaposing the thinking and activities of members of the UK Parliament and other legislatures, who are expected to think and act politically, with the thinking and activities of judges, who, according to many critics, are not supposed to act politically. We found that, in many instances, judges must, and do, legislate, such as when they are developing the common law or are putting a gloss on a statute. These instances were labelled in this book as examples of 'judicial legislating' and 'judicial law-making'. If one wanted to, one could label all such activity 'political' because all of this activity is value-laden and could be undertaken by legislative bodies in the first instance.

Equating putting a gloss on statutes and pronouncing common law rules with political activity would, in effect, mean that a substantial portion of the activity of appellate judges—perhaps most of their activity—would be political.

Reviewing the cases that have been discussed so far in this book, the following judicial rulings would be considered political using this definition:

- an owner of a licensed tavern who serves alcoholic beverages to an obviously intoxicated patron is negligent;
- in case of an injury caused by a product, the burden of proof shall be shifted to the producer to prove that the product was not defective;
- a landlord may only refuse an application for a new lease by the tenant if the landlord has a bona fide intention to occupy the holding for the purposes of a business coupled with a real possibility of starting the business;
- one may demand compensation for slander, libel, or other nonpecuniary injury to one's reputation (*Ehrverletzung*);
- there is no common-law tort of harassment;
- there is a duty to act honestly in the performance of contractual obligations;
- if the only reason for a vendor's failure to perform a contract for the sale of land, or an interest in land, was his or her inability, through no fault of her own, to provide good title, then the vendee may only recover his or her expenses.

All of these judicial rulings were accepted as statements of the law within the jurisdictions of the appellate courts that pronounced them, so they should arguably be included within the definition of political judging in the sense of law-making. In one of the above rulings (there is no common-law tort of harassment), the appellate court refused to recognize a new tort of harassment. In other words, the court refused to redefine or change the law. Should this ruling be excluded from the list of 'political' (employing the definition of 'political' above) pronouncements of common-law rules? Why? Because it is conservative in the sense of not changing the law? But acting conservatively in this sense is also value-laden. Yet, if changing the law is considered to be political, then the ruling concerning the limitation of damages for non-performance of a contract for the sale of land would necessarily be political because it did change the law. So, too, the ruling that limits the right of a landowner to refuse an application for a new lease and the other rulings listed above.

In conclusion, labelling judicial pronouncements on the common law and on statute law as political activity is accurate in the sense that such pronouncements are value-laden and, as such, legislative in nature.

C. Fact-finding and 'hunches' as political judging

In section B, it was concluded that equating the term 'political judging' with judicial law-making would mean that putting glosses on statutes and pronouncing common-law rules would consist of political activity because they are value-laden. This is, indeed, a very broad definition and probably not the one that most critics of political judging would employ. But as broad as this definition is, it is also narrow because it excludes judicial activity that can also sometimes be criticized for being political, in particular fact-finding.

Consider a judge who imposes tougher sentences on offenders whose motives or crimes he particularly dislikes. Or who imposes a lenient sentence on an offender whom the judge admires or identifies with.[2] The judge's bias may even be unconscious, such as a bias against a racial or ethnic group or against the ideology of communists or Neo-Nazis.[3] These conscious and unconscious biases, political and other, can influence fact-finding and the balancing of interests necessary to decide whether an action or result is, for example, fair, reasonable, or in the best interests of the child in a family-law dispute.[4]

These unconscious biases can also colour judicial 'hunches'. As described in Chapter 2, judicial hunches are the intuitions that judges sense when they set about deciding a case. These hunches are primarily a product of judges' training and experience.[5] Judges might describe these hunches as an exercise in judgment: they

[2] See e.g. Liam Stack, 'Light Sentence for Brock Turner in Stanford Rape Case Draws Outrage' *New York Times* (6 June 2016).

[3] See Dan Kahan, David A. Hoffman, and Donald Braman, 'Whose Eyes Are You Going to Believe? Scott v. Harris and the Perils of Cognitive Illiberalism' (2009) 122 Harv L Rev 837.

[4] On the role of emotions in this process, see Adam Smith, *The Theory of Moral Sentiments* (A. Millar 1761); Neil MacCormick, 'Particulars and Universals' in Zenon Bankowski and James MacLean (eds), *The Universal and the Particular in Legal Reasoning* (Aberdeen University Press 2006) 3; Thomas Lundmark, 'Die Rolle von Emotionen in juristischen Entscheidungsprozessen' (2018) 49 Rechtstheorie 243.

[5] See generally Max Radin, *Law as Logic and Experience* (Yale University Press, 1940) and Max Radin, 'Theory of Judicial Decision' (1925) 2 Am BAJ 359. See also Gary Klein, *Intuition At Work: Why Developing Your Gut Instincts Will Make You Better at What You Do* (Doubleday Business 2002); Jack Katz, *How Emotions Work* (University of Chicago Press 1999).

get a sense of how the case should be judged. Llewellyn writes, 'Good hunching power is a resultant of good sense, imagination, and *much* knowledge. The *more* knowledge of what courts have done, the more skilful the hunch.'[6]

But there is more to hunches than merely training, experience, and knowledge of the law and of precedents. Indeed, people with a great deal of experience do not necessarily have more accurate intuition.[7] In addition, hunches draw on associations, even unconscious associations. And hunches—and what we call logical reasoning—are sparked and influenced by emotions.[8]

Judge Joseph C. Hutcheson Jr was a very enthusiastic exponent of judicial hunches.[9] In his 1929 article 'Judgment Intuitive: The Function of the Hunch in Judicial Decision', Hutcheson wrote,

> [W]hen the case is difficult or involved, and turns upon a hairsbreadth of law or of fact, ... I, after canvassing all the available material at my command, and duly cogitating upon it, give my imagination play, and brooding over the cause, wait for the feeling, the hunch—that intuitive flash of understanding which makes the jump-spark connection between question and decision, and at the point where the path is darkest for the judicial feet, sheds its light along the way.

While Hutcheson's colourful description of hunches may well be accurate as far as it goes, one should notice that his description does not mention the role played in hunching by predilections and prejudices, including those of a political (i.e. value-laden) nature. Of course, that was not the topic of Hutcheson's article. Critically, however, these hunches—and the biases and other factors that inform them—are almost invariably omitted from the decisions that the judges announce. Hutcheson was well aware of this. He wrote that the process used to decide a case—'the judgment or decision, the solution itself'—is not revealed in the judge's 'reasoned' ruling. Here, Hutcheson is employing the word 'reasoned' in the sense of giving reasons: Hutcheson candidly describes the judgment or decision as 'the rationalization by the judge on that pronouncement' or, more memorably, 'the apologia for that decision'.[10]

This dichotomy between the motivations for the judge's decision, on the one hand, and the justifications or apologia for the decision on the other, was described by Justice Holmes in 'The Path of the Law':

[6] K.N. Llewellyn, *The Bramble Bush: On Our Law and Its Study* (Oceana Publications 1951) 98.

[7] Eugene Sadler-Smith, *Inside Intuition* (Routledge 2008).

[8] See generally Antonio Damasio, *Descartes' Error: Emotion, Reason and the Human Brain* (Vintage 2006); Pavel Vasilyev, 'Beyond Dispassion: Emotions and Judicial Decision-Making in Modern Europe Rechtsgeschichte—Legal History Rg 25' (2017).

[9] Joseph C. Hutcheson Jr, 'Judgment Intuitive: The Function of the Hunch in Judicial Decision' (1929)14 Cornell L Rev 274. Hutcheson also refers to the faculty of hunching as 'feeling' the correct decision.

[10] Ibid n. 10.

> The language of judicial decision is mainly the language of logic. And the logical method and form flatter that longing for certainty and for repose which is in every human mind. But certainty generally is illusion and repose is not the destiny of man. Behind the logical form lies a judgment as to the relative worth and importance of competing legislative grounds, often an inarticulate and unconscious judgment, it is true, and yet the very root and nerve of the whole proceeding.[11]

To this point, in this book, we have considered very broad definitions of political judging, some so broad that they might extend to every judicial act that is in any way value-laden, even if the judge's motive or bias is unconscious. But what of more conscious judicial decision-making? What effect do the political and other conscious preferences of the judge have on legal reasoning? This topic is explored in section D.

D. Judicial 'lurches' as political judging (and judicial activism)

In Chapter 2, it was stated that judges sometimes announce major changes to the existing legal order, a phenomenon referred to in this book as 'lurches'. What changes are major? They may well be in the eye of the beholder, but they would all seem to share a perception by a wide swath of people in the legal population that a particular judicial ruling has caused a major change in the law.

The category of lurches would encompass the 'great cases' that Hutchinson discusses in *Is Eating People Wrong?: Great Legal Cases and How they Shaped the World*.[12] According to Hutchinson, 'What counts as a great case is simply whatever people agree to designate as a great case.' Hutchinson's great cases include *Hadley v. Baxendale*, which introduced limits on damages awarded for breach of contract; *Donoghue v. Stevenson*, which announced the neighbour principle in tort law; *Brown v. Board of Education*, which outlawed the racial segregation of schools in the United States; *Roncarelli v. Duplessis*, which held that administrative discretion in Canada must be exercised in good faith; *Miranda v. Arizona*, which ruled that suspects in the United States must be informed of their rights before questioning; and *Mabo v. Queensland*, which recognized native title in favour of Indigenous Australians.

All of the cases just mentioned could be styled examples of judicial activism. That being said, judicial activism is arguably even harder to define than political

[11] O.W. Holmes, 'The Path of the Law' (1897) 10 Harv L Rev 457.

[12] Allan C. Hutchinson, *Is Eating People Wrong?: Great Legal Cases and How They Shaped the World* (Cambridge University Press 2010). See generally Lord Walker of Gestingthorpe, 'How Far Should Judges Develop the Common Law?' (2014) 3 Cambridge J Int'l Comp L 124; Alan Paterson, Decision-Making in the UK's Top Court' (2014) 3 Cambridge J Int'l Comp L 77.

judging. In its broadest sense, judicial activism would encompass all concretizations and changes in the law, however small, including judicial glosses and pronouncements on the common law. Yet, often, what the law actually is on a particular point is unclear. That is why we need judges. Judges can only decide cases that are presented to them; and, when deciding these cases, they can only rule for one party or the other. Consequently, on these questions of so-called first impression, no matter how the court decides, the losing party will be entitled to criticize the result as an example of judicial activism.

Hellman defines judicial activism as 'judicial review with an outcome adverse to the result reached through the political process'.[13] Of the Hutchinson's 'great cases', *Hadley* and *Donoghue* did not involve law that had been established through the political process. They were pronouncements of common law. Consequently, they would presumably not qualify as judicial activism under this definition. *Roncarelli* held that the Premier of the Province of Quebec had acted beyond his authority (ultra vires), which meant that the outcome was arguably not 'adverse to the result reached through the political process'. Consequently, *Roncarelli* might not satisfy Hellman's definition of judicial activism. Whether *Miranda* meets this definition is arguable since the political process had not (yet?) established any law against advising suspects of their constitutional rights. On the other hand, *Mabo* would arguably meet Hellman's definition. So where are we left: *Roncarelli*, which held an action of the Premier to be ultra vires, was possibly political, but *Miranda*, which had far-reaching consequences for all questioning by the police, is not political?

Perhaps the epithet 'judicial activism' should be reserved for cases that had a direct and immediate effect on a considerable number of people. *Miranda* had a direct and immediate effect on all police departments, but the effect on the general public was much smaller. Indeed, of all the 'great cases' mentioned above, only *Brown v. Board of Education* was likely to have had such a direct and immediate effect on a large number of people. The other decisions probably had a weaker, more diffuse, effect. However, the effects of decisions in *Hadley* and *Donoghue* have been felt around the English-speaking world. So, which cases are examples of judicial activism or political judging, those with an immediate effect, those with far-reaching effect, or both?

Tamanaha identifies another theme involving politics and the courts: 'when judges step into the middle of major contested political issues of the day, issues that many people believe elected representatives should decide rather than unelected judges'.[14] This definition holds more promise than the previous definitions. Healthcare reform, same-sex marriage, campaign finance restrictions, affirmative (or 'positive') action, and environmental regulation are issues that Tamanaha identifies

[13] Arthur D. Hellman, 'Judicial Activism: The Good, the Bad, and the Ugly' (2002) 21 MC L Rev 253.

[14] Brian Z. Tamanaha, 'The Several Meanings of "Politics" in Judicial Politics Studies: Why "Ideological Influence" Is Not "Partisanship" (2012) 61 Emory LJ 759 at 15.

as 'major contested political issues of the day'. He writes, 'When the issues at stake are widely seen as a political matter, then almost by definition the decision is political.' The conclusion seems inescapable: judicial decisions that are condemned as being political, in this sense, can only be identified in the same way as those judicial decisions condemned as being activist: they are decisions that people do not like. After rehearsing the extensive literature on the topic of judicial activism,[15] one is left with the impression, shared by Justice Anthony Kennedy of the US Supreme Court and others, that 'An activist court is a court that makes a decision you don't like.'[16]

Perhaps the overturning of laws as unconstitutional is a more objective measure of the political nature of judicial decisions. This measure is objective in the sense that the instances can be readily identified, at least in countries such as Germany and the United States, where judges enjoy this power. The United States provides so many examples of legislation being ruled unconstitutional because there are so many statutes enacted by the fifty states and by the Commonwealth of Puerto Rico:[17] fifty-two jurisdictions, when one includes federal law.

Here is one example from Puerto Rico: a Puerto Rican statute authorized the police to search the luggage of passengers arriving from the mainland United Sates. Unsurprisingly, since Puerto Rico is part of the United States, this statute was held to be unconstitutional.[18] This, of course, is an example or an 'outcome adverse to the result reached through the political process'. Does this mean that all rulings of unconstitutionality constitute judicial activism?

If so, then judicial activism has a venerable and muscular history in the United States for constitutional challenges to state legislation in the United States are plentiful. The website *Justia* lists nearly 1,000 instances, going back to 1809, in which the US Supreme Court has held state laws and state constitutional provisions to be unconstitutional.[19] Some of these instances are unanimous decisions of all nine judges on the Court. And a great many of the cases appear, at least at first blush, to be uncontroversial. One such example was a provision of the Constitution of the State of Alabama that was adopted in 1901 for the purpose of racial discrimination.[20]

[15] See e.g. Christopher Wolfe, *Judicial Activism: Bulwark of Freedom or Precarious Security?* (2nd edn, Rowman & Littlefield 1997); Keenan D. Kmiec, 'The Origin and Current Meanings of "Judicial Activism"' (2004) 92 Calif L Rev 1441; Bradley C. Canon, 'Defining the Dimensions of Judicial Activism' (1983) 66 Judicature 236; David A. Strauss, 'The Death of Judicial Conservatism' (2009) 4 DJCLPP 1; Richard A. Posner, *The Federal Courts: Challenge and Reform* (Harvard University Press 1996) 314.

[16] Frederick P. Lewis, *The Context of Judicial Activism: The Endurance of the Warren Court Legacy in a Conservative Age* (Rowman & Littlefield 1999).

[17] For examples of rulings by the state courts invalidating state legislation, see Hellman, 'Judicial Activism'. See generally William J. Brennan Jr, 'State Constitutions and the Protection of Individual Rights' (1977) 90(3) Harv L Rev 489.

[18] *Torres v. Puerto Rico*, 442 U.S. 465 (1979).

[19] See <https://law.justia.com/constitution/us/state-laws-held-unconstitutional.html#:~:text=State%20or%20local%20laws%20held,operation%20of%20the%20Supremacy%20Clause> accessed 22 November 2023.

[20] *Hunter v. Underwood*, 471 U.S. 222 (1985).

Unsurprisingly, this statute was found to be unconstitutional on the basis of the 14th Amendment to the United States Constitution, which reads: 'No state shall ... deny to any person within its jurisdiction the equal protection of the laws.' Should this decision be classified as an example of judicial activism? Many other cases concern attempts by one state to gain a competitive advantage over another state or to protect state-owned businesses. This was the situation in *Deukmejian v. National Meat Association*,[21] where California imposed a tax only on out-of-state processors of beef, not on in-state processors.

Cases such as *Deukmejian v. National Meat Association* are not likely to provoke public outcries and charges that the judges are overstepping their bounds, at least not outside the jurisdictions whose legislation was ruled unconstitutional. However, a great number of declarations of unconstitutionality of state statutes have involved very contentious political issues. Take the recent case of *Obergefell v. Hodges*.[22] At issue were statutes in the states of Michigan, Kentucky, Ohio, and Tennessee that defined marriage as a union between one man and one woman. A divided Supreme Court of the United States invalidated these laws, holding that all states must allow civil marriage for same-sex couples.

When it comes to federal statutes, as opposed to state and territorial statutes, one finds comparatively few cases of Supreme Court invalidation on constitutional grounds. By far the most well-known is the 1803 decision in *Marbury v. Madison*,[23] the first case in which the Supreme Court ruled an Act of Congress to be unconstitutional. The most notorious case of unconstitutionality was the third case in which the Supreme Court invalidated an Act of Congress: *Dred Scott v. Sandford*.[24] At issue was the constitutionality of the Missouri Compromise, a federal statute that prohibited slavery within the Louisiana Territory that was owned and controlled by the federal government of the United States. In a very contentious ruling, the Supreme Court held that the Congress did not have the authority to prohibit slavery.

It is unnecessary to cite additional examples from the United States, or from other countries, to make the following point. When judges hold statutes to be unconstitutional, they are invalidating the decisions of legislators. When enacting the statute, the legislators were acting politically. Consequently, the judicial act of invalidating acts of the legislatures can be considered, at least to this extent, political in nature. Judicial, constitutional review is, therefore, anti-democratic. This is a feature that prompts some academics to oppose judicial review on constitutional grounds.[25]

[21] *Deukmejian v. National Meat Ass'n*, 469 U.S. 1100 (1985).

[22] *Obergefell v. Hodges*, 576 U.S. 644 (2015).

[23] *Marbury v. Madison*, 5 U.S. (1 Cr.) 137 (1803).

[24] *Scott v. Sandford*, 60 U.S. (19 How.) 393 (1857).

[25] Jeremy Waldron, *Law and Disagreement* (OUP 1999); Larry Alexander, *Constitutionalism: Philosophical Foundations* (Cambridge University Press 1998); Jeremy Waldron, 'A Rights-Based Critique of Constitutional Rights' (1993) 13 OJLS 18. Others are on the same warpath.

E. Judicial overruling as political judging

Some commentators, including the author of this book, have suggested that a court may be acting politically when overruling its own precedents. The author has compared the overruling practices of the German Federal Constitutional Court with the US Supreme Court. The purpose of this comparison is to provide objective evidence of the relative political-ness of these two courts.

After identifying the instances of overruling over specific time periods, the author divided the overrulings—departures from precedent—into three groups: corrective, renovative, and political. These groups are based on categories ascertained by Lewis A. Kornhauser.[26] A 'corrective' departure is one in which the earlier case was decided wrongly or, as is sometimes said, *per incuriam*. Departures that reflect changes in society are referred to as 'renovative'. Departures that cannot be explained as being corrective or renovative are styled 'political'. Political departures, for the purposes of this study, are those that are presumed to reflect the adjustments in basic values that are only felt when new judges are appointed to a court. Put another way, political departures, for the purposes of this study, are those that the judges who decided the precedential case would have disagreed with.

Applying these definitions to the instances of departures from precedent over a certain period of time, the author found that over half (58 per cent) of the departures from precedent by the German Federal Constitutional Court were political in nature, meaning that they were presumably due to the appointment of new judges to the court. The percentage for the US Supreme Court (42 per cent) was somewhat lower.

Does this mean that the German Federal Constitutional Court is more political (in this sense) than the US Supreme Court? Or would it be more accurate to compare the rate of political departures to the total number of departures? For the time periods studied, the German Federal Constitutional Court overruled at a rate of 0.63 per cent, and the US Supreme Court overruled at a rate of 1.13 per cent, almost twice as often as the German Court. This difference might suggest that the German Court is approximately half as political as the US Court. But these percentages include overrulings for corrective or renovative purposes, which are not political in the sense used here. In order to arrive at a rate of political rulings, it is necessary to

See e.g. Larry D. Kramer, *The People Themselves: Popular Constitutionalism and Judicial Review* (Oxford University Press 2004); M. Tushnet, *Taking the Constitution Away from the Courts* (Princeton University Press 2000). See critically Larry Alexander, 'What Is the Problem of Judicial Review?' (2006) 31 Aust J Legal Phil 1.

26 See Lewis A. Kornhauser, 'An Economic Perspective on Stare Decisis' (1989) 65 Chi-Kent L Rev 115. Kornhauser actually identifies four reasons for departures from previous precedents: changes in values, here called 'political' departures; changes in the world, here called 'renovative' departures; improvements in information; and improvements in imperfect decision-making, the latter two referred to here as 'corrective' departures.

multiply the rate of all overrulings (0.63 per cent and 1.13 per cent, respectively) by the rate of political overrulings (58 per cent and 42 per cent, respectively). Doing so, we find that the German Federal Constitutional Court is only slightly less likely than the US Supreme Court to engage in political overruling (0.37 per cent and 0.47 per cent, respectively). Bearing in mind that the rates of overruling, and the numbers of overruling cases, are small, and that the classification between political and non-political overrulings is inexact, it would be misleading to generalize further than to conclude, on the basis of this study, that the overruling practices of the two courts are markedly similar.

For the purposes of this comparison, it was the appointment of one or more new judges to the court that presumably caused the courts to discard precedents for reasons described as political. This usage of the adjective 'political' is arguably a broad one: the actual factors that motivated the new judges need not have been political in nature. However, the appointment of these judges did have a political effect in these few cases, and presumably in cases of first impression, where there was no need to overrule precedent because a change in the law is political in the sense of being legislative and value-laden.

F. Ideological bias as political judging

Whether judges are newly appointed, as discussed in section E, or have been on the bench for a considerable amount of time, they will, from time to time, be presented with cases of first impression.

Cases of first impression are the bread and butter of the appellate courts, making the decisions of these courts a fruitful source for the detection of evidence of the ideological leanings of various judges. And it is often the dissenting opinion that exposes these leanings. Perhaps the most well-known dissent in the jurisprudence of the US Supreme Court is that of Justice Holmes in the 1905 case of *Lochner v. New York*.[27] At issue was the constitutionality of a statute of the State of New York from the year 1895 that limited the working hours for bakery workers. The majority held that the New York statute was unconstitutional.

The justification adopted by the majority in *Lochner* was that the state law constituted 'an unreasonable, unnecessary and arbitrary interference with the right and liberty of the individual to contract in relation to labor'. We saw, in the discussion above regarding fact-finding and 'hunches', that the justification that is recorded in the court's decision is merely Hutcheson's 'apologia' or Holmes's 'logical form'. It is not necessarily, or not at all, the motivation for the decision. So, what

[27] *Lochner v. New York*, 198 U.S. 45, 75 (1905). In 1898, the Supreme Court upheld the constitutionality of a state law that limited the working hours of miners and smelters because of the inherent danger of such work: *Holden v. Hardy*, 169 U.S. 366 (1898).

was the motivation for the majority's decision in *Lochner*? Justice Holmes, who participated in the deliberations, claimed, in his short dissenting opinion, that the majority was motivated by 'an economic theory'. Tellingly, and predictably, this theory is not mentioned or even hinted at in the majority's very long decision. According to Holmes, the economic theory that motivated the majority was the strict laissez-faire philosophy advocated by Herbert Spencer in his book *Social Statics, or The Conditions Essential to Happiness Specified, and the First of Them Developed*.[28]

Whether Holmes was right or not need not concern us here. For the purposes of this discussion, the moral of the story is that judging the constitutionality of the statute at issue in *Lochner*, and the constitutionality of other statutes, is a product of many factors, such as particular economic theories or political ideologies, and that these factors are almost never revealed by the court's justifications, even if the judges are conscious of these factors.

The potential motivational factors are legion. They include concerns for the environment and climate change, respect for entrepreneurship, sympathy for minorities and the poor, preference for local and state decision-making, interest in education, disregard for religion, belief in rehabilitation, distrust of experts, admiration for creativity and invention, qualms about the reliability of eye-witness testimony, dislike of politicians, and a host of other concerns. And the motivational factors may include, or be influenced by, the personal characteristics and qualities of the judge, such as his or her compassion, arrogance, intelligence, maturity, experience, thoughtfulness, seriousness, laziness, selfishness, slyness, and inquisitiveness, to name just a few. And the judge's emotional state may also play a role.

While few of these, and other, motivational factors would ordinarily be described as ideological in the sense of belonging to a system of ideas and ideals, these motivational factors can, nevertheless, influence a judge's ideology and, in turn, how the judge will decide cases. Before emigrating to England in the 1930s, Professor Kahn-Freund[29] served as a judge on the Labour Court in Berlin. In an interview years later, Kahn-Freund recalled that the Supreme German Labour Court 'bent over backwards in all questions of individual employment to be helpful to the individual'. But the Court was 'as restrictive as possible' when it came to labour disputes. What motivated these decisions, according to Kahn-Freund, was 'the ideology of the fascist labour legislation of 1926'.[30]

[28] Herbert Spencer, *Social Statics, or The Conditions Essential to Happiness Specified, and the First of Them Developed* (John Chapman 1851).

[29] Otto Kahn-Freund, 'The Study of Labour Law—Some Recollections' (1979) 8 Indus LJ 197.

[30] See also Otto Kahn-Freund, *Das soziale Ideal des Reichsarbeitsgerichts: Eine kritische Untersuchung zur Rechtsprechung des Reichsarbeitsgerichts* (Bensheimer 1931) and Otto Kahn-Freund, 'Der Funktionswandel des Arbeitsrechts' (1932) 67 Archiv für Sozialwissenschaft und Sozialpolitik 146.

G. Summary

In trying to understand what critics of political judging mean by the term 'political judging', this chapter explored various definitions or themes of the political role of judges. Equating political judging with legislative activity, which is indisputably value-laden, would mean that all judicial glosses and statements of common law rules are legislative in nature and therefore political because they, too, are value-laden. Judicial intuition, here referred to as 'hunching', is also value-laden but generally unconscious. Fact-finding is also influenced by value-laden factors.

The 'lurches' that were discussed in this chapter are more obvious examples of value-laden judging because the changes that they make in the law are major.

The practice of judicial overruling brings the political-ness of judging into clearer focus. Some overruling is due to a perceived need to correct a precedent or to renovate the law in cases where the precedent was decided against a legal or factual background that no longer exits. However, some instances of overruling can only be explained by the ascension of a new judges to the court, resulting in political (value-laden) overruling.

Finally, this chapter discussed the issue of ideological judging. It was seen that a judge's ideology, whether conscious or unconscious, can have a substantial influence on the judge's decision-making. Critically, this influence, and the influence of other factors discussed, is seldom revealed in the rationalization of the judge's decisions, that is, in the so-called reasoning of the court.

What role does political judging play in legal reasoning? The conclusion of this brief chapter is that politics, by any definition, has at least the potential to influence almost all judicial activity, including how judges reason in all permutations of the word 'reason'.

4
Rules from Statutes and Cases

A. Introduction

The first section (B) of this chapter sketches the status of academic and judicial enquiry on the topic of the methodology of the use of rules from statutes and judicial case decisions and exposes the lack of a methodology for the use of *ratios* from statutory glosses and from common law (*Richterrecht*). Section C demonstrates how the Savigny canons of textual, historical, and purposive interpretation can be utilized to justify different solutions to a simple factual scenario. Section D illustrates the indistinguishability between judicial *ratios* and statutory rules. Section E discusses statutory analogies and section F discusses case-law analogies. The topic of analogies is discussed further in Chapter 8 (System-Contextual Argument).

B. The methodological deficit for statutory glosses and common law (*Richterrecht*)

In Germany, the methodology of statutory interpretation has been a subject of study for centuries. As noted in Chapters 1 and 2, Friedrich Carl von Savigny dealt with the ways in which a legal norm could be interpreted in the nineteenth century.[1] Savigny's interpretative canon, refined by Karl Larenz,[2] has become so widely accepted in Germany today that academic debates on statutory interpretation are largely confined to fringe issues (such as the handling of foreign, European, and international law),[3] although some academics still pose questions about the

[1] Carl Friedrich von Savigny, *System des heutigen Römischen Rechts* (Veit 1840) Bd. 1, §33, 212ff: '*Soweit ist die Auslegung der Gesetze von der Auslegung jedes anderen ausgedrückten Gedankens (wie sie z.B. in der Philologie geübt wird) nicht verschieden. Das Eigenthümliche derselben zeigt sich aber, wenn wir sie in ihre Bestandtheile zerlegen. So müssen wir in ihr Vier Elemente unterscheiden: ein grammatisches, logisches, historisches und systematisches.* For the transatlantic reception of von Savigny's work, see Edward Geoffrey de Montmorency, 'de Montmorency' in Sir John MacDonnell, Edward Manson, and Van Echten Veeder (eds), *Great Jurists of the World*, vol. 2 (Little, Brown and Company 1914) 447; Friedrich Müller and Ralph Christensen, *Juristische Methodik* (11th edn, Duncker & Humblot 2013) 128; Christian Baldus, *Europäische Methodenlehre* (Karl Riesenhuber ed., De Gruyter 2015) 31, 35.

[2] Karl Larenz, *Methodenlehre der Rechtswissenschaft* (1st edn, Springer Verlag 1960) 8; Karl Larenz and Claus Wilhelm Canaris, *Methodenlehre der Rechtswissenschaft* (3rd edn, Springer 1995) 133, 141 *et seq.*

[3] For comparative law as a potentially separate method of interpretation, see e.g. Peter Häberle, 'Grundrechtsgeltung und Grundrechtsinterpretation im Verfssungsstaat' (1989) 20 JZ 913. For comparative law interpretation in uniform international law, see Claudia Rudolf, *Einheitsrecht*

Universals of Legal Reasoning by Judges. Thomas Lundmark, Oxford University Press.
DOI: 10.1093/oso/9780198785675.003.0004

demarcation between the four interpretive methods. For example, academics ask: do the third-party effect of fundamental rights (*Drittwirkung*),[4] the application of general clauses like *Treu und Glauben*,[5] and the observance of principles of the European Human Rights Convention[6] belong to the contextual (systematic) interpretation method? Or should not the contextual (systematic) method of interpretation be merged with the purposive?[7] Or could not the contextual (systematic) be better combined with the textual interpretative method?[8]

Compared to the dense thicket of academic publications in German on the interpretation of statutes, the literature in German concerning the interpretation of judicial decisions is more or less a desert. While most German legal theorists and the German Federal Constitutional Court[9] agree that judicial decisions in the sense of *Richterrecht*[10] can constitute a proper source of law,[11] these theorists and judges have failed to develop methods of interpretation to be employed for rules

für internationale Forderungsabtretungen (Mohr Siebeck 2006) 33. On the interpretation and further training of European Union primary law, see e.g. Matthais Pechstein and Carola Drechsler, 'Die Auslegung und Fortbildung des Primärrechts' in Riesenhuber, *Europäische Methodenlehre*, 126. For a 'substantiation of EU Law' building upon one of von Savigny's canons of interpretation, see Sebastian Martens, *Methodenlehre des Unionrechts* (Mohr Siebeck 2013) 294, 331. On the interpretation of international treaties in the context of constitutional norms, see e.g. Georg Ress, Christoph Schreuer, and C.F. Müller, 'Wechselwirkungen zwischen Völkerrecht und Verfassung bei der Auslegung völkerrechtlicher Verträge' (1982) 23 BDGV 61.

[4] In the affirmative, pointing out that a classification into the teleological criterion could also be made, see Oliver Raabe, Richard Wacker, Daniel Oberle, Christian Baumann, and Christian Funk, *Recht ex machina: Formalisierung des Rechts im Internet der Dienste* (Springer 2012) 63.

[5] For example, on the ineffectiveness of the usual interpretation tools to capture the informative content of general clauses, see Sudabeh Kamanabrou, 'Die Interpretation zivilrechtlicher Generalklauseln' (2002) 202 AcP 663, 670.

[6] Affirmatively, Ilka Klöckner, *Grenzenüberschreitende Bindung an zivilgerichtliche Präjudizien* (Mohr Siebeck 2006) 76.

[7] On the overlap of the systematic and teleological method (for Swiss law), see Carl Baudenbacher, *Lauterkeitsrecht in Europa: Eine Sammlung von Länderberichten zum Recht gegen unlauteren Wettbewerb* (Martin Schmidt-Kessel and Silva Schubmehl eds, European Law Publishers 2011) 589. On the relationship and selective overlaps between systematic and teleological methods in European law, see e.g. Walter Frenz, *Handbuch Europarecht, Band 5: Wirkungen und Rechtsschutz* (5th edn, Springer 2010) paras 388, 389, 416, 417; Heike Völter, *Der Lückenschluß im Statut der Europäischen Privatgesellschaft (Rechtsfragen der Handelsgesellschaften)* (Otto Schmidt 2000) 56.

[8] Cf. e.g. Larenz and Canaris, *Methodenlehre der Rechtswissenschaft*, 142, which, in the context of determining the meaning of the word, already takes into account (among other things) the entire 'context of meaning of the law'.

[9] The Federal Constitutional Court does not consider that *Richterrecht* has the same binding quality as statute law (BVerfGE 84, 212, 227); it nonetheless recognizes the authority of the courts to 'creatively develop' (*schöpferische Rechtsfindung*) the law. Ulfrid Neumann, *Theorie der juristischen Argumentation, in Einführung in Rechtsphilosophie und Rechtstheorie der Gegenwart* (Arthur Kaufmann, Winfried Hassemer, and Ulfrid Neumann eds, 8th edn, C.F. Müller 2011) 337 n. 11.

[10] For examples of *Richterrecht* from German case law, see Hans-Bernd Schäfer, 'The Relevance of Law and Economics for the Development of Judge-Made Rules: Examples' (1996) 40 EER 989.

[11] Franz Bydlinski and Peter Bydlinski, *Grundzüge der juristischen Methodenlehre* (3rd edn, Facultas 2018) 120; Franz Bydlinski, *Juristische Methode und Rechtsbegriff* (Springer 1983), 255; Müller and Christensen, *Juristische Methodik*, 138ff; Riesenhuber, *Europäische Methodenlehre*, 138; Bernd Rüthers, Christian Fischer, and Axel Birk, *Rechtstheorie* (6th edn, C.H. Beck 2011) 149 *et seq*.

articulated in those decisions.[12] Even the book with the very promising title *The Development and Interpretation of Richterrecht* ('*Die Entwicklung und Auslegung von Richterrecht*') disappoints in this respect, as Professor Langenbucher merely employs the traditional methods of interpretation to determine the *rationes decidendi* implicit in judicial decisions but not to apply those *rationes* to factual scenarios. Similarly, Professor Picker, in his article '*Richterrecht* and Legal Doctrine' (*Richterrecht und Rechtsdogmatik*), recognizes that *Richterrecht* can, indeed, produce a 'rule' but only after the rule has been 'examined by legal experts and consequently accepted by the legal community'. How the legal community is to apply these accepted rules to factual scenarios is not discussed.

Furthermore, these publications by Picker and Langenbucher are limited, both in their titles and their content, to *Richterrecht*, which are only those judgments whose legal basis is so remote from statute law that one cannot draw an analogy to a statute, let alone employ textual, historical, or purposive arguments based on a statute. These publications consequently overlook the extremely prevalent phenomenon of judicial glosses on statutes.

Where to mark the exact boundary between *Richterrecht* ('pure' common law) and judicial decisions interpreting statute is a matter of diverging opinion in Germany. One academic would classify the law of industrial action (*Arbeitskampfrecht*), for example, as *Richterrecht*; others classify this area of law as statutory and constitutional interpretation. Yet, no observer of the German legal system would contend that most judicial decisions can be classified as *Richterrecht*. Indeed, the vast majority of judicial decisions are based on statute law, albeit usually statute law as interpreted by previous judicial decisions.

This observation leaves open the question of how lawyers should use not only the rules that comprise *Richterrecht* but also the rules that are found in, or are distilled from, judicial decisions—the glosses—that are based on statute or constitutional law as these glosses vastly outnumber rules from *Richterrecht*. In addition, these glosses cover far more areas of law than *Richterrecht* and not just in Germany. The use of rules from both *Richterrecht* and from judicial glosses is, of course, a major topic of this book.

In England, textbooks on the English legal system generally present the traditional rules of interpretation—the literal rule, the golden rule, and the mischief rule—together with the more recent purposive rule or approach, sometimes referred to as the teleological approach.[13] The teleological rule or approach is often reserved for European-based law and for law potentially affecting rights guaranteed by the Human Rights Act 1998.[14] According to §3(1) of the Human Rights

[12] One of the few authors who have identified this deficit is Fritz Jost, 'The Adjudication of Law and the Doctrine of Private Law' in Mark van Hoecke and François Ost (eds), *The Harmonisation of European Private Law* (Bloomsbury Publishing 2000)167 at 177.

[13] Gary Slapper and David Kelly, *The English Legal System* (Routledge 2020).

[14] Alisdair Gillespie and Siobhan Weare, *The English Legal System* (8th edn, Oxford University Press 2021) 38 *et seq.*; Emily Allbon and Sanmeet Kaur-Dua, *Elliott and Quinn's English Legal System* (21st

Act, 'So far as it is possible to do so, primary legislation and subordinate legislation must be read and given effect in a way which is compatible with the Convention rights.' Although this provision is usually described as mandating purposive interpretation, it is more appropriately delegated to the category of system-contextual arguments, where it will be discussed in this book (see Chapter 8).

At first glance, it might appear that the traditional rules of interpretation—the literal rule, the golden rule, and the mischief rule—correspond to the categories employed in this book; but this is not the case. While the literal rule does, indeed, correspond to the category of argument described in this book as textual, and sometimes literal, the golden and mischief rules are another story.

The golden rule is basically an extension or gloss on the literal rule.[15] The golden rule was first stated in 1857 in the case of *Grey v. Pearson*:[16]

> The grammatical and ordinary sense of the words is to be adhered to, unless that would lead to some absurdity, or some repugnance or inconsistency with the rest of the instrument, in which case the grammatical and ordinary sense of the words may be modified so as to avoid that absurdity, but no further.

The classic case employed to illustrate the application of the golden rule is the 1872 case of *Regina v. Allen*. The defendant in that case was charged with bigamy under a statute that stated, 'Whosoever being married shall marry any other person . . . shall be guilty of bigamy.' The defendant claimed that he could not be guilty because, legally, someone who is already married cannot marry again. Most, if not all, readers will agree that one does not need a separate rule of interpretation to decide this case in favour of the prosecution, for, if one were to accept the interpretation of the statute, the statute would be meaningless. But if one were looking for a rule or an argument, as they are termed in this book, either a historical or purposive argument would do the job: a historical argument because the defendant's claim would mean that no one could be convicted of bigamy, and this could not have been Parliament's intent, or a purposive argument because the purpose of this prohibition is to prevent exactly what happened in the case of the defendant. There is no need for a separate 'golden rule'.

The next traditional rule of interpretation in England is the mischief rule. This rule is sometimes referred to as the rule in *Heydon's Case*,[17] a case from 1584, in which the

edn, Pearson 2020) 57 *et seq*; Colin Manchester, *Exploring the Law* (3rd edn, Sweet & Maxwell 2006) 40 *et seq*; Emily Finch and Stefan Finski, *Legal Skills* (7th edn, Oxford University Press 2019) 58 *et seq*; Slapper and Kelly, *The English Legal System*, 94 *et seq*.

[15] See Slapper and Kelly, *The English Legal System*, 103: the golden rule 'is generally considered to be an extension of the literal rule'.

[16] *Grey v. Pearson*, 6 HL cas. 61 (1857).

[17] *Heydon's Case* (1584) 76 ER 637.

Court of Exchequer was called on to interpret the Suppression of Religious Houses Act 1535. This Act ordered the expropriation of property above a certain value, like the Manor of Ottery, owned by religious orders. However, a 'lease or grant for life, or for term of years' was exempt from expropriation, provided that the lease or grant had been made more than a year before the passage of the Act. *Heydon's Case* was concerned with how the exemption for a 'lease or grant for life, or for term of years' should be understood in the context of a grant that was not in the form of a lease.

Some years before the passage of the Act, the Manor of Ottery made a grant of land to a father and son named Ware 'for their lives, at the will of the lord, and according to the custom of the said manor'. The grant was in the form of a copyhold, a medieval form of tenancy, which is also referred to in the report of the case as a customary estate. From all appearances, the grant of the copyhold was an arms-length transaction, with no hint of the 'mischief' that the Act sought to remedy, such as the making of 'long and unreasonable leases'.

The problem for the Wares was that copyholds were not explicitly mentioned in the Act. Consequently, the question for the Court of Exchequer was: does a customary estate constitute a 'lease or grant for life, or for term of years' for the purpose of the exception from expropriation?

Even though copyholds were not mentioned in the Act, the Barons (i.e. judges) of the Court of Exchequer unanimously ruled in favour of the Wares, holding 'that the said copyhold estate was an estate for life, within the words and meaning of the said Act'. This holding is an example of a teleological extension: the Court extended—one could also say 'stretched'—the words 'lease or grant' to include customary copyhold estates.[18]

How is the ruling in *Heydon's Case* to be understood in the matrix of arguments extolled in this book? The description above of the holding of *Heydon's Case* as a 'teleological extension',[19] from the Greek word for 'purpose', suggests the answer: purposive. Holland and Webb agree. They note that the purpose of the Act was stated in the preamble.[20] 'Thus', according to Holland and Webb, 'the judge did

[18] The oft-quoted language of the so-called mischief rule announced in *Heydon's Case* is: And it was resolved by them, that for the sure and true interpretation of all statutes in general (be they penal or beneficial, restrictive or enlarging of the common law,) four things are to be discerned and considered: 1st. What was the common law before the making of the Act. 2nd. What was the mischief and defect for which the common law did not provide. 3rd. What remedy the Parliament hath resolved and appointed to cure the disease of the commonwealth. And, 4th. The true reason of the remedy; and then the office of all the Judges is always to make such[7] construction as shall suppress the mischief, and advance the remedy, and to suppress subtle inventions and evasions for continuance of the mischief, and *pro privato commodo*, and to add force and life to the cure and remedy, according to the true intent of the makers of the Act, *pro bono publico*. See generally Robert F. Williams, 'Statutes as Sources of Law beyond Their Terms in Common-Law Cases' (1982) 50 Geo Wash L Rev 554.

[19] See generally E.T. Feteris, 'The Pragma-Dialectical Analysis and Evaluation of Teleological Argumentation in a Legal Context' (2008) 22 Argumentation 489.

[20] 'An Acte wherby all Relygeous Houses of Monkes Chanons and Nonnes whiche may not dyspend Manors Landes Tenementes & Heredycaments above the clere yerly Value of ij C Li are geven to the Kinges Highnes his Heires and Successours for ever.'

not have to go beyond the bounds of the Act to discover the mischief it sought to remedy'.[21]

After a review of other cases employing the mischief rule, Holland and Webb conclude that today, 'the distinction between the mischief and golden rules is, in the minds of some judges, so fine as to be virtually non-existent'. They also suggest that the mischief rule might be subsumed under 'a general purposive approach'.[22] While it might well be subsumed under such an approach, Holland and Webb would presumably agree that, even if the golden rule were combined with the mischief rule, they would not add up to the category of purposive argument as used in this book.

Before addressing the English understanding of the use of rules from case law, we should mention additional arguments that are referred to in English textbooks as secondary aids to the interpretation or construction of statutes. Holland and Webb have compiled a lengthy list of what they refer to as 'rules of grammar': the title of the act, inclusive words and lists, *expressio unius est exclusio alterius*, *ejusdem generis*, and *noscitur a sociis*.[23] These 'rules of grammar' are all textual arguments as defined in this book.

Regarding case law, Holland and Webb provide an excellent explication of the English understanding of many aspects of case law. Written with students in mind, Holland and Webb begin with a discussion of judicial precedent in chapter 6 ('The Doctrine of Judicial Precedent'), in which they explain the origin of the doctrine of *stare decisis* and how the principle of a case is established before introducing students to the hierarchy and procedures of the various courts in the United Kingdom. In chapter 7 ('How Precedent Operates: *Ratio Decidendi* and *Obiter Dictum*'), Holland and Webb walk the reader through the steps of defining and perceiving the *ratio* before turning their attention briefly to the interpretation of the *ratio*. At this point, the reader is presented with a short exercise to show that a hypothetical *ratio* can be inferred or restated by later judges in at least four different ways. But what do the judges do with the *ratio* that they have inferred or restated? That is not explained.

Another excellent book on the topic, a book that is also addressed to students, is Twining and Miers's *How to Do Things with Rules: A Primer of Interpretation*. In chapter 9 ('Reading Cases'), the authors remind readers that, while judges in subsequent cases 'do not consider themselves necessarily bound by the explicit wording [of the *ratio* in a precedential case,] ... there is a tacit convention that special attention should be paid to the words used by judges in prior cases and often a

[21] James Holland and Julian Webb, *Learning Legal Rules: A Students' Guide to Legal Method and Reasoning* (Oxford University Press 2022) 206.

[22] Ibid 208.

[23] Ibid 270–274. At 275–279, Holland and Webb also list *ignorantia leges non excusat*, other statutes, the Interpretation Act 1978, punctuation and marginal notes, explanatory notes, dictionaries, and *travaux préparatoires*.

passage from a judgment in the prior case is treated as an adequate formulation of the *ratio*'.[24] Much of the discussion following this quotation in Twining and Miers's book deals with arguments for avoiding precedential cases and in identifying, and rehearsing, five usages of the term '*ratio decidendi*', although at one point, in a footnote, the authors write: 'One area of controversy is what weight to give to the actual words by a judge in this context. Few consider that courts are formally bound by the precise wording but in practice great weight is quite often given to such formulations.'[25] Other than these brief allusions to what could correspond to the textual arguments based on the *ratio*, Twining and Miers go no further to describe what judges actually do with the *ratio*, which is all the more disappointing considering the title of their book: *How to Do Things with Rules*.[26]

Having reviewed two leading and excellent textbooks on the subject of legal rules and interpretation, and having seen that they do not have much to say about what to do with the *ratio* after having found it, we should not be surprised that books on the general topic of the English legal system (books that need not be mentioned here)[27] run out of steam at the very point that they are most needed in showing what judges do with the *ratio*.

C. Savigny's canons in action: Textual, historical, and purposive

At this juncture, it would be useful to look at how the traditional interpretive methods developed by Savigny are employed. For this purpose, we will first use a hypothetical example from the German Product Liability Act (*Produkthaftun gsgesetz*).[28] For this first hypothetical, we will content ourselves with a threefold canon: the textual (what was said), the historical (what was meant), and, third, the purposive (what is reasonable). A different, second hypothetical will be used to illustrate system-contextual argumentation.

The first hypothetical case concerns a 'mom-and-pop' bicycle shop that buys bicycle parts, assembles bicycles from those parts, and sells the assembled bicycles.

[24] William Twining and David Miers, *How to Do Things with Rules* (5th edn, Cambridge University Press 2010) 313–314. At 339, the authors write: 'Common law rules are not rules in fixed verbal form. [Judges of inferior courts] may, and often do, give such formulations very considerable weight, but they also sometimes reformulate the rules more widely or narrowly in their own words.'

[25] Ibid 340 n. 92.

[26] The authors write: '[T]he main aim of this book has been to help to understand some of the difficulties in the way of interpreting rules rather than to provide a recipe, if such were possible': William Twining and David Miers, *How to Do Things with Rules* (4th edn, Butterworths 1999) 373.

[27] One such book claims: 'The use of ratios, and the use of precedent generally, is just as puzzling as is identifying a ratio': Fiona Cownie, Anthony Bradney, and Mandy Burton, *English Legal System in Context* (4th edn, Oxford University Press 2007) 101.

[28] The wording of the German Product Liability Act is nearly identical to the UK Consumer Protection Act 1987. They are both based on the EU Product Liability Directive [85/374/EEC].

Assume that a customer buys one of these bicycles and drives it to work every workday. Two weeks later, while cycling to work, the customer pushes on the pedals, and one pedal suddenly breaks off. The customer loses her balance, falls to the ground, and breaks her arm. A court-appointed expert examines the chain using x-rays and concludes that the accident was caused by a latent defect in the chain of the bicycle that could not have been detected by those who assembled the bicycle. In other words, the people in the 'mom-and-pop' bicycle shop were not at fault.

In harmony with the European Product Liability Directive, the German Product Liability Act reads: 'The producer shall be liable for damage caused by a defect in his product.'[29] A claim under the Product Liability Act therefore does not require proof of fault: it is sufficient to prove that there was a defect in the product, which is the case here. Notice that sellers, like the 'mom-and-pop' bicycle shop in our hypothetical scenario, are not mentioned in the German Product Liability Act: by its terms, the Act only applies to 'producers'. Who, then, are producers? The German Product Liability Act defines a 'producer' as 'the manufacturer of a finished product, the producer of any raw material or the manufacturer of a component part'.[30] Notice that the definition does not mention assembly.

Back to our hypothetical case: is our hypothetical 'mom-and-pop' bicycle shop a producer for purposes of the German Product Liability Act? Beginning with the text, one might consult the German dictionary, *Duden*. There, the verb 'to produce' is defined as 'to make' or 'to create'. If we were to employ a textual argument of statutory interpretation, we might well conclude that mere assembling does not rise to the level of making or creating a bicycle, and, as a consequence, that no liability would attach to the bicycle shop.

However, we might proceed to ask ourselves what the legislator intended (what was meant). Assume, for the purpose of our hypothetical scenario, that we find a legislative committee report with this sentence: 'The producer of the final product also includes ... one who only provides the final assembly of the product whose parts have been supplied to him by another producer.' If we allow ourselves to be persuaded by this historical argument, we would conclude that the bicycle shop is, indeed, liable as a producer.

The third type of interpretative argumentation considered here is the purposive argument: what is reasonable? The two purposes most often advanced for the no-fault product liability are (1) compensation for losses; and (2) internalization of costs, also called loss-spreading.[31] Using purposive arguments, one could conclude that liability should attach to the owners of the bicycle shop because (1) doing so

[29] Article 1, Directive 85/374/EEC.

[30] §4 Abs. (1) Produkthaftungsgesetz.

[31] Thomas Lundmark, 'The Restatement of Torts (Third) and the European Product Liability Directive' (1996) 5 JILP 239.

would allow an injured person to be compensated and (2) the cost could be passed on to consumers by charging a higher price for bicycles in the future.

Before moving on to the next hypothetical, which will illustrate one of the categories of 'system-contextual' argumentation as the term is used in this book, we should pause to consider the relevance of the above discussion to a few of the major theses of this book, namely that the methodology of interpretation of the statutory law and of case law are basically identical; that, in both cases, one starts with a 'rule', which can also be a definition; that one applies the rule by using identical arguments, whether it is a statutory norm or a *ratio decidendi*; and that there is no distinction to be made between the use of *ratios* that result from statutory interpretation and those that result from *Richterrecht*.

This last point—*ratios* that result from statutory interpretation are used in the same way as those resulting from *Richterrecht*—should be a very gratifying observation for most of us because commentaries, practice books, encyclopaedias, and other secondary sources will collect and report these *ratios* identically, regardless of their source, just as they report statutory norms. And, furthermore, as illustrated in this book, *ratios* are employed just like statutory norms. This is a win–win situation.

This observation—*ratios* are employed like statutory norms—can be demonstrated by revealing that, in the example above regarding historical argumentation, the statement that is said to be taken from a legislative committee report ('The producer of the final product also includes … one who only provides the final assembly') is not from a legislative committee at all: it is a *ratio* from a decision of the German Federal Supreme Court.[32] And the quotation of that *ratio* is taken not directly from the decision itself but from the leading commentary on civil law, *Palandt*.[33]

Interestingly, the judicial decision from which this *ratio* was taken predated the enactment of the Product Liability Act. That means that this *ratio* is (or at least, at one time was) 'pure' common law or *Richterrecht*.[34] Yet, in *Palandt*, the decision is quoted in a discussion regarding the meaning of the word 'producer' as employed in the Product Liability Act. And, crucially, this quotation from *Palandt* was cited by the Higher Regional Court in Dresden as authority for holding that the 'mom-and-pop' bicycle shop, which merely assembled the bicycle, was liable as a 'producer' for the injuries caused be the defective bicycle part.[35]

[32] Urt. v. 14 June 1977, VI ZR 247/75.

[33] *Palandt-Sprau*, 78. Aufl. 2019, §4 ProdHaftG, Rn. 3.

[34] Before the enactment of the Product Liability Act, in cases involving a defective product, German courts, without legislative authority, had been shifting the burden of proof from the plaintiff to the producer, saddling the producer with the practically impossible task of proving that it was not negligent in producing the defective product. For a discussion in English of this judicial law-making, see H. Duintijer Tebbens, *International Product Liability: A Study of Comparative and International Aspects of Product Liability* (Sijthoff & Noordhoff 1979) 76 *et seq*.

[35] *OLG Dresden*, Versicherungsrecht 1998, 59.

To avoid confusion, perhaps it should be noted that the decision of the Higher Regional Court in Dresden employed the *ratio*, as found in *Palandt*, textually, just as it was quoted in the commentary: the term 'producer' includes one who assembles; the bicycle shop assembled the bicycle, therefore, the bicycle shop is a producer; and as a producer of a bicycle with a defect, the bicycle shop is liable.

Note that the Higher Regional Court in Dresden might have employed the *ratio* according to its history, just as if the *ratio* had been a statute. Of course, unlike with a statute, there are no legislative reports and other *travaux préparatoires* to consult. Rather, the court would need to consult the precedential judicial decision of the German Supreme Court itself and perhaps other judicial decisions that discuss the precedential decision. If the Dresden court had, indeed, read the precedential decision, it would have learned that the German Supreme Court, in fact, refused to impose liability on a company that had merely assembled a defective crane. The reason for the Supreme Court's refusal was that, while the assembler could, indeed, be considered a producer for purposes of product liability, the assembler can only be considered to be the producer of the entire product (the crane), not of the component parts of the crane; and it was a component part of the crane—the hook—that was defective, not the crane as such; therefore, the assembler of the crane was not liable.

To repeat: the *ratio* from the precedential decision of the German Supreme Court was employed in a textual manner by the Higher Regional Court in Dresden. Since the *ratio* was employed in a textual manner, there was no reason to read the precedential decision. If the judges of the Higher Regional Court in Dresden had, indeed, read the precedential decision, they would have seen that the *ratio* quoted in *Palandt* was an *obiter dictum*, that is, something said in passing.[36] The fact is that judicial rules (*ratios* and definitions) are, for the most part, indistinguishable from statutory rules and definitions; and if one does not know that the rule is judicial in origin, one will automatically use the rule in the same way that one would ordinarily use a statutory rule.

D. The indistinguishability between *ratios* and statutory rules

To illustrate the indistinguishability between judicial *ratios* and statutory rules, consider the following examples from Germany,[37] some of which have their origins in judicial decisions and some in statutes. In perusing these examples, the reader is asked to try to distinguish the statutory rules from the case-based rules:

[36] R. Kent Greenawalt, 'Reflections on Holding and Dictum' (1981) 39 J Leg Ed 431 and sources cited at n. 45.

[37] See generally Thomas Lundmark and Sebastian Herrmann, 'Auslegung von Richterrecht' [2020] NJW 28–34.

> Collateral agreements must be in writing if they concern the content of the tenancy agreement and they are of substantial importance to the parties. (*Nebenabreden unterliegen dann der* Schriftform, *wenn sie den Inhalt des Mietverhältnisses gestalten und nach dem Willen der Parteien wesentliche Bedeutung haben.*)[38]
>
> If the aggrieved party cannot use the article of property that has been damaged, the person who caused the damage must reimburse the aggrieved party for the costs of renting an article of equivalent value. (*Kann der Geschädigte wegen des schädigenden Ereignisses die Sache nicht nutzen, hat ihm der Schädiger die Kosten für die Anmietung einer gleichwertigen Sache zu ersetzen.*)[39]
>
> If the application to lodge an appeal is rejected, the judgment becomes binding. (*Wird der Antrag auf Zulassung der Revision abgelehnt, so wird das Urteil rechtskräftig.*)[40]

A waiver is only effective if it is directed to a concrete matter, and it has been explained clearly and unmistakably (*Ein Verzicht ist nur wirksam, wenn er sich auf eine konkrete Angelegenheit bezieht und eindeutig und unmissverständlich erklärt wurde*):[41]

> If a public authority fails to provide a factually necessary statement of facts, then there is a procedural error. (*Unterlässt* die *Behörde eine sachlich notwendige Aufklärung des Sachverhalts, liegt ein Verfahrensfehler vor.*)[42]
>
> The employer cannot reprimand or terminate an employee merely because the employee participated in a strike. (*Wegen der* bloßen *Teilnahme an einem Streik darf der Arbeitgeber nicht abmahnen oder kündigen.*)[43]

> If a party to a wedding ceremony dies before the officiating registrar of marriage has declared the marriage to be legally valid, the marriage will nevertheless be valid. (*Stirbt ein Ehegatte vor dem Ausspruch des Standesbeamten, dass die Verlobten nunmehr kraft Gesetzes rechtmäßig verbundene Eheleute seien, ist die Eheschließung gültig.*)[44]

> A judgment that does not contain findings of fact and conclusions of law, and that has been fully recorded in the protocol of the hearing, cannot be amended if it has left the inner service area of the court unless allowed by §77b Abs. 2 OWiG. (*Ein vollständig in das Sitzungsprotokoll aufgenommenes, nicht mit Gründen versehenes*

[38] Vgl. *BGH*, Urt. v. 25 November 2015—XII ZR 114/14 im Anschluss an *BGH*, Urt. v. 22. December 1999—XII ZR 339/97.

[39] *OLG Rostock*, Urt. v. 11 March 2011—5 U 122/10.

[40] §566 Abs. 6 ZPO.

[41] *VG Köln*, Urt. v. 5 February 2010—27 K 4398/08.

[42] Vgl. *VGH Baden-Württemberg*, Beschl. v. 10 June 2011—1 S 915-11.

[43] Vgl. *BAG*, Urt. v. 11 August 1992—1 AZR 103-92.

[44] Otto Palandt, *Bürgerliches Gesetzbuch* (78th edn, C.H. Beck 2019) §1312 n. 2.

Urteil, das den inneren Dienstbereich des Gerichts bereits verlassen hat, darf nicht mehr verändert werden, es sei denn, die nachträgliche Urteilsbegründung ist gemäß §77b Abs. 2 OWiG zulässig.)[45]

A church is free to hold and administer all of the facilities associated with the church, regardless of their legal form. (*Alle der Kirche zugeordneten Einrichtungen sind ohne Rücksicht auf ihre Rechtsform Objekte, bei deren Ordnung und Verwaltung die Kirche frei ist.*)[46]

In payment transactions that are not in euros, the payment service user and the payment service provider can agree that §675t Abs. 1 Satz 3 und Abs. 2 BGB be inapplicable in whole or in part. (*Für Zahlungsvorgänge, die nicht in Euro erfolgen, können der Zahlungsdienstnutzer und sein Zahlungsdienstleister vereinbaren, dass §675t Abs. 1 Satz 3 und Abs. 2 BGB ganz oder teilweise nicht anzuwenden ist.*)[47]

The period in which an employee [of a company being taken over] must object to working with new management cannot begin before transfer of ownership [of the company]. (*Der für die Erfüllung des Zeitmoments maßgebliche Zeitraum der widerspruchslosen Weiterarbeit bei dem neuen Betriebsinhaber beginnt frühestens mit dem Betriebsübergang.*)[48]

An operator of a web search engine need only take action to rectify an illegality when it has knowledge of the illegality. (*Den Betreiber einer Internet-Suchmaschine trifft grundsätzlich erst dann eine Prüfungspflicht, wenn er Kenntnis von der Rechtsverletzung erlangt.*)[49]

One who is not qualified, or does not himself train apprentices, may not employ apprentices unless he retains persons who are personally and professionally qualified to provide training in the training facility, and who are responsible to train the apprentices personally, and to a significant extent. (*Wer fachlich nicht geeignet ist oder wer nicht selbst ausbildet, darf Auszubildende nur dann einstellen, wenn er persönlich und fachlich geeignete Ausbilder oder Ausbilderinnen bestellt, die die Ausbildungsinhalte in der Ausbildungsstätte unmittelbar, verantwortlich und in wesentlichem Umfang vermitteln.*)[50]

One who infringes an ancillary copyright by selling copyrighted goods is obliged to divulge his supplier to the copyright holder. (*Wer* durch *den Vertrieb einer Ware ein ergänzendes wettbewerbsrechtliches Leistungsschutzrecht verletzt, ist dem Berechtigten zur Nennung der Bezugsquelle verpflichtet.*)[51]

[45] Vgl. *BGH*, Beschl. v. 8 May 2013—4 StR 33612.
[46] Vgl. *BVerfG*, Beschl. v. 11 October 1977—BvR 209/76.
[47] Vgl. §675e Abs. 3 BGB.
[48] Vgl. *BAG*, Urt. v. 24 August 2017—8 AZR 265-17.
[49] Vgl. *BGH*, Urt. v. 14 May 2013—VI ZR 269/12.
[50] §28 Abs. 2 BBiG.
[51] Vgl. *BGH*, Urt. v. 24 March 1994—I ZR 42/93.

Although the rules quoted above all look like statutes, in fact, every one of them is a case-based rule, that is, a *ratio*. These rules look so much like statutes that one of these rules has, in fact, been codified by the *Bundestag* virtually word for word.[52] The fact that one of these case-based rules has been codified does not indicate that the phrasing of this particular rule is in any way exceptional for it is not. The rule that has been codified, and all of the other rules quoted above, are merely examples of the innumerable legal rules that have been pronounced by judges, either in the course of applying statutes or in the course of announcing rules that are not based on statute, that is, pure judge-made law (*Richterrecht*).

The point of this exercise is this: without knowing the source of these rules, it is impossible to distinguish the rules that are articulated in judicial decisions from those that are articulated in statutes.

E. Statutory analogies

The fourth of Savigny's canons, the system-contextual element, is employed in this book as a category of arguments that includes analogical arguments. Analogical arguments, as the term is employed in this book, are those that cite rules from other areas of law. To employ an analogical argument for a particular fact pattern before the court, the judge must identify a rule that cannot be applied to the fact pattern in a textual, historical, or purposive manner. This limitation is crucial for if the fact pattern could be subsumed under the rule in a textual, historical, or purposive manner, there would be no need to employ an analogical argument with the rule. Having identified this rule, the judge, either consciously or unconsciously, fashions a broader, overriding principle that encompasses both the fact pattern before the court and the fact pattern of the identified rule.[53]

This style of argument is easier to understand when there is an example. The example here is a hypothetical one. The example employs a rule from an equally hypothetical Unwholesome Food Ordinance (UFO):

> It is illegal to sell any food that is diseased, unwholesome, or injurious to health. Anyone who violates this ordinance is liable for the injury caused.

[52] Section 2 of the UK Health and Safety at Work etc. Act 1974 contains a list of duties that employers owe their employees. That list basically mirrors the descriptions of a safe workplace as listed in *Wilsons & Clyde Coal Co. Ltd v. English* [1938] AC 57.

[53] 'A judge who reasons by analogy has to have an organizing theory that explains why the facts of the instant case are similar … to the facts of the precedent cases': Michael McHugh, 'The Judicial Method' (1999) 73 ALJ 37, 45; Carmine Conte, 'From Only the "Bottom-Up"? Legitimate Forms of Judicial Reasoning in Private Law' (2015) OJLS 1, 11.

Assume, for the purposes of this hypothetical scenario, that Mary buys a hamster from Hamsters-R-Us and gives it to her friend Zara as a pet. Zara becomes seriously ill from a strange disease. Expert testimony establishes that Zara contracted the disease from her pet hamster and that the hamster had the disease when it was sold.

Can Zara bring a claim against Hamsters-R-Us on the basis of the UFO? From a textual standpoint, is a hamster sold as a pet 'food'? While hamsters can be, and are, eaten by humans in some places, very few people would consider them to be food. Can a hamster be considered food for a pet, perhaps for a snake? The name of the rule—the Unwholesome Food Ordinance—sounds like a reference to human food. If pets were intended, one would probably expect the rule to be styled the Unwholesome Human and Pet Food Ordinance. And, anyway, Zara did not get sick by ingesting the hamster.

If one looks at the legislative history of the UFO, assume that a careful search of the historical record fails to uncover any suggestion that pets should be included within the ambit of the UFO. Indeed, all of the available records speak of consumption by humans.

Could a purposive argument be made, a so-called teleological extension? This would be a real stretch as most of us would probably infer that the purpose of the UFO is to protect consumers from diseased, unwholesome, and injurious things that they eat, not that they pet. Consequently, the judge who heard Zara's claim would, in all likelihood, reject it.

If the judge who heard the claim wanted to rule in Zara's favour, the judge might consider other possible causes of action, such as negligence. But, in our scenario, there is no reason to suggest that Hamsters-R-Us was negligent, and proof of negligence is a prerequisite to a successful claim.

However, if the judge were determined to rule in Zara's favour, perhaps because a great number of other people had contracted the same strange disease from a hamster, the judge might resort to making an analogical argument. In this instance, the judge would look for a broad, overriding principle that encompasses both the fact pattern before the court and the fact pattern of the UFO. In this instance, the judge might argue that the overriding principle behind the UFO is the protection of (human) consumers from diseased animals that are sold to them.

Statutory analogies are employed in Germany to recognize causes of action on behalf of claimants who are only remotely related to the class of claimants that the identified statute, from a textual standpoint, intends to protect. For example, there is no statute in Germany that can be textually, historically, or purposively construed to require an employer to compensate his or her employees for damage to the employees' own property in the course of employment. Yet, the Federal Labor Court imposes such a requirement by analogy to §670 of the Civil Code, which, by its terms, only applies to unpaid agents. The overriding principle that encompasses both factual patterns—the one in the statute and the one before the Court—might be articulated as follows: unpaid agents and (underpaid?) employees deserve to be compensated or, more broadly, people who are following instructions from another person in a personal contractual relationship may recover their losses. This latter principle is roughly the justification fashioned by the Federal Labor Court when it first applied §670 to the employer/employee relationship:

> Section 670 applies to [unpaid] agency agreements. One sees the same general idea of activity on behalf of another person. But even if one follows the weight of authority and refuses to classify an employment contract as an agency agreement, and only sees it as an independent activity of an economic nature within the sphere of influence of another's economic activity, the result cannot be otherwise. For the principle [of reimbursement] behind Civil Code section 670 is so obvious and in the nature of things so necessary that it is to be applied even without express legislation.[54]

The dividing line between a teleological extension and a statutory analogy is a blurred one: one could view the different arguments—teleological extension and statutory analogies—as lying on a continuum.[55] And, unsurprisingly, examples of teleological extensions that significantly stretch the language of the statute are sometimes referred to as statutory analogies, at least in the common-law world.[56] This is probably due to a number of reasons. For one thing, statutory analogies, in the sense used in this book, are extremely rare in common-law jurisdictions,[57] probably, in part, because judges in those jurisdictions can often fall back on the common law. Another reason is that the word 'analogy' in law is used in so many different ways in English,[58] causing significant confusion among judges and scholars alike.

The topic of analogies will be revisited in Chapter 8 on system-contextual arguments.

[54] BAGE 12, 15; see also BAG (1962) NJW 411, 414; Roland Rixecker *et al.* (eds), '§670 BGB' *Münchener Kommentar* (6th edn, C.H. Beck 2012) margin note no. 3.

[55] See C.W. Maris, 'Milking the Meter: On Analogy, Universalisability and World Views' in Patrick Nerhot (ed.), *Legal Knowledge and Analogy: Fragments of Legal Epistemology, Hermeneutics and Linguistics* (1st edn, Springer 1990) 77 *et seq*.

[56] See *Estate of Mary Mason v. Fairbank*, 62 Cal. 2d 213 (1965) 217, discussed below: 'Accordingly, we adopt for the distribution of the estate in such a case the rules set forth in sections 750–753 of the Probate Code.'

[57] The one exception to this statement is perhaps the practice of borrowing a statute of limitations when none can be found that expressly applies to the factual situation before the court. But these borrowings do not go so far as to create new causes of action, as do statutory analogies in Germany.

[58] See the excellent discussion in Stephen Utz, 'Problems in American Legal Methodology' in Martin Häublein and Stephen Utz (eds), *Rechtsgeschäft, Methodenlehre und darüber hinaus* (De Gruyter 2012) 295. See also Grant Lamond, 'Analogical Reasoning in the Common Law' (2014) 34(3) OJLS 567; E.H. Levi, *An Introduction to Legal Reasoning* (University of Chicago Press 1948) 1–3; Edward H. Levi, 'An Introduction to Legal Reasoning' (1948) 15(3) Univ Chic Law Rev 1–3; Lloyd L. Weinreb, *The Use of Analogy in Legal Argument* (Cambridge University Press 2005) 1–5.

F. Case-law analogies and the importance of facts in judicial decisions

In section E, and in the remainder of this book, the term 'analogical argument' is used to describe an argument that cites a rule from another area of law, similar to the usage of the term in civil-law jurisdictions.[59]

The source of the cited rule is irrelevant: the rule may find its source in a statute or judicial decision. The definition of 'analogical argument' employed in this book is, consequently, limited to rules, not arguments, and not references to the facts of a judicial decision. The definition of analogy employed in this book is admittedly a very narrow one. In fact, it is so narrow that, as will be shown in Chapter 8, the author has been unable to find many examples of case-law analogies in common-law jurisdictions that can be squeezed into this admittedly narrow definition.[60]

Common-law authors tend to employ the term 'analogy' expansively, more in line with its dictionary definition of 'comparison'. At the extreme, these authors simply equate the entire process of judicial reasoning in common-law jurisdictions with analogy.[61] In their textbook *The English Legal System,* Gary Slapper and David Kelly come close to this extreme. There, they state that judicial reasoning 'tends to be carried out on the basis of analogy, and judges have a large degree of discretion in selecting what are to be considered as analogous cases'.[62]

Professor Stephen Utz, on the other hand, correctly observes that the 'obsession of common-law scholars and jurists with analogy has obscured our vision of the actually quite varied patterns of legal reasoning'.[63] For example, the process of 'selecting what are considered to be analogous cases', as mentioned by David Kelly, turns out to be identical to the process of selecting statutes. If a lawyer's client is injured by a product, a California lawyer will immediately think of case law, such as the seminal case of *Greenman v. Yuba Power Products*.[64] The English lawyer will think of the Consumer Protection Act 1987, and the Irish lawyer will think of the Liability for Defective Products Act 1991. The thinking process is identical: all three have the client's factual situation in mind, and all three know that there is law on the subject that is helpful to the client. But whereas the California lawyer thinks of case-law, the English and Irish lawyers think of statutory law. How can the thinking process of the California lawyer be properly described as 'on the basis

[59] '[O]ne has become inclined, in civil law countries, to apply a legal precept or rule established in a statutory provision by way of analogy to a similar constellation of interests presented in the situation at bar where the words of the codes seem to provide for it': Arthur Lenhoff, *Comments, Cases and Other Materials on Legislation* (Dennis & Co. 1949) 946.

[60] See Chapter 8, section E.

[61] See also the discussion of deduction in Chapter 2 at nn. 55–66.

[62] Slapper and Kelly, *The English Legal System*, 314.

[63] Stephen Utz, 'Problems in American Legal Methodology' in Häublein and Utz, *Rechtsgeschäft, Methodenlehre und darüber hinaus*, 296 at n. 46.

[64] *Greenman v. Yuba Power Products* (1963) 59 Cal. 2d 57.

of analogy' without describing the thinking processes of the English and Irish lawyers in the same way? Yet, the author of this book has only ever encountered descriptions of the search for applicable case law as analogous, never as a search for applicable statute law.

This is puzzling because, as emphasized in Chapter 2 regarding the *Normsuche*, statutes are also factual in nature. Indeed, statutes are hypothetical judgments. But the infatuation of common-law scholars with analogy obscures this identicalness.

While no one knows what obscuration lurks in the minds of juristic mankind, nor why it lurks there, one can distinguish at least three 'patterns of legal reasoning' (to use Utz's terminology) that can be discerned if one's 'vision' is not obscured by one's obsession with analogy.

One 'pattern' is the tantamount importance of the use of the holding or *ratio*. The *ratio* is the case-based rule that can be employed by using the arguments described in the following chapters. We will see, in those chapters, that, ordinarily, the arguments used by judges in employing both statutory and case-based rules are the textual, historical, and purposive arguments.

A second 'pattern' of a case that is often employed in legal reasoning are the facts. What often confuses students is that the facts of a case are employed in several ways. The most obvious way that facts are employed is as an aid to the *Normsuche* of finding a case that has a rule that may apply to the case at hand, that is, a precedential case. To use another example, if a student in England is confronted with a hypothetical factual situation in which a person suffers psychiatric harm from witnessing a shocking event on television, the student will recall the case of *Alcock v. Chief Constable of South Yorkshire*.[65] The facts of the case, which concerned the Hillsborough stadium disaster in Sheffield, imprint a powerful memory that helps students feel their way to this precedential case, thus speeding the process of the *Normsuche*.

Having found the case of *Alcock*, the student in England will be able to find the *ratios* of the case. (The word '*ratios*' is plural here because *Alcock* sets out a scheme of rules, referred to as control mechanisms, that are akin to a statutory scheme.) This presents another instance in which the facts of a case—here, the *Alcock Case*—can be employed. Most of the *ratios* set out in *Alcock* constitute control mechanisms for so-called secondary victims, defined as those victims who cannot show 'direct impact or fear of immediate personal injuries for oneself'. In order for these secondary victims to recover, they must show, among other things, that they 'actually witness[ed] the event or its immediate aftermath'. Some of the claimants whose children and other close relatives died in the Hillsborough stadium disaster had watched the event live on television. The House of Lords dismissed the claims of

[65] *Alcock v. Chief Constable of South Yorkshire* [1992] 1 AC 310.

these claimants. This fact would be relevant to the English students' hypothetical factual situation.

Another way in which the facts of a precedential case can be relevant is when one is determining the *ratio*. The ratio can be articulated in various ways.

Rupert Cross[66] proposed a definition that reflects the judge's train of thought in the original case. He took the term *ratio* to mean 'any rule of law expressly or impliedly treated by the judge as a necessary step in reaching his conclusion, having regard to the line of reasoning adopted by him, or a necessary part of his direction to the jury'. Arthur Goodhart, on the other hand, stressed the essential facts,[67] and Edward H. Levi essentially adopted the perspective of a judge who looks on the case retrospectively.[68]

The most elegant—and accurate—elucidation of the art of determining the *ratio* is that of Lewis A. Kornhauser.[69] According to Kornhauser, one can expand or contract the *ratio* of the case depending on whether one chooses to use the *result* of the judicial decision (i.e. the fact-based holding), the *rule* as announced in the decision itself, or some broader *principle* under which the decision can be subsumed. In most cases, the result (fact-based holding) will be narrower than the rule announced in the decision. And, of course, the statement of the result can vary considerably depending on how many factual details one chooses to add to the statement of the result.[70]

There is also flexibility in determining the *rule* that is announced in the decision. The rule might be articulated more than once, with slightly different nuances, or there might be concurring opinions (also called 'judgments') with different articulations of the rule. In a lawyer's everyday practice, 'finding' the *ratio* usually involves merely looking in a book or on the internet to see how the *ratio* has been reported by other judges and practitioners. In a good many cases, the restatement of the rule in the headnote will prove to be the generally accepted articulation of the *ratio* of the case. The *principle* may be stated broadly or narrowly, depending on the circumstances and needs of the interpreter.

The following example, taken from a judicial decision in Germany, illustrates Kornhauser's three approaches to articulating a *ratio*. In 1984, an enterprising Bavarian T-shirt salesman printed T-shirts with a picture of Adolf Hitler in uniform on the front. Above Hitler's picture were the words, in Gothic script: 'Adolf Hitler, European Tour, 1939–1945'. After selling 153 of these T-shirts, the man was charged and convicted of violating German §86a(1) of the Penal Code, which

[66] Rupert Cross and J.W. Harris, Precedent in English Law (4th edn, Clarendon Press 1991) 72.

[67] Arthur L. Goodhart, 'Determining the Ratio Decidendi of a Case' (1930) 40 Yale LJ 161, 182.

[68] Levi, *An Introduction to Legal Reasoning*, 2.

[69] Lewis A. Kornhauser, 'Stare Decisis' in Peter Newman (ed.), *New Palgrave Dictionary of Economics and the Law* (Palgrave Macmillan 1998) 509.

[70] As discussed below, adding facts to the statement of the result is a common way of distinguishing precedents.

prohibits distributing 'symbols of a prohibited organization'. The salesman appealed to the German Federal Constitutional Court, alleging that his conduct was protected by the 'artistic freedom' clause of article 5(3) of the German Basic Law.[71] The German Federal Constitutional Court agreed and reversed the salesman's conviction.

What is the *ratio* (i.e. the *rule*) of the case? Let us start with the headnote of the Court's decision, which reads: 'Satirical representations of National Socialist symbols are protected by art. 5(3) of the Basic Law.' This headnote comports with the reasoning of the Court. The fact-based holding (the *result*) would be narrower. One could state the fact-based holding as 'Satirical depictions of Hitler are protected.' One could state the fact-based holding even narrower still: 'Satirical depictions of Hitler on T-shirts are protected.' A *principle* that could be induced from the decision, one that is broader than the *ratio*, might be: 'Critical representations of National Socialist symbols are protected.' The idea here is that satire is only one form of criticism. An even broader principle might be: 'Representations of National Socialist symbols are protected if they are presented in a way that expresses opposition to the National Socialist organization, and that attacks its ideology.'

The distinction between principle, *ratio*, and fact-based result becomes critical when one is faced with another, similar case. Such came to pass a few years later, when a man was convicted of selling stickers with black swastikas superimposed with red circles with a line drawn through them. Swastikas are, of course, symbols of the National Socialist Party, which is a 'prohibited organization' for purposes of §86a(1) of the German Penal Code. How could one apply the T-shirt decision of the German Federal Constitutional Court to the swastika case? Let us start with the *ratio*, which is the typical, almost exclusive, way that precedents are applied in Germany. As will be recalled, the *ratio* from the headnote of the T-shirt decision reads: 'Satirical representations of National Socialist symbols are protected.'

Is a crossed-out swastika satirical? In common parlance, satire usually implies humour. Is a crossed-out swastika humorous? Most people would probably not think so. We do not know from the record whether the trial judge even considered the T-shirt decision of the Federal Constitutional Court, nor do we know whether the trial judge considered the crossed-out swastika to be humorous. However, assuming that the judge did consider the decision of the Constitutional Court, and assuming that the trial judge did not find that crossed-out swastika to

[71] Article 5 [Freedom of expression]
(1) Every person shall have the right freely to express and disseminate his opinions in speech, writing, and pictures and to inform himself without hindrance from generally accessible sources. Freedom of the press and freedom of reporting by means of broadcasts and films shall be guaranteed. There shall be no censorship.
(2) These rights shall find their limits in the provisions of general laws, in provisions for the protection of young persons, and in the right to personal honor.
(3) Art and scholarship, research, and teaching shall be free. The freedom of teaching shall not release any person from allegiance to the constitution.

be satirical, he or she might have distinguished the T-shirt decision on the basis of the Constitutional Court's *ratio*: the crossed-out swastika is not satirical. The fact-based result of the T-shirt decision would similarly be of little help to the swastika-sticker salesman. Indeed, it might have been the case that the trial judge, mindful of the T-shirt decision, felt that the case should be resolved by a higher court, so he or she convicted the salesman so that the case would be appealed.

While a crossed-out swastika might not be satirical, it certainly is critical. At least, that is what the Federal Supreme Court (not the Federal Constitutional Court) thought for the Federal Supreme Court held that distribution of the cross-out swastika sticker is protected by the Basic Law. The Court's *ratio*, citing the T-shirt decision: Section 86a(1) was 'obviously' not intended to cover the use of National Socialist symbols 'in a way that expresses opposition to the organization and that attacks its ideology'. This, of course, is one of the principles of the T-shirt case that we articulated above.

Before moving on to the next chapters, in particular the chapter on historical arguments, we should mention that the facts in precedential decisions can be employed in yet another, very important, way: as if they are *travaux préparatoires* (the legislative record). Of course, judicial decisions are not legislation in the strict sense, so a better term would be *travaux juridiques*. But the truth is that recitations of facts in judicial decisions are sometimes used in exactly the same way as the factual situations mentioned in the historical legislative record. The facts in the legislative record often illustrate what the legislators had in mind when enacting the statute, which, in turn, enables judges to predict how the legislators who enacted the statute would likely decide the case at bench. The facts of precedential cases can help judges predict how the judges who decided the precedential cases would likely decide the case at bench.

G. Summary

The first part of this chapter reviewed the academic literature on the methodology of using of rules from cases and exposed a lack of a comprehensive methodology for the use of *ratios* from statutory glosses and from pure common law (*Richterrecht*).

The second part of the chapter employed the Savigny canons of textual, historical, and purposive interpretation to justify different solutions to a simple factual scenario. It was seen that the approach is identical when employing a statutory rule and a judge-made rule.

The next section of the chapter quoted a number of rules from German law to illustrate the indistinguishability between *ratios* and statutory rules.

Statutory analogies were explained and illustrated by means of an example. Analogical arguments are those that identify a rule that cannot be applied to the fact pattern before the court in a textual, historical, or purposive manner. The topic of analogies is discussed further in Chapter 8 on system-contextual arguments.

Finally, the chapter discussed case-law analogies and the importance of facts in judicial decisions. The term 'analogy' is commonly used in legal writing to mean any comparison whatsoever, such as the process of the *Normsuche* of comparing the facts before the court to various rules in order to select the most appropriate rule, whether the rule be statutory or case-based.

The facts of a precedential case may also be relevant to the ascertainment of the *ratio*. One can expand or contract the *ratio* of a case, according to Lewis A. Kornhauser, depending on whether one chooses to use the result of the judicial decision (i.e. the fact-based holding), the rule as announced in the decision itself, or some broader principle 'under which the decision can be subsumed'.

5
Textual Argument

A. Introduction

Textual arguments focus on the wording of the rule in question. To make this style of argument pictorial, imagine that the rule in question is a template, such as one that is used by pupils at school to draw various shapes, such as circles, triangles, and squares. By using a pencil to trace the edges of the perforations in the template, the pupils can draw the shapes more accurately than would have been possible without the template. The template provides precision.

Precision is also one of the values being sought by judges who use textual arguments. But instead of having circles, these judges' templates have legal terms carved into them. And just as the perforations in pupils' templates have different shapes and sizes, so too do the terms on the judges' legal templates have different shapes and sizes. Some of these terms, such as 'speech', require very large perforations in the legal template; others, such as 'mortgage', can be represented by comparatively smaller perforations. Some of the legal templates may have perforations with smooth edges, such as when there is a reference to a quotation from a statute or constitutional provision. But most will have ragged edges, serrated edges, and even indistinct edges. In any event, figuratively speaking, the task of the judge is to scrutinize the facts of the case while looking through the perforations in the legal template he or she has chosen to use. This requires defining—and often redefining—terms.[1]

When referring to rules in statutes, this style of argumentation is usually called the 'literal rule' in English, although it is also often referred to as the 'plain-meaning rule'.[2] In other languages, this style of argument can be referred to as 'linguistic', 'grammatical',[3] or even 'logical-grammatical'.[4] This book employs the term 'textual

[1] This, in turn, can result in changing the shape and size of the imaginary templates.

[2] Different styles of argumentation are usually referred to as 'rules' in English. Remember that these styles of argument are not rules in the sense that the word 'rule' is used in this book.

[3] Patrick Melin, *Gesetzesausgesauslegung in den USA und in Deutschland* (Mohr Siebeck 2005) 253: 'Die grammatische Auslegung hat zum Ziel, den sich aus dem Sprachgebrauch und den Regeln der Grammatik und Syntax ergebenden sprachlinceen Sinn einer Norm zu ermitteln' ('The grammatical interpretation aims to determine the linguistic meaning of a norm resulting from the use of language and the rules of grammar and syntax').

[4] Stig Strömholm, *Rätt, Rättskällor och Röttstillämpning: En lärobok i allmän rättslärä* (2nd edn, Norstedts Juridik 1984) 397; Stig Strömholm, Max Lyles, and Filippo Valguarnera, *En lärobok i allmän rättslärä* (2nd edn, Norstedts Juridik AB 1984) 397.

Universals of Legal Reasoning by Judges. Thomas Lundmark, Oxford University Press.
DOI: 10.1093/oso/9780198785675.003.0005

argumentation' regardless of whether the rule is found in a statute or a judicial decision.

The person who employs a textual argument may focus on individual words, a sentence, or a group of sentences. In so focusing, the person aims to ascertain and elaborate what the rule states, that is, how the rule is written. This textual focus differs from historical argumentation, which aims to reconstruct what the legislator or precedential judges intended. This textual focus also differs from purposive argumentation, which aims to enforce the policies behind the statute or case-based rule instead of employing the rule's wording or its historical background. Finally, textual argumentation differs from system-contextual argumentation, as the term is used here, because system-contextual argumentation, including analogical argumentation,[5] employs other rules and principles to, in effect, modify the text of the rule at hand.

Interpreting the words of a rule is usually the starting point for legal interpretation,[6] and it is sometimes the ending point. In other cases, judges will redefine a word so that it can serve to support the outcome that they desire, such as in the example below that redefines 'weapon' to include hydrochloric acid. But employing textual arguments encompasses more than merely defining or redefining words. As with all of the styles of argument (see Chapter 2), the use of a textual argument is merely a justification for a decision that has 'been reached on other, unarticulated grounds'.[7]

As mentioned above, there are various ways of defining this category of argument, with various nuances. Some of these ways are presented and discussed in section B. Section C provides examples of textual argument based on the wording of statutory rules. Section D does the same for judicial glosses. Section E presents examples of rules articulated in judicial decisions, here referred to as pure common law. It will be seen that the source of the rule is irrelevant: the process of argumentation is identical.

B. Textual argumentation in general

The quotations below are short descriptions of the literal rule of statutory interpretation. These descriptions have been extracted, in large part, from judicial

[5] In this book, analogical argumentation refers to the fashioning of a broader, overriding principle that encompasses two or more fact patterns, where only one of the fact patterns can be subsumed under a previously articulated rule. In effect, analogical argumentation posits a wholly novel rule.

[6] 'Every interpretation begins with the wording': Guy Beaucamp and Lutz Treder, *Methoden und Technik der Rechtsanwendung* (C.H. Beck 2011) 34; See also Bernd Rüthers, Christian Fischer, and Axel Birk, *Rechtstheorie mit Juristischer Methodenlehre* (7th edn, 2013 C.H. Beck) para 731; Georg Bitter and Tilman Rauhut, 'Grundzüge zivilrechtlicher Methodik—Schlüssel zu einer gelungenen Fallbearbeitung' (2009) JuS 289–298; Hans-Werner Laubinger, 'Höchstrichterliche Rechtsprechung zum Verwaltungsrecht' (1989) 80 VerwArch 261–301; Uwe Diederichsen and Gerhard Wagner, *Die BGB-Klausur* (8th edn, C.H. Beck 1994) 169.

[7] Carl F. Stychin and L. Mulcahy, *Legal Methods and Systems: Text & Materials* (Sweet & Maxwell 2010) 106.

decisions and from introductory texts intended for law students. Some of the descriptions are from the English-speaking legal world, others are translations from the German original.

Notice that some of the descriptions include a justificatory clause for why this particular style of argument is thought to be preferable. These justificatory clauses are not strictly relevant to the thesis and coverage of this book and are consequently not generally discussed, other than to point out that a few of the descriptions state or suggest that, if the application of the literal 'rule' affords an answer, then the judge may not consider the rule's history or purposes.

The purported pros and cons of the various styles of argument have been rehearsed in innumerable books and articles.[8] The author of this book does not contend that any style of argument is preferable to another. Indeed, he contends that all of the arguments should be available but that each one should be used transparently and candidly: the person interpreting should explain why he or she chose the particular argument or arguments and why he or she rejected other arguments that, at first glance, appeared to be more obvious choices. In other words, the person must explain why he or she prefers the result that the chosen argument or arguments allowed him or her to reach.

Some legal commentators note that the textual style of argumentation is frequently employed in other subjects in the humanities, where it is referred to as 'interpretation'.[9] In part because this style of argumentation is readily accepted in other disciplines, the view is taken that the textual approach should prevail over other methods or styles of legal interpretation.[10] For the purposes of this book, the fact that textual interpretation is practiced in other subjects merely suggests that this style of argumentation is universal but not that it is preferable.

The following are descriptions of the so-called plain-meaning rule or literal method of statutory interpretation:[11]

> The literal rule provides that words must be given their plain, ordinary, and literal meaning.[12]

[8] The author therefore rejects any notion of transcendent or inherent integrity as advocated by Dworkin and others. For an excellent expose of the debate between Ronald Dworkin and Duncan Kennedy on this issue, see Raef Zreik, Ronald Dworkin, and Duncan Kennedy, 'Two Views of Interpretation' (2019) XXXII CJLJ 195.

[9] Norbert Horn, *Einführung in die Rechtswissenschaft und Rechtsphilosophie* (3rd edn, C.F. Müller in Hüthig Jehle Rehm 2004) mn. 178.

[10] Rüthers *et al.*, *Rechtstheorie*, mn. 731.

[11] A few of the quotations literally exhort judges to reach results that the judges believe to be absurd. This is a very odd exhortation in any context but especially so when it is made in the context of a 'rule'. Although these exhortations smack of the discredited defence of 'just following orders', in fact, it is very difficult to find examples in which judges have taken their own advice literally, so to speak. In fact, such utterances entered into jurisprudential discourse during times in history in which there was a hypersensitivity among judges that their role in interpreting statutes would be construed as a political activity. While one can still, today, find references to these exhortations, particularly in academic literature, it is doubtful that they have any currency.

[12] Emily Finch and Stefan Fafinski, *Legal Skills* (Oxford University Press 2021) 59.

The first principle in interpretation is that the judge should apply the words according to their 'ordinary, plain and natural meaning'.[13]

To use the literal rule, 'take only the plain, literal meaning of the words used because those are the words the draftsman chose to employ'.[14]

The wording of a statute has a double function: it is the starting point of judicial perception of purpose and defines the limits of interpretation.[15]

The essence of the literal rule is that the courts simply look at the words and apply them as they are written with the suggestion that Parliament must have known what they meant.

[The literal rule] gives all the words in a statute their ordinary and natural meaning, on the principle that the best way to interpret the will of Parliament is to follow the literal meaning of the words they have used.[16]

If the language of the statute be plain, admitting of only one meaning, the Legislature must be taken to have meant and intended what it has plainly expressed, and whatever it has in clear terms enacted must be enforced though it should lead to absurd or mischievous results.[17]

The literal rule seeks to give the words a meaning which equates with their ordinary meaning in the context of the Act, whether that is a popularly understood meaning or a technical meaning.[18]

This view of judicial interpretation holds that the judge should look primarily to the words of the legislation in order to construe its meaning and, except in the very limited circumstances considered below, should not look outside of, or behind, the legislation in an attempt to find its meaning.[19]

The general approach which is said to be the primary method of common-law statutory interpretation is usually referred to as the literal approach. The classic statement of this technique is found in The Queen v Judge of the City of London Court [1892] 1 QB 273: If the words of an Act are clear, you must follow them, even though they lead to a manifest absurdity. The Court has nothing to do with the question whether the legislature has committed an absurdity. The literal approach demands that the court apply the ordinary, natural meaning of the words used.[20]

[13] Penny Darbyshire, *Darbyshire on the English Legal System* (Sweet & Maxwell 2020) 30.

[14] James Holland and Julian Webb, *Learning Legal Rules: A Student's Guide to Legal Method and Reasoning* (Oxford University Press 2022) 258.

[15] Arthur Meier-Hayoz, *Der Richter als Gesetzgeber* (Juris-Verlag 1951) 43.

[16] Emily Allbon and Sanmeet Kaur-Dua, *Elliott & Quinn's English Legal System* (1st edn, Pearson 2020) 57–58.

[17] John N. Adams and Roger Brownsword, *Understanding Law* (Sweet & Maxwell 2006) 105, quoting Lord Atkinson in *Vacher & Sons v. London Society of Compositors* (1912) HL 18.

[18] Colin Manchester and David Salter, *Manchester and Salter on Exploring the Law: The Dynamics of Precedent and Statutory Interpretation* (Sweet & Maxwell 2011) 40.

[19] Gary Slapper and David Kelly, *The English Legal System* (Routledge 2020) 96.

[20] Peter Goodrich, *Reading the Law: A Critical Introduction to Legal Method and Techniques* (Blackwell Publishers 1986) 54.

> The only rule for the construction of Acts of Parliament is that they should be construed according to the intent of the Parliament which passed the Act. If the words of the statute are in themselves precise and unambiguous, then no more can be necessary than to expound those words in that natural and ordinary sense. The words themselves alone do, in such a case, best declare the intention of the law giver.[21]

The quotations above evince a number of assumptions. The first assumption, at least from the chronological standpoint of legal reasoning, is that the interpreter of the statute has already chosen which rule to apply, that is, the statute for purposes of the above quotations. As was shown in Chapter 2 ('Making, Finding, Applying, and Justifying'), the choice of which rule to apply is not a logically deductive process. And the choice sometimes involves the exercise of a high degree of discretion, meaning that the choice, in such instances, is subjective, not objective. Second, in the quotations above, the interpreter of the rule has already chosen a statutory rule to apply, not a rule drawn from a case decision for none of the sources cited here, or known to the author, mentions the plain-meaning rule in the context of interpreting judicial precedents. Further, some of the quotations above imply, or even expressly state ('defines the limits of interpretation'), that statutory rules, at least, cannot be employed for argumentation beyond their texts, which would presumably not allow for so-called teleological extensions, teleological reductions, and other argumentative devices that will be discussed later in this book.

Another assumption evidenced by the above quotations—the most important for the purposes of this book—is that the words of a rule can, at least in certain circumstances, be 'clear' or 'precise and unambiguous'. However, the words used in rules are not like numerical terms (like the numbers 1, 2, and 3) that have stable meanings.[22] In fact, legal words are (almost?) never endowed with a clear-cut, or even a static, meaning. Rather, their meaning is influenced by dynamic social conventions.

The meaning of words arises through a natural, evolutionary process in which the language gradually adapts itself to the needs, desires, and conventions of the people who employ the word. The determination of linguistic conventions (which is the subject of empirical linguistics) can therefore help find the meaning of a word, or at least 'a' meaning of a word. However, while scholars of language regard linguistic conventions as equivalent to facts, scholars of law, including judges, tend to rely on their intuition as to what the words 'really' mean in the context of the case before them.

[21] William Twining and David Miers, *How to Do Things with Rules* (Cambridge University Press 2010) 340 n. 92 also turn to a case decision for a 'standard definition', citing *Sussex Peerage Case* per Tindal CJ (1844) 11 Cl & Fin 85.

[22] Rolf Wank, *Die Auslegung von Gesetzen* (3rd edn, C.H. Beck 2005) 60.

It is often said that ambiguous and vague terms present a particularly difficult challenge in interpreting the meaning of words. A term is said to be ambiguous if it is capable of two or more different meanings. One such example is the word 'term' itself, which, in legal English, can mean a word, a contractual condition, a period of time, or perhaps something else. The word 'law' has many meanings, including a statute, rule, a system of rules, a court decision, or unwritten custom. And if one leaves the confines of legal terminology, 'law' can also mean a body of divine commandments or a scientific phenomenon that always occurs if certain conditions are met.

Since the words 'term' and 'law' are capable of two or more different meanings, they are considered to be ambiguous as defined above. In the case of ambiguous words, the meaning can only be determined by reference to context. This may prove to be fairly simple in the examples just referred to, but other terms and contexts can cause difficulties. Indeed, there are also cases where even the context does not help in ascertaining the meaning of an ambiguous word. According to some commentators, it is only when textual interpretation does not succeed in producing a clear result that one may resort to the historical and purposive interpretative methods.[23] But notice that the person interpreting the word is the one who has the last word, so to speak, on whether the result is clear or not.

Whereas ambiguous terms are said to be capable of more than one meaning, terms are said to be vague if they are uncertain in meaning and indefinite in scope.[24] Vague terms are sometimes said to have 'blurred edges'. In legal discussions, a term is often said to be vague when it is very broad in its reach. Accordingly, so-called vague terms can be found in general clauses in German law, such as the term *Treu und Glauben* in §138 of the German Civil Code, which roughly translates as 'unconscionability'.[25] Lawyers talk about 'concepts', by which they often mean something more abstract than the dictionary denotation of a legal term.[26] For example, the word 'freedom' is a legal term with certain denotations in various contexts. But, according to some, 'freedom' is also a concept that captures reflections or emanations from all the various imaginable usages of the

[23] For examples, see the various articulations in Chapter 5 of the literal rule of statutory interpretations at nn. 241–250.

[24] See generally William Van Orman Quine, *Word and Object* (MIT Press 1960) 85, 129.

[25] In fact, the doctrine of *Treu and Glauben* was the inspiration for the American Germanophile Karl Llewellyn to incorporate a doctrine of unconscionability into §2-302 of the Uniform Commercial Code in the United States.

[26] On the role of dictionaries in statutory interpretation argument in Canada, see Ruth Sullivan, *Statutory Interpretation* (2nd edn, Irwin Law Inc. 2007) 53 *et seq*. For the experience in the United States, see e.g. A. Raymond Randolph, 'Dictionaries, Plain Meaning, and Context in Statutory Interpretation' (1994) 17 Harv J Law Public Policy 71; Lawrence Solan 'When Judges Use the Dictionary' (1993) 68 Am Speech 1; Note, 'Looking It Up: Dictionaries and Statutory Interpretation' (1994) 107 Harv L Rev 1437; William N. Eskridge, Jr and Philip P. Frickey, 'Foreword, Law as Equilibrium' (1994) 108 Harv L Rev 26, 74 *et seq*. discussing dictionary shopping.

term, and from any similar, related terms, such as liberty and right. Consider, for example, the 'concept of ordered liberty', which has been held by the US Supreme Court to allow the Court to apply the protections of the first ten amendments to the US Constitution, which are textually directed to the federal government to the state governments.[27]

In 1914, the German jurist Philipp Heck, founder of interest-based jurisprudence (which will be discussed in section C 'Textual argumentation using statutes'), wrote that, with 'vanishing few' exceptions, every word is ambiguous (*mehrdeutig*). Yet, according to Heck, every word has a certain terminological core (*Begriffskern*) that is surrounded by the word's periphery (*Begriffshof*), which gradually disappears.[28] H.L.A. Hart echoes this distinction when he writes that 'all rules have a penumbra of uncertainty where the judge must choose between alternatives'.[29] Yet Hart, like Heck before him, insists that there is no such uncertainty—and thus no judicial discretion—when a case falls within the core of a rule, that is, in cases 'in which no doubts are felt about its application'.[30] Thus, according to Heck and Hart, those factual situations that fall within the core meaning of the word or rule are, more often than not, unambiguous, whereas those situations that fall outside the terminological core are ambiguous.

Consider, for example, the German word *Mensch*, which means 'human being'. Section 212 of the German Penal Code, discussed in Chapter 2, provides that any person who kills a human being but who is not guilty of murder is guilty of manslaughter. Putting aside the question of whether suicide constitutes manslaughter in a literal reading of this provision, we can agree with Hart that 'no doubts' would be 'felt about' concluding that a thirty-year-old healthy and alert woman would qualify as a human being for the purposes of §212. In case of her death at the hand of another, we would conclude that the person who killed her is guilty of at least manslaughter. And we would not expect the judge, in pronouncing judgment, to make a special point of explaining why the victim fits the definition of 'human being' because 'no doubts are felt about its application'.

But what if the thirty-year-old woman, before she was killed, had lain for years in a hospital bed with no discernible brain activity, in other words, she was brain dead in common parlance? Is the person who killed her guilty of manslaughter? Was this actually a killing within the meaning of the statute? Do we 'feel doubts … about its application' in this situation? If so, does this woman belong within the penumbra of the term '*Mensch*' and of §212? Further with this scenario, what if the female

[27] Jacob W. Landynskii, 'Due Process and the Concept of Ordered Liberty: "A Screen of Words Expressing Will in the Service of Desire"?' (1974) 2 Hofstra L Rev 1.

[28] Philipp Heck, 'Gesetzesauslegung und Interessenjurisprudenz' (1914) 112 AcP 1, 173.

[29] H.L.A. Hart, Leslie Green, Joseph Raz, and Penelope A. Bulloch, *The Concept of Law* (3rd edn, Oxford University Press 2012) 12.

[30] H.L.A. Hart, 'Positivism and the Separation of Law and Morals' (1958) 71 Harv L Rev 593, 607.

victim was not yet born? Would she be a *Mensch* the moment after conception, or shortly before birth, somewhere in between, or not until she is born? German case law points to the beginning of the birth pangs in the case of natural birth and the opening of the womb in the case of Caesarean section. The reader can see the problems presented by the core/penumbra distinction.

Allan C. Hutchinson takes Hart—and, by extension, Heck—to task for Hart's core/penumbra distinction regarding the interpretation of the prohibition 'no vehicles in the park'.[31] In explaining the distinction, Hart writes that this prohibition 'plainly ... forbids an automobile'. In other words, 'no doubts are felt about [the prohibition's] application' to an automobile. Hutchinson points out that 'vehicle' existed as a word long before automobiles were invented so that the word 'vehicle' 'presumably had some different core and settled meaning at that time' it was invented. And, of course, the core and settled meaning at the time the word 'vehicle' was invented could not have been 'automobile' because automobiles did not exist. Consequently, when construing legal terms and rules, one needs to pay careful attention to the historical context and also to the present-day cultural and regional context for, as stated above, words are not like numbers. To quote Hutchinson again, it is all penumbra.[32]

C. Textual argumentation using statutes

In this part, we will look at judicial case decisions that employ textual arguments to decide the following questions: (1) Is electricity a 'movable thing'? (2) Are opaque glass blocks 'windows'? (3) Are the parents of a bridegroom 'parties to a contemplated marriage'? (4) Do cleaning and oiling constitute 'repairing'? and (5) Is hydrochloric acid a 'weapon'?

All of these case decisions hinge on the definitions of the words in quotation marks. And, in all of these cases, it will be seen that judges sometimes employ other arguments, such as purposive arguments, in addition to textual arguments to justify their judgments. It will also be seen that the judges could have decided the cases a different way if they had chosen to do so.

[31] Allan C. Hutchinson, *Toward an Informal Account of Legal Interpretation* (Cambridge University Press 2016) 32–33, reviewed by Thomas Lundmark, 'Hutchinson, Toward An Informal Account of Legal Interpretation' (2017) 80 MLR 1178.

[32] Hutchinson, *Toward an Informal Account*, 35. See also David Mellinkoff, 'The Myth of Precision and the Law Dictionary' (1983) 31 UCLA L Rev 423. The complexity of such enquiries is magnified enormously in international law in light of the scores of languages involved. On the topic in general, see Heikki E.S. Mattila, *Comparative Legal Linguistics* (Ashgate 2006); Marcus Galdia, *Legal Constructs Reflections on Legal-Linguistic Methodology* (Faculty of Modern Languages and Literature (UAM) Poznan 2021).

(1) Is electricity a 'movable thing'?

One classic example of a statute being construed textually is provided by §242(1) of the German Penal Code:

> Whosoever takes from another person a movable thing [*bewegliche Sache*] that belongs to that person with the intent to unlawfully appropriate it for himself or a third person shall be punished by imprisonment not exceeding five years or by fine.

Is electrical current a 'movable thing' for the purposes of §242(1)? In a well-known case from 1899, the *Reichsgericht*, the predecessor of the German Federal Supreme Court, held:

> The term 'thing' [*Sache*] is to be understood as a physical thing. It is commonly understood in this way in [legal] science and case decisions, and as repeatedly expressed by the *Reichsgericht*... According to the prevailing natural understanding [of the term], which understanding corresponds to the findings and the terminology of the natural sciences, the nature of a physical thing implies substance, matter that fills space, that is the body [*Körper*] in a physical sense. [Consequently, on this textual approach, electrical current cannot qualify as a 'thing' for the purposes of the section.]

As this example shows, textual argumentation ostensibly searches for the true meaning of the statute by defining terms in the manner that Heck described in section A of this chapter. This type of argument superficially means taking the legislators at their word. And, like all statutory interpretation or construction, this argument results in a judicial concretization, refinement, or re-articulation of the statute, something that is referred to in this book as a 'gloss' and which is discussed further in section C below. Occasionally, the concretization is implicit so that it must be induced from the result. But in this case, and in most cases, the concretization is explicit: electrical current is not a physical 'thing' for the purposes of §242(1). In any future case in which someone taps electricity from someone else, the gloss will be applied textually, and no prosecution under §242(1) will succeed.

Sticking closely to the text of the statute is said to limit judicial discretion. After all, the argument goes, the legal terms themselves will only bear a certain amount of linguistic re-defining—of stretching and contracting—before they completely lose their meaning. The best counter-argument to this purported limitation on judicial discretion is to point out that judges *choose* to employ non-textual arguments when they are convinced that the result they would otherwise reach is incorrect, unreasonable, unjust, or not what was intended. In the case of the purloined electrical current, the purpose of the statute was to deter and punish people for taking something of value from another person. Because electricity is something of value, the person who siphoned electricity could be found guilty, and the judges would employ a purposive argument to uphold and justify the conviction. Indeed, construing a similar statute that criminalized theft, the Supreme Court of the Netherlands held, in 1921, that the appropriation of electricity was punishable as a theft of property.[33]

The electricity example shows that textual arguments can sometimes be employed to support curious results. Most members of the public would probably have difficulty understanding why siphoning off electricity from one's neighbour is not a crime, but syphoning off the neighbour's water is. Nevertheless, from a legal standpoint, the decision cannot be dismissed as being patently wrong for courts from other countries have reached the same result.[34] But the *Reichsgericht* might well have decided the case otherwise: it might have decided, as did the Supreme Court of the Netherlands, that electricity is, indeed, a 'thing' for the purposes of the statute. And it is arguable that this latter construction would have been the 'true' meaning of the statute, that is to say the true meaning as intended by members of the German legislature, the *Reichstag*, the Imperial Parliament. For one year after the *Reichsgericht's* decision in the electrical current case, the *Reichstag* specifically criminalized the theft of electrical current in what is now §248c of the German Penal Code.[35] If statutory interpretation is supposed to anticipate how the legislature would decide, then the *Reichsgericht* got it wrong.

(2) Are opaque glass blocks 'windows'?

An interesting usage of textual arguments can be found in a case by the German Federal Supreme Court in 1960 that was faced with the construction (i.e. interpretation) of the word 'window' in a covenant between two adjoining landowners.[36]

[33] HR 23-05-1921, NJ 1921, 564 (*Elektriciteitsarrest*), discussed in Geert Corstens and Rteinder Kuiper, *De Rechter Grijpt de Macht: En andere misvattingen over de democratische rechtsstaat* (Prometheus 2020) and C.W. Maris, 'Milking the Meter: On Analogy, Universalisability and World Views' in Patrick Nerhot (ed.), *Legal Knowledge and Analogy: Fragments of Legal Epistemology, Hermeneutics and Linguistics* (Springer 1991) 71 et seq.

[34] A similar approach can be seen in England, as discussed in Holland and Webb, *Learning Legal Rules*, 267 and n. 14. In *Low v. Blease* (1975) Crim. L.R. 513, 'the Division Court held that electricity was not "appropriated" . . . by switching on the current, nor, the court said, could electricity constitute "property" within s.4 of the Theft Act'.

[35] Section 248c(1) of the German Penal Code:

> Whosoever taps the electrical energy of another from an electrical facility or installation by means of a conductor which is not intended for the regular withdrawal of energy from the facility or installation, shall, if the offence was committed with the intent of appropriating the electrical energy for himself or a third person, be liable to imprisonment not exceeding five years or a fine.

[36] *BGH*, Urt. v. 13 July 1960—V ZR 90/59.

According to this covenant, if any building were to be constructed on the property line with the neighbour's property, then no window shall be installed that faces the neighbour's property. In alleged violation of this covenant, the defendant installed a number of glass blocks in the wall facing her neighbour's land. The blocks were recessed into the wall, similar to windows, but the surface of the glass had grooves so as to let in light, similar to windows. But, unlike windows, the grooves in the glass obscured the view.

Were these glass blocks 'windows' in the sense of the covenant? This case is particularly interesting because of §133 of the German Federal Civil Code, which applies to declarations of intent in contracts, such as the covenant here. Section 133 reads: 'When a declaration of intent is interpreted, it is necessary to ascertain the true intention rather than adhering to the literal meaning of the declaration.' In the context of interpretation, ascertaining the 'true intention' is attempting to discern the historical, subjective intent of the people who composed the covenant. It is not clear, from the reports of the case, whether the parties to this lawsuit were the ones who composed the covenant. But if they were, it seems safe to assume that neither one had given any thought whatsoever to the question of whether glass blocks should be prohibited for if one of the parties had given thought to the question, he or she could have provided for this eventuality by inserting language into the covenant to allow or to prohibit such blocks.[37]

Because it is not possible to 'ascertain the true intention' of the parties in this case, who should win? The court cannot split the difference. The answer should arguably turn on the purpose of the prohibition against windows. If the purpose was aesthetic, then anything that looks like it might be a window, such as these glass blocks, should be prohibited. If the reason is privacy, then only transparent materials should be prohibited, which would mean that the translucent glass blocks in this case were not offensive. But notice that the latter interpretation—translucent materials are inoffensive—might open up the door for the adjoining landowner to install window frames with glass that is merely translucent but not transparent.

No matter which way the case is decided, the judge needs a reason or, better, an argument. And there are only four in this example: textual, historical, purposive, and system-contextual (including analogical). The historical argument has been dealt with: it is impossible to know the 'true intention', and, as far as we know, there are no *travaux préparatoires*-like documents to add credence to the judge's decision one way or the other. On the other hand, there are purposive arguments to

[37] Notice that the interpretational conundrum for the judges in this case would be the same if the prohibition against windows were contained in a municipal ordinance or building code. However, a building code might contain a definition of the word 'window'. Also, there might be committee reports or other *travaux préparatoires* that would evidence the subjective intentions of the drafters or adopters of the code.

support either decision, depending upon whether aesthetics is seen as the purpose or whether the purpose is privacy. No system-contextual-analogical argument presents itself, nor was one needed in this case. For the judges decided to employ a textual argument:

> In common usage, a window's essential characteristic is its translucency. Consequently, one can still speak of a 'window' if openings in a wall are filled with glass blocks that are opaque and allow neither air nor noises to pass through.[38]

Notice that, if the court had wanted to decide the case the other way, it could simply have stated that, 'in common usage', the essential characteristic of a window is its transparency.

(3) Are the parents of a bridegroom 'parties to a contemplated marriage'?

A textual argument was also employed in a California case where the court was called upon to decide whether an intended bride was entitled to keep two engagement presents given to her at the time of her engagement. One present was the diamond ring that the bridegroom had given to her, and the other present was an expensive wristwatch, set in diamonds, that the bridegroom's mother had given the intended. The trial court found that it was the bridegroom who broke off the engagement, not his intended bride; further, that the gift from the mother was nonrevocable under the applicable statute. At issue was the proper construction of §1590 of the Civil Code, which reads:

> Where either party to a contemplated marriage in this State makes a gift of money or property to the other on the basis or assumption that the marriage will take place, in the event that the donee refuses to enter into the marriage as contemplated or that it is given up by mutual consent, the donor may recover such gift or such part of its value as may, under all of the circumstances of the case, be found by a court or jury to be just.

Although §1590 speaks of a 'party to a contemplated marriage', the would-be bridegroom urged the court to apply the statute liberally to allow him also to recover for the expensive wristwatch that had been a gift from his mother and father. In the terminology employed in this book, the son was urging the judges to extend the

[38] *BGH*, Urt. v. 13 July 1960—V ZR 90/59.

statute according to its purpose or to extend the statute by analogy. The purposive argument would look to the purposes behind the statute, that is, to avoid unjust enrichment and to encourage engagement presents. The analogical argument would be that the bridegroom's parents should be allowed to step into their son's shoes as both the son and his parents found themselves in the same predicament; but, unlike the son, the parents did not break off the engagement. The bridegroom may well have argued that allowing his parents to recover the watch would be 'just' in the words of the statute, 'under all of the circumstances of the case', which could also be termed a textual argument.[39]

The California Court of Appeal refused to depart from what it perceived to be the clear language of the statute:

> The clear meaning of [§1590] is that the donee of an engagement ring is entitled to retain possession thereof when the marriage contract is breached by the donor without any fault on the donee's part ... [As to the gift from the appellant's parents], appellant could not in any event recover the watch as it was not a gift made by a party to the contemplated marriage.[40]

Is it clear that the bridegroom's parents are not 'parties to the contemplated marriage'? Could it not be argued, with a straight face, that, by accepting the very expensive gift of a wristwatch set in diamonds, the fiancée was embracing the bridegroom's parents as 'parties'? And, since the parents did not 'breach' the 'marriage contract', should they not be able to recover this very expensive gift? Or, if the judges in this case had wanted to, they could have ruled that one of the purposes of the statute was to avoid unjust enrichment, which would justify a court order that the wristwatch be returned.

(4) Do cleaning and oiling constitute 'repairing'?

Berriman v. London & North Eastern Railway Co.[41] is a good example of a court concealing behind textual arguments the real motivations that led to their judgment. While the judgments or 'speeches' of the five British Law Lords who decided the case are almost exclusively devoted to textual arguments about the

39 Although the arguments of the parties are not discussed in detail in the case report, it is reported that the would-be bridegroom contended that

> his refusal to celebrate the marriage does not entitle respondent to the ring for the reason that a marriage was a necessary prerequisite to the passing of the title of the ring—in other words, an implied condition to the vesting of the title to the ring in respondent, citing Ruehling v. Hornung, 98 Pa. Super 535.

40 *Simonian v. Donoian*, 96 Cal. App. 2d 259, 262 (1950).

41 *Berriman v. London & North Eastern Railway Co.* (1946) AC 278.

meaning of the terms 'permanent way', 'permanent way man', and 'repairing', their speeches also contain certain passages which demonstrate that the judges did, indeed, take matters other than terminology into account, as one would expect. Textualism does not prohibit judges from thinking about the purposes served by a rule or about the effect of their judgment on the public at large; rather, textualism simply places limits on the arguments that judges may use in crafting their judgment.

Berriman concerned a fatal accident that occurred in the early afternoon of 17 December 1943 along the rail line between the town of Brough and Kingston upon Hull, a port city in northeastern England. The decedents, Frederick Berriman and Mr Rowe, were cleaning and oiling the metal connections leading from a signal cabin up to the 'slide chair' that moves a piece of track, which, in turn, determines the direction the next train will take. This piece of track is moved by pulling a lever in the signal cabin.

Berriman's widow sued her late husband's employer, the railroad company, alleging that the company had violated Rule 9 of the Prevention of Accidents Rules 1902, which had been promulgated pursuant to the Railway Employment (Prevention of Accidents) Act 1900. This Act provides for criminal penalties for violation of the rules promulgated pursuant to the Act. Section 1(1) of this Act, which is still in force, provides:

> The Board of Trade may ... make such rules as they think fit with ... the object of reducing or removing the dangers and risks incidental to railway service.

The rule at issue in this case—Rule 9—provided at the time:

> With the object of protecting men working singly or in gangs on or near lines of railway in use for traffic for the purpose of relaying or repairing the permanent way of such lines, the railway companies shall, ... in all cases where any danger is likely to arise, provide persons or apparatus for the purpose of maintaining a good look-out or for giving warning against any train or engine approaching such men so working.

As stated above, Berriman and Rowe were engaged in cleaning and oiling, which are activities that are undertaken to forestall the need for repairs. The two were working on and alongside the railroad tracks, which is a place 'where any danger is likely to arise'. It was agreed that Berriman and Rowe were not 'relaying' track for the purposes of Rule 9. But were they 'repairing the permanent way', as contended by Berriman's widow?

The trial judge ruled that the two workmen were not engaged in repairing for the purposes of Rule 9 and therefore denied recovery to their widows. The Court of Appeal reversed, holding 3:0 that cleaning and oiling did, indeed, constitute 'repairing'.[42] What followed on appeal to the House of Lords was a 13,500-word decision in which all 5 Law Lords delivered their own judgment. Three Law Lords—the majority—agreed with the trial judge that cleaning and oiling did not amount to repairing. Consequently, they restored (reinstated) the judgment of the trial court. Two Law Lords agreed with the three Lord Justices of Appeal. Accordingly, these two Law Lords dissented.

The opinions or 'speeches' of the dissenters, like those of the majority, consist primarily of textual arguments. However, both dissenting judges also made a purposive argument.[43] Lord Jowitt, in dissent, concludes:

> Having regard to the fact that the primary intendment of the Act in question was to provide more adequate protection for railway servants, I think it should be so construed in this case.[44]

The argument of Lord Jowitt can be described as an argument in favour of a teleological extension in that it would extend or stretch the word 'repair' to cover maintenance. Teleological extensions are discussed in Chapter 7. The other dissenter, Lord Wright, insisted that the 'construction adopted by the Court of Appeal ... [is] in accordance with good sense, and everyday use of language'. Lord Wright added a policy-orientated argument that discloses his motivation:

> [The] object [of this measure] is to protect and save human life. Least of all in such a measure can technical subtleties prevail, where the issue is between men's life and death. If it is necessary to take the specified precautions, when the work on which the man is engaged on the permanent way is renewing or replacing bolts or the like, surely it is equally necessary to impose the same safeguards when the man is cleaning and oiling. In each case, there is danger and the danger is the same.[45]

One can also find passages in the judgment of the majority that illustrate that extra-terminological considerations entered into the judges' thinking. Bear in mind that what was at stake was much more than the compensation for Berriman's widow for this precedent would extend to future spouses of employees who were injured.

[42] *Berriman v. London and North Eastern Railway Company* [1945] KB 462.

[43] Lord Wright, in dissent, made a policy-orientated, cost-spreading argument: '[T]he construction which I adopt ... would impose some additional burden on the railway company. That drawback must yield to the purpose of saving life, which must outweigh some small extra expense or trouble to the company': [1946] AC 278, 301.

[44] Lord Jowitt, ibid 291, remarked: 'At one moment of time a man might merely be oiling and cleaning and at another moment he might be doing something which is repair in the narrow sense of the word that is in making good something which has developed a fault.'

[45] Ibid 300.

As is stated in Lord Jowitt's judgment, all of the connections at all railroad junctions need to be cleaned and oiled weekly. This work was accomplished by two men (at the time), working together. Lord MacMillan, who was also in the majority, warned:

> If the word 'repairing' were to be extended to include the simple and routine matter of oiling and cleaning, the railway companies would require to provide persons or apparatus for the purpose of maintaining a good look-out or for giving warning of an approaching train or engine every time one of their servants oiled a single bearing in the system of points and connecting rods and this under the sanction of prosecution and penalties.

Lord Porter, also in the majority, perceived what he, at least, believed to be a substantial difference between cleaning and oiling, on the one hand, and relaying and repairing on the other:

> [M]en relaying or repairing ... will for extended periods be concentrated on their work and unable to watch for oncoming trains whilst so engaged, whereas men cleaning, oiling or changing points by hand are only momentarily engaged and can insure their own safety by looking to see the state of the line or lines before they undertake their job.

Finally, the Law Lords in the majority all made one purposive or policy-orientated argument, reminding readers that §11 of the Railway Employment (Prevention of Accidents) Act 1900 provides for criminal penalties:[46]

> Where penalties for infringement are imposed it is not legitimate to stretch the language of a rule, however beneficent its intention, beyond the fair and ordinary meaning of its language [MacMillan L].

In light of the fact that five of the judges who heard this case (three Lord Justices of Appeal and two Law Lords) would have ruled in favour of the widow and only four judges (one trial judge and three Law Lords) ruled against her, it should be obvious that the case might well have been decided the other way.

[46] Section 11 of the Railway Employment (Prevention of Accidents) Act 1900:

1) If any railway company or other company or person acts in contravention of, or fails to comply with, any rule under this Act, then—(a) the company or person shall be liable for each offence on conviction under the Summary Jurisdiction Acts to a fine not exceeding fifty pounds, or in the case of a continuing offence to a fine not exceeding ten pounds for every day during which the offence continues after conviction.

(5) Is hydrochloric acid a 'weapon'?

In late 1949 or early 1950, in a small city in northern Germany, a fifteen-year-old girl set out on foot to take a large sum of money to the bank. She carried the money in her purse, which was tucked tightly under her arm inside her coat. The girl had to pass an apartment building. A woman who was standing outside the apartment building lured the girl, by some artifice, into the entryway of the building. Once there, the woman took a bottle containing a solution of hydrochloric acid out of her own purse and splashed the liquid onto the girl's face. While the girl was distracted, the woman snatched the girl's purse and disappeared with the money. The girl suffered shock. Her eyes were inflamed. The acid burned a hole in the skin of the girl's face, leaving a small scar. Expert testimony established that the girl could have been blinded had the woman splashed the entire amount of the bottle into the girl's eyes.

The acid-splashing woman was charged with causing grievous bodily harm in violation of former §223a(1) of the Penal Code,[47] which read, at the time, as follows:

> If the bodily injury is inflicted by a weapon, especially by a knife or other dangerous instrument (*Werkzeug*), or by stealth, or by acting jointly with another, or by methods that pose a danger to life, [then the penalty shall be increased].

The German Federal Supreme Court was asked to decide whether hydrochloric acid can be considered a weapon for the purposes of §223a(1) of the Penal Code.[48]

A judge who is inclined to employ a textual argument would notice that, in mentioning 'a knife or other dangerous instrument', the Penal Code provision does not limit the definition of 'weapon' to such instruments; rather, knives and other dangerous instruments are not merely examples of weapons, they are also examples of particularly dangerous weapons. By singling out knives and other 'dangerous' instruments, this provision suggests, by way of *argumentum e contrario*, that there must be other instruments that are not as dangerous as knives but that can still be considered to be weapons. Further, the judge who is inclined to employ a textual argument must also consider that at least some items do not rise to the level of weapons at all since there is also a crime of (simple) bodily harm, which is found in §223, that does not require that a weapon be used. A consideration of such textual arguments might very well assist the judge in this case in concluding that acid is a weapon for the purposes of §223a(1) of the Penal Code. And, in fact, this is how the Federal Supreme Court decided in this case in 1950: acid is a dangerous instrument for the purposes of §223a of the Penal Code.

47 Now found in §224 of the Penal Code. The new version incorporates the holding of this case by adding the following: 'by employing poison or other substances dangerous to health'.

48 *BGH*, 21 November 1950—4 StR 20/50.

The reader might well ask why this case was even appealed all the way to the Federal Supreme Court. Is it not clear that acid attacks are just as dangerous as knife attacks, perhaps even more so? The answer lies in the history of this provision, which was enacted in 1871 as part of a comprehensive German Penal Code. A decade after its enactment, in 1882, the Imperial Court (*Reichsgericht*), the predecessor of the Federal Supreme Court, held, in a similar case, that sulphuric acid was not a dangerous instrument for the purposes of §223a of the Penal Code,[49] meaning that the defendant in that case could only be convicted of causing bodily harm, not the more serious crime of causing grievous bodily harm. Interestingly, the Imperial Court in 1882 reached its decision on the basis of the legislative record, which showed that the *Reichstag* had 'mechanical' weapons in mind, that is, weapons that could slash, thrust, stab, or be thrown or shot. This interpretation of the statute had been accepted as binding law for decades. However, the judges of the Federal Supreme Court chose not to follow the precedents and the generally accepted interpretation of the statute. Consequently, the judges needed to overrule the 1882 case in order to find that splashing acid qualifies as a dangerous weapon. In doing so, the Federal Supreme Court acknowledged and dismissed the legislative history, opting instead to construe the statute textually but using a modern understanding of dangerous instrument instead of the historical understanding of the term:

> As the technology of war has increasingly produced and used weapons to burn, stun, and poison, and even created weapons much more horrific than mechanical weapons, the clear distinction between mechanical and chemical agents, as was assumed in earlier times ... can no longer be maintained. This development has long been followed in the common usage of what is meant by 'weapon.'

This case neatly illustrates two things: that the meaning of words changes over time and that judges are the ones who define the words that are found in statutes.

D. Textual argumentation using judicial glosses on statutes (statutory precedents)

Judicial glosses are concretizations of statutes that explain or modify the statute. Glosses look like subsidiary legislation and can be understood as such.

The cases below all construe judicial glosses in a textual manner (i.e. they use textual arguments) to answer the following questions: (1) Does a landlord who cannot obtain financing still have a 'reasonable prospect' of carrying out a

[49] RG Rspr. Bd. 4 S. 298.

business? (2) Can in vitro fertilization constitute 'palliative treatment for an illness'? and (3) Is being pulled behind a boat in an inner tube a 'sporting activity'? These questions are discussed in order.

(1) Does a landlord who cannot obtain financing still have a 'reasonable prospect' of carrying out a business?

Section 30(1)(g) of the Landlord Tenant Act 1954 in the United Kingdom expressly allows a landlord to refuse to renew a lease to a business tenant if the landlord 'intends to occupy the holding for the purposes of a business carried on by him'. Contrary to what might appear to be the plain language of the statute, the courts, beginning with the Court of Appeal, have held that a mere intent on the part of the landlord is insufficient. In 1962, the Court of Appeal decided the case of *Gregson v. Cyril Lord Ltd.*[50] In that case, the Court of Appeal put a 'gloss' on §301(1)(g) by announcing two tests for judging intent in such cases:

> The question whether the landlords intend to occupy the premises is primarily one of fact, but the authorities establish that, to prove such an intention, the landlord must prove two things. First, a genuine bona fide intention on the part of the landlords that they intend to occupy the premise for their own purposes. Second, the landlords must prove that, in point of possibility, they have a reasonable prospect of being able to bring this occupation by their own act of volition.

This gloss on the statute—reasonable prospect of putting his intention into effect—amounts to a judicial modification of the statute in what can be termed a teleological reduction: the gloss reduces the potential breadth of the word 'intent'.

Forty years after *Gregson*, in the case *Zarvos v. Pradhan*,[51] the trial court ruled that the landlord in the case had failed to satisfy the second test; that is, he failed to show that he had a 'reasonable prospect', in the words of the gloss announced in *Gregson*, of being able to occupy the premises 'for the purposes of a business carried on by him', in the words of the statute. The trial judge justified his ruling textually, relying on the gloss announced by the Court of Appeal in *Gregson v. Cyril Lord Ltd*:

> I regard [this case] as one where the reasonable prospect of putting the intention into effect does not exist ... despite the fact the Mr Zarvos is experienced in this kind of business and once carried it out on the property. There is simply too

[50] *Gregson v. Cyril Lord Ltd* [1962] 3 All ER 907.

[51] *Zarvos v. Pradhan* [2003] EWCA (Civ.) 208. See Michael Haley, 'Section 30(1)(g) of the Landlord and Tenant Act of 1954: The Unjust Relegation of Renewal Rights' (2012) 71 Cambridge LJ 118, 146.

much money that will have to be borrowed in order to get the business up and running.

Note that the trial judge could have ruled that Zarvos did, indeed, 'in point of possibility, . . . have a reasonable prospect of being able to bring this occupation by [his] own act of volition': the judge could have ruled that Zarvos had a reasonable prospect of borrowing less money to set up some less costly business on the property.

Mr Zarvos appealed the judgment against him to the Court of Appeal, which affirmed the trial court's judgment.[52]

(2) Does in vitro fertilization constitute 'palliative treatment for an illness'?

In 1986, the German Federal Supreme Court was faced with having to decide what constituted 'treatment for an illness' for the purposes of health insurance. The insurance provisions at issue in the case are those that apply to health-insurance contracts covering Bavarian public officials. These provisions at the time obligated insurance companies to reimburse the costs incurred in the 'medically necessary treatment' of an insured person 'due to illness'. At stake in this case were the medical costs that had been incurred by the petitioner for an unsuccessful in vitro fertilization (IVF).

Some years before she turned to IVF, the petitioner had suffered a tubal (ectopic) pregnancy, necessitating the surgical removal of her left fallopian tube. Unfortunately, the petitioner's right fallopian tube was congenitally malformed. Consequently, the only possibility for the petitioner to conceive a child was through IVF.

The legal issue was whether the tubal pregnancy constituted an 'illness' for which IVF was a 'medically necessary treatment'. The trial court entered judgment in favour of the petitioner, but the intermediate appellate court reversed, holding, in effect, that infertility is not an illness.

On appeal, the Federal Supreme Court reinstated the trial court's judgment.[53] According to the Federal Supreme Court, the intermediate appellate court employed an overly narrow understanding of the term 'treatment for an illness' in that it had failed to employ a definition—a gloss—that had been announced by the Federal Supreme Court in 1977.[54]

In the 1977 case, the Federal Supreme Court held that necessary treatment includes 'palliative treatment for an illness'. The illness being treated by IVF in this

52 *Zarvos v. Pradhan*, 208. See Haley, 'Section 30(1)(g) of the Landlord and Tenant Act', 146.

53 *BGH*, 17 December 1986—IVa ZR 78/85; BGH Z 99, 228 (1986).

54 *BGH*, Urt. v. 14 December 1977 IV ZR 12/76.

case was, according to the Federal Supreme Court, not infertility as such but rather the cause of the infertility, that is, the tubal pregnancy which, as a side effect of that pregnancy, resulted in the removal of the petitioner's only functioning fallopian tube. In the case before the court, IVF was employed as a medical procedure that was necessary to take the place of the fallopian tube and thereby palliate this side effect.

This justificatory argument of the Federal Supreme Court is basically textual: what does palliate mean in this context? However, as is common practice, the Federal Supreme Court also went on to employ another argument. In this case, it was a policy argument, which is referred to in this book as a purposive argument. In this purposive argument, the court wrote that infertility often has a substantial negative effect on the self-image of the affected person and can lead to very serious conflicts between married couples, which can lead to mental illness.

Notice that the judges of the intermediate appellate court had decided the case differently. This fact indicates that the judges of the Federal Supreme Court could have decided the case against the petitioner, had they wanted to.

(3) Is being pulled behind a boat in an inner tube a 'sporting activity'?

Section 1714 of the California Civil Code is the general tort statute in California. Section 1714(a) reads as follows:

> Everyone is responsible, not only for the result of his or her willful acts, but also for an injury occasioned to another by his or her want of ordinary care or skill in the management of his or her property or person, except so far as the latter has, willfully or by want of ordinary care, brought the injury upon himself or herself.

According to what might appear to be the plain language of this statute, an injured person need only prove 'want of ordinary care or skill' (i.e. negligence) in order to recover. Does this standard also hold true for participants in sporting activities? That was the question facing the California Supreme Court in 1992, in the case *Knight v. Jewett*.[55] Recognizing that participating in sporting activities involves inherent risks, risks that participants have presumably accepted, the Supreme Court held, in that case: 'a participant in an active sport breaches a legal duty of care to other participants … only if the participant intentionally injures another player or engages in conduct that is so reckless as to be totally outside the range of the ordinary activity involved in the sport'.[56] Applying the gloss that it had pronounced,

[55] *Knight v. Jewett*, 3 Cal. 4th 296 (1992).
[56] Ibid.

the California Supreme Court in *Knight* ruled that participating in American-style touch football was such a sport. Consequently, the plaintiff was denied recovery because he failed to prove that the conduct that caused his injury was intentional or reckless.

But what of 'tubing', which involves riding on an inner tube while being towed behind a motorboat? The trial court in *Record v. Reason*[57] ruled that tubing was 'an active sport' and accordingly entered judgment for the defendant because the conduct of the defendant was not intentional or reckless. The Court of Appeal affirmed the judgment, employing textual arguments to support its judgment and by putting its own gloss on the Supreme Court's opinion in *Knight v. Jewett* by supplying a definition of 'sport' in this context:

> Compiling all of the distinguishing factors, it appears that an activity falls within the meaning of 'sport' if the activity is done for enjoyment or thrill, requires physical exertion as well as elements of skill, and involves a challenge containing a potential risk of injury . . . From the evidence presented, tubing meets these criteria.[58]

Notice that the Court of Appeal felt it necessary, or at least desirable, to define what 'sport' means in this context; for the word 'sport' often connotes that a person is involved in competition with another person or persons, which is not the case with tubing. In other words, the Court of Appeal, if it had wanted to, could have defined 'sport' differently, justifying the Court in reversing the judgment of the trial court, thus allowing the plaintiff's case to proceed.

E. Textual argumentation using 'pure' common-law precedents

The term 'common law' can have any number of meanings. In the English-speaking legal world (i.e. the common-law tradition), the statutory glosses discussed in section D would ordinarily be referred to as statements of case law or common law in the simple sense of judge-made law for the judges are 'making' amendments to the statute. However, in the civilian tradition, the glosses in the cases above would be referred to simply as statutory interpretation. In this section, we are considering a narrower category of case law. These are cases in which the judges do not purport to be construing statutes at all: they are announcing and developing law without the involvement of the legislature. To promote clarity, law in the absence of statute

57 *Record v. Reason*, 73 Cal. App. 4th 472 (1999).
58 Ibid.

is referred to here as 'pure' common law, which is termed *Richterrecht* (judges' law) in German.[59]

The following discussion will identify rules of 'pure' common law, that is, rules that are announced by judges in areas of law in which there is no statute that provides a rule of decision, and, of course, in which there are no judicial glosses on a statute that provides a rule of decision. After identifying these pure common-law rules, the discussion will cite examples in which these rules have been applied by other courts in a textual manner.

In the United States, the textual approach is probably the most common approach employed with rules derived from pure common law. One need only read the (usually brief) recitation of jurisdiction in the opinions of the US Supreme Court to see this phenomenon. Here is an excerpt from a recent decision of the US Supreme Court, *Department of Commerce v. New York*:[60]

> We begin with jurisdiction. Article III of the Constitution limits federal courts to deciding 'Cases' and 'Controversies.' For a legal dispute to qualify as a genuine case or controversy, at least one plaintiff must have standing to sue. The doctrine of standing 'limits the category of litigants empowered to maintain a lawsuit in federal court to seek redress for a legal wrong' and 'confines the federal courts to a properly judicial role.' Spokeo, Inc. v. Robins, 578 U. S. ___, ___ (2016) (slip op., at 6). To have standing, a plaintiff must 'present an injury that is concrete, particularized, and actual or imminent; fairly traceable to the defendant's challenged behavior; and likely to be redressed by a favorable ruling.' Davis v. Federal Election Comm'n, 554 U. S. 724, 733 (2008).
>
> The District Court concluded that the evidence at trial established a sufficient likelihood that the reinstatement of a citizenship question would result in noncitizen households responding to the census at lower rates than other groups, which in turn would cause them to be undercounted and lead to many of respondents' asserted injuries. For purposes of standing, these findings of fact were not so suspect as to be clearly erroneous. We therefore agree that at least some respondents have standing.

Judicial holdings on issues of pure common law are also applied textually in the United Kingdom, in California, and in Germany. For the United Kingdom, this phenomenon is illustrated below by the textual use of the common-law rule of the venerable case of *Rylands v. Fletcher*, decided in 1868. For California, there is an example below in which the common-law rule on product liability, which was announced by the California Supreme Court in *Greenman v. Yuba Power Products,*

[59] This is also the definition employed in Konrad Zweigert and Hans-Jürgen Puttfarken, 'Statutory Interpretation—Civilian Style' (1969–1970) 44 Tul L Rev 704, 717.

[60] 588 U.S. (2019).

Inc., is applied textually. The examples from Germany are two court decisions that announce, and apply, the judicially created cause of action for violation of a person's right of personality.

The following questions will be explored by way of illustration of the phenomenon that rules of 'pure' common law can be, and are, applied textually: (1) Does the rule in *Rylands v. Fletcher* apply to damage caused on the landowner's own land? (2) Is a pedestrian pathway and cycle path a 'product'? and (3) Does a magazine article that describes a woman as a 'milked-out goat' violate the woman's right of personality?

(1) Does the rule in *Rylands v. Fletcher* apply to damage caused on the landowner's own land?

In *Rylands v. Fletcher*, Fletcher built a reservoir on his land. The reservoir burst and flooded Rylands' land. Even though there was no negligence on Fletcher's part, according to the Law Lords, Fletcher was nonetheless (strictly) liable. The House of Lords, adopting the reasoning of Mr. Justice Blackburn of the Court of Exchequer Chamber, held:

> [T]he neighbour who has brought something on his own property (which was not naturally there), harmless to others so long as it is confined to his own property, but which he knows will be mischievous if it gets on his neighbour's, should be obliged to make good the damage which ensues if he does not succeed in confining it to his own property.[61]

The elements of a *Rylands* cause of action are consequently (1) bringing something onto one's property, (2) while knowing that it will be mischievous if it gets onto a neighbour's property, and (3) causing damage when it escapes from one's property.

The 1947 case of *Read v. Lyons*[62] concerned an explosion during the Second World War in a munitions factory on the respondent's land. The explosion killed a man and injured the appellant and others. The trial judge awarded damages to the appellant on the authority of *Rylands v. Fletcher*, but the Court of Appeal reversed, holding that *Rylands* did not apply. The House of Lords agreed with the Court of Appeal. In his judgment, Viscount Simon employed a textual argument as to why *Rylands* did not apply:

> [I]n the case now before us the first essential condition of 'escape' does not seem to me to be present at all. 'Escape', for the purpose of applying the proposition in

[61] *Rylands v. Fletcher* [1868] LR 3 HL 330, 339–340.
[62] *Read v. Lyons* [1947] AC 156.

> *Rylands v. Fletcher*, means escape from a place where the defendant has occupation of, or control over, land to a place which is outside his occupation or control.

In conclusion, it was held that there could be no liability under *Rylands* for there had been no 'escape' from the land since the explosion occurred on the defendant's land and remained within its boundaries.[63]

Notice that the Law Lords in this case could have extended the rule of *Rylands* to encompass the present case as there was no legislation on the issue of occupiers' liability at the time. The Occupiers' Liability Act 1957 had not yet been proposed.

(2) Is a pedestrian pathway and cycle path a 'product'?

In the United Kingdom, the European Union, and some states in the United States,[64] product liability law is statutory. In California, product liability law is not statutory. It proceeds from the holding of the California Supreme Court in *Greenman v. Yuba Power Products, Inc.* This holding is employed by the California courts as if it were a statute. Here is the holding of *Greenman*:

> A manufacturer is strictly liable in tort when an article he places on the market, knowing that it is to be used without inspection for defects, proves to have a defect that causes injury to a human being.[65]

To award damages under this holding, an injured person who has been injured due to a defect must prove that (1) the manufacturer of the article (2) that has a defect (3) placed the article on the market (4) knowing that the article was to be used without inspection for defects. For the record, *Greenman* involved injuries to a man in San Diego by an allegedly defective Shopsmith, which is a combination power tool that can be used as a saw, drill, and wood lathe. While the injured man could not prove negligence at trial, he did successfully prove that the Shopsmith was defective.

The plaintiffs in *Fisher v. Morrison Homes, Inc.*[66] were the parents of a six-year-old boy who was killed when he rode his bicycle off a pedestrian pathway and cycle path onto a street in City of Pleasanton, California, which is near the San Francisco Bay area. The alleged defect was the absence of a barrier between the pedestrian

[63] Ibid 168.

[64] See Geraint Howells and David G. Owen, 'Products Liability Law in America and Europe' in Geraint Howells, Iain Ramsay, and Thomas Wilhelmsson (eds), *Handbook of Research on International Consumer Law* (2nd edn, Edgar Elgar 2018) 202 n. 37, listing Maine, Oregon, South Carolina, Alabama, Arkansas, Georgia, Indiana, Louisiana, Oklahoma, and Washington as states with statutes establishing liability for defective products.

[65] 59 Cal. 2d 57 (1963) 62.

[66] *Fisher v. Morrison Homes, Inc.*, 109 Cal. App. 3d 131 (1980).

pathway and street. While the action was allowed to proceed on a negligence claim, the California Court of Appeal rejected the product liability claim that was based on *Greenman*, the prevailing law in California. In rejecting the product liability claim, the court employed a textual argument:

> [P]athways . . . are not 'products' placed in the stream of commerce for profit, but are more akin to a service. Strict liability principles are therefore inapposite.[67]

Had the Court of Appeal wanted to rule the case in favour of the plaintiffs, it would have been hard pressed to fashion a textual argument that a pathway is a 'product placed on the market'. The Court of Appeal might, however, have employed language from the *Greenman* decision and from an earlier concurring opinion[68] of Chief Justice Traynor as a historical argument that the Supreme Court would also likely rule in favour of the plaintiffs, and the Court of Appeal could have constructed a purposive argument employing the policies behind product liability, such as the principle of compensating the injured, the advantage of internalizing the loss (cost-spreading), and the deterrence effect of such a ruling.

(3) Does a magazine article that describes a woman as a 'milked-out goat' violate the woman's right of personality?

In 1958, the First Civil Senate of the German Federal Supreme Court decided the famous *Herrenreiter*[69] *(Dressage rider) Case*, which involved advertising posters showing a photograph of a dressage rider astride his jumping horse. The product being advertised was an over-the-counter patent medicine to alleviate male sexual impotence. The horseman in the photograph was the plaintiff in the trial court. The photograph, which had been taken by a press photographer at an equestrian competition, had been used without the plaintiff's permission. While the poster caused no measurable financial detriment to the plaintiff or to his brewery in Cologne, it was insulting in that it implied that the plaintiff suffered from impotence. This exposed the plaintiff to public ridicule among the members of his social sphere. Further, an award to the plaintiff of a licensing fee, which might be permitted under existing law, would not compensate the plaintiff for his pain, suffering, and loss of amenity (*Schmerzensgeld*).[70]

The judges of the First Civil Senate might easily have ruled against the plaintiff on his claim for pain, suffering, and loss of amenity, for there is no statute

[67] Ibid n. 2.
[68] *Escola v. Coca Cola Bottling Co.*, 24 Cal. 2d 453, 461 (1944).
[69] This case will be discussed in more detail in Chapter 8 ('System-Contextual Argument').
[70] P.R. Handford, 'Moral Damage in Germany' (1978) 27 Int'l & Comp LQ 849.

in the German Civil Code that allows for an award of damages under these circumstances; and §253 of the German Civil Code states that no damages shall be awarded for non-financial loss (*immaterieller Schaden*) unless expressly provided for by statute.[71] Notwithstanding §253, which the judges (conveniently) failed even to cite in their decision,[72] the judges of the First Civil Senate of the Federal Supreme Court announced a new rule: 'Damages shall be awarded for substantial injury to the right of personality of another.'[73]

Five years after *Herrenreiter*, the Sixth Civil Senate of the same court, the German Supreme Court, considered a case in which a television newscaster from Berlin was criticized and ridiculed in a series of articles in the magazine *Stern*.[74] The articles insinuated that she engaged in deviant sexual behaviour and described her appearance as that of a 'milked-out goat' (*ausgemolkene Ziege*). The articles caused the woman mental distress and allegedly led to her dismissal from the television station where she worked at the time. The courts below awarded the newscaster damages for pain, suffering, and loss of amenity. After discussing the *Herrenreiter* and other decisions, the Sixth Civil Senate agreed:

> The intermediate appellate court correctly accepted that the prerequisites set out for entitlement to payment of compensation are met in the present case. It rightly pointed out that the violation of the law for which the defendants are responsible is particularly serious in view of the type of defamation and the substantial interference in the private sphere, with the widespread circulation of the magazine being of particular significance.

[71] Section 253 of the German Civil Code reads: '(1) For an injury that is not a financial injury, damages can be claimed only in cases determined by statute. (2) If damages are awarded for bodily injury, or for injury to health, liberty, or sexual self-determination, a claim for damages can also be made for non-financial injury.'

[72] The judges justified their ruling by citing Articles 1 and 2 of the German Basic Law, the Constitution, and by employing an analogy to §847, which has since been repealed; Huw Beverley-Smith, Ansgar Ohly, and Agnes Lucas-Schloetter, *Privacy, Property and Personality: Civil Law Perspectives on Commercial Appropriation* (Cambridge University Press 2006) 101. In 1958, when the *Herrenreiter Case* was decided, §847 read:

> (1) In a case of bodily injury or injury to health, as well as in a case of deprivation of liberty, the injured person can also claim damages for non-financial injury. (2) The same claim may be made by a female person against whom a felony or a crime against morals was committed, or who has been forced to co-habit through deceit, threat, or abuse of a relationship of dependence. Arguments by analogy will be discussed in Chapter 8 ('System-Contextual Arguments').

[73] BGHZ 26, 349 (1958). Another translation: 'The Civil Code … must also be construed to protect against injury to the "undisturbed exercise of decision-making" which constitutes the "freedom of self-determination over his personal sector of life"'; Paul M. Schwartz and Karl-Nikolaus Peifer, 'Prosser's Privacy and the German Right of Personality: Are Four Privacy Torts Better Than One Unitary Concept?' (2010) 98 Calif L Rev 1925, 1951. For an English translation of the decision, see Basil S Markesinis, *A Comparative Introduction to the German Law of Tort* (Clarendon Press 1986) 195–201. For an early discussion of 'personality' rights, see Roscoe Pound, 'Interests of Personality' (1915) 28 Harv L Rev 343.

[74] Fernsehansagerin: *BGH*, Urt. v. 5 March 1963—VI ZR 55/62 ausgemolkene Ziege.

This is a textual argument.

If the judges of the Sixth Civil Senate had wanted to deny recovery to the television newscaster, they might have encountered difficulties. For one thing, the decision of the First Civil Senate in *Herrenreiter* is formally binding on the Sixth Senate and the other eleven civil senates of the Federal Supreme Court.[75] Section 132(2) of the Court Constitution Act (*Gerichtsverfassungsgesetz*), which is applicable to the civil senates of the Federal Supreme Court, reads in relevant part: 'If one senate wishes to depart from the decision of another senate on an issue of law, the Grand Senate for Civil Matters shall decide.'[76] In other words, if the Sixth Civil Senate had wanted to deny recovery to the television newscaster because the judges of the Sixth Civil Senate disagreed with the law as stated in *Herrenreiter*, they would have had to refer the case to the Grand Senate for Civil Matters, which consists of the President and one other judge of each of the thirteen civil senates.[77]

F. Summary

This chapter, like the rest of the book, adopts an elastic interpretation of textual argument as an argument that focuses, either sharply or fuzzily, on one or more words of the rule that is sought to be employed. Whether one adopts an elastic interpretation or a strict interpretation, the illustrations in the chapter prove that the style of textual argument is exactly the same regardless of whether the rule derives from a statute, from a judicial gloss on a statute (statutory precedents), or from 'pure' common-law rules, that is, rules that are pronounced by judges in areas of law in which there is no statute that provides a rule of decision.

Various authorities insist that textual arguments are superior to other arguments because there are instances when the text is clear. Hutchinson counters these authorities by drawing attention to the fact that, unlike numbers, words must be understood in their historical and cultural context. Crucially for the purposes of this book, none of these authorities contend that textual arguments are superior to other arguments when applying rules from case law. Indeed, as will be illustrated in Chapter 6 'Historical Argument', the authorities universally embrace the use of historical argument when interpreting and applying the *ratios* and holdings of judicial precedents.

[75] Each of the federal courts in Germany (the federal courts are the highest in the court hierarchy) has a statute that forbids the senates of those courts from deciding cases in contravention of the holdings of previous cases of the other senates: Thomas Lundmark, *Charting the Divide between Common and Civil Law* (Oxford University Press 2012) 357.

[76] *Gerichtsverfassungsgesetz*, §132. As a procedural prerequisite, the Sixth Civil Senate would first have to enquire of the First Civil Senate whether the First Civil Senate still stood by its decision.

[77] *Gerichtsverfassungsgesetz*, §132(5).

6
Historical Argument

A. Introduction

Historical arguments highlight occurrences and circumstances—the historical setting[1]—before, during, and sometimes after the making[2] of the rule in question. At their core, historical arguments employ the historical setting to divine the subjective intent of the people who drafted the rule.[3] Elizabethan legal theorist Edmund Plowden (1518–1585) described this process as using one's imagination:

> And in order to form a right Judgment when the Letter of Statute is restrained, and when enlarged, by Equity, it is a good Way, when you peruse a Statute, to suppose that the Law-maker is present, and that you have asked him the Question you want to know touching the Equity, then you must give yourself such an Answer as you imagine he would have done, if he had been present.[4]

This imagination or divination of the subjective intent of the law-giver is not always articulated: often, the judges who employ historical arguments will merely speak generally about how the rule was understood in the past, or they will speak of the historical context. But the premise of the argument is the same: the historical law-giver, 'if he had been present', would agree with the decision that the judges have reached.

[1] Rupert Cross, John Bell, and Sir George Engle, *Statutory Interpretation* 141 (Butterworths 1987).

[2] As illustrated in this chapter, the rule may be a statute, judicial gloss on a statute, or a common-law rule.

[3] Because it attempts to reconstruct what the legislators would have done if confronted with the factual situation before the court, some commentators in Germany refer to this approach as the 'subjective method'. See Bernd Rüthers, *Die unbegrenzte Auslegung: Zum Wandel der Privatrechtsordnung im Nationalsozialismus* (2012) 182.

[4] Edmund Plowden, *The Commentaries, or Reports of Edmund Plowden, of the Middle-Temple, Esq; and Apprentice of the Common Law* [electronic resource]: *Containing Divers Cases upon Matters of Law, Argued and Adjudged in the Several Reigns of King Edward VI. Queen Mary, King and Queen Philip and Mary, and Queen Elizabeth. Originally Written in French, and Now Faithfully Translated into English, and Considerably Improved by Many Marginal Notes and References to All the Books of the Common Law Both Ancient and Modern. To Which Are Added, the Quæries of Mr. Plowden, Now First Rendered into English at Large with References, and Many Useful Observations. In Two Parts. With Two New Tables, More Compleat Than Any Yet Published; the One, of the Names of the Cases, the Other of Principal Matters* (1816) at 467 <https://archive.org/details/commentariesorre00grea/page/n11/mode/2up?view=theater> accessed 13 January 2024. Actually, as indicated in the title, this is a translation from the original, published in law French.

Universals of Legal Reasoning by Judges. Thomas Lundmark, Oxford University Press. © Thomas Lundmark 2024.
DOI: 10.1093/oso/9780198785675.003.0006

When making historical arguments about the application of a rule, judges often speak of the rule's 'context'. This can be confusing to the reader for the word 'context' can be used not only in the sense of 'historical context' but also with the other categories of argumentation as well. A quick search of academic articles reveals a myriad of usages of the terms 'textual context',[5] 'purposive context',[6] 'functional context',[7] and 'teleological context',[8] among many other usages of the term 'context'.[9] However, when the expression 'historical context' is being used, it invariably signals that a historical argument is being made.

There are various ways of defining this category of argument, with various nuances to the definitions. One academically prominent nuance concerns the use of legislative materials. When dealing with statutes and statutory instruments, this nuance of argument is characterized by references to the legislative record or *travaux préparatoires*. These references are usually to pre-enactment printed materials from the legislative bodies, such as the Parliament in the United Kingdom, the Congress of the United States, and the *Bundestag* and *Bundesrat* in Germany. In Germany and elsewhere, courts will also occasionally consider post-enactment evidence of legislative intent.[10]

Another nuance involving historical arguments is the 'originalist' or 'intentionalist' debate that is particularly conspicuous in the United States. In the United States, this debate is disputed most passionately by those advocating, and those opposing, the use of arguments about the original intent of the drafters of the Constitution of the United States. But, interestingly, this debate does not extend to the drafters of statutes or judicial case decisions.[11]

Of course, courts always consider the historical setting, even though this consideration remains customarily unspoken. If the issue before the court involves a rule

[5] See e.g. Leonid Sirota and Benjamin Oliphant, 'Originalist Reasoning in Canadian Constitutional Jurisprudence' (2017) 50 UBC L Rev 516 at n. 44.

[6] G.E. Devenish, 'Department of Land Affairs v. Goedgelegen Tropical Fruits—A Triumph for Teleological Interpretation, an Unqualified Contextual Methodology and the Jurisprudence of Ubuntu' (2008) 125 S African LJ 231.

[7] Jerzy Wroblewski, 'Problems of Judicial Reasoning in Civil Law and Common Law Systems—Some Reflections on Julius Stone's Approach' (1986) 10 Bull Austl Soc Leg Phil 187.

[8] Jorge M. Farinacci-Fernos, 'Looking for the Correct Tool for the Job: Methodological Models of Constitutional Interpretation and Adjudication' (2017–2018) 52 Rev Juridica U Inter PR 213.

[9] However, 'historical context' appears to be the most common usage.

[10] See Holger Fleischer, 'Comparative Approaches to the Use of Legislative History in Statutory Interpretation' (2012) 60 Am J Comp L 401, 434, citing 81 RGZ 276 (1913) at 292. The latter case is discussed in Thomas Finkenauer, *Das entstehungsgeschichtliche Argument als Etikettenschwindel: Zwei Beispiele aus der Rechtsprechung des Reichsgerichts zum Bereicherungsrecht, Das Bürgerliche Gesetzbuch und seine Richter: Zur Reaktion der Rechtsprechung auf die Kodifikation des deutschen Privatrechts (1896–1914)* (Max Planck für europäische Rechtsgeschichte 2000) 305.

[11] See generally Frank H. Easterbrook, 'The Role of Original Intent in Statutory Construction' (1988) 11 Harv J Law Public Policy 59, 61; Dennis J. Goldford, *The American Constitution and the Debate over Originalism* (Cambridge University Press 2005); Mitchell N. Berman, 'Originalism Is Bunk' (2009) 84 NYUL Rev 1; Robert W. Bennett and Lawrence B. Solum, *Constitutional Originalism: A Debate* (Cornell University Press 2011). See also Raoul Berger, *Government by Judiciary: The Transformation of the Fourteenth Amendment* (Harvard University Press 1977).

from an older statute or case decision,[12] the judge will unquestionably be receptive to an argument that the rule was understood differently when it was promulgated than it is today. And if the rule has just been promulgated, whether in a statute or case decision, the judge will instinctively, and unconsciously, consider the present (historical) context.

This chapter, by contrast, addresses instances in which judges do, indeed, mention the historical context for whether the judges consider the historical context or not is not the purpose of this inquiry. Rather, the purpose of this inquiry is to depict how judges wield historical arguments to fortify the plausibility and, thereby, the persuasiveness and acceptance of the results that they have reached.

Some of the ways of defining this category of argument when dealing with statutory rules are presented and discussed in section B. Section C provides examples of historical argument based directly on the wording of statutory rules. Section D does the same for historical argument based on judicial glosses on statutes, in other words, argument based upon precedents that have construed specific statutes. Section E considers historical arguments based on precedents that articulate rules of 'pure' common law, that is, where there is no statute or statutory gloss that provides the rule of decision.

One might wonder why it is necessary to distinguish between precedents based on statutory glosses (section D) and precedents based on 'pure' common law (section E). In fact, it is not necessary, as such, for the source of the rule is irrelevant: the processes of argumentation are identical regardless of the source of the rule. In the discussion that follows, it will be seen that this insight is a demonstrable fact. Nevertheless, there is an abundance of confusion in the legal literature on this point. And, in conversations and correspondence with the author, numerous academics have voiced their disbelief of this insight. In fact, one very prominent legal scholar wrote to the author: 'we find it difficult to accept ... that judges follow precedents as if they were following a binding statement in a text', by which the scholar presumably meant 'text of a statute'. Consequently, it seems essential to provide illustrations of the widespread, incontrovertible phenomenon that judges follow both judicial glosses on statutes (which are rules in themselves), as well as rules stated in precedential cases, based on 'pure' common law 'as if they were following a binding statement in a text' of a statute.

It should be remembered that all common law (i.e. judge-made law), including all judicial pronouncements that are based more or less directly on statutory or constitutional law, is embedded in, and limited by, the particular legal system. Indeed, until the middle of the nineteenth century in England and elsewhere in the common-law world, common-law judges were bound by the system of writs that only conferred jurisdiction upon them to decide certain standardized conflicts.

[12] In this book, the term 'judicial history' will be used when dealing with rules from judicial decisions, including judicial glosses on statutes.

And today, of course, judges in all of the examples addressed in this book are bound by a system of law and convention that limits their law-making prerogative. The US Supreme Court has the authority, for example, to declare acts of Congress and of the President to be unconstitutional, but the US Supreme Court, unlike the Supreme Court of the United Kingdom, has no general common-law jurisdiction.[13] Consequently, and in contrast to the UK and Californian Supreme Courts, more or less all of the decisions of the US Supreme Court (with extremely few exceptions) will contain citations to federal statutes, treaties, and constitutional law.[14]

B. Historical arguments in general

The following are descriptions of historical methods of statutory interpretation, quoted in part from introductory texts intended for students. Notice that the method of historical argumentation is often confounded with other methods. Some of the descriptions include a justificatory clause for why this argument should be used.

> In addition to the ordinary meanings of a text, its context includes precedent cases interpreting and applying the text, uncontroversial hypothetical cases, cases or situations governed by other rules within the same enactment, historical events or situations linked to enactment of the rule, contemporary historical, economic, and social practices at the time of enactment, and the examples given in the legislative history.[15]
>
> Statutes are to be read in the light of conditions at the time of their enactment. A new meaning is sometimes given to the words of an old statute because of changed conditions. The scope of a statute may appear to include conduct that did not exist when the statute was enacted—for example, certain activity related to technological progress. Such a case does not preclude the application of the statute thereto.[16]
>
> The philosophy [of the historical school of law] emphasizes the continuity in the law and believes that current laws should be constructed on that which has been done in the past. One can see the influence of this school of law in our system's reliance on case law and precedence. Also, so judges rely on the original intent of our Constitution's authors when attempting to interpret the Constitution.[17]

[13] *Erie Railroad Co. v. Tompkins*, 304 U.S. 64 (1938), overruling *Swift v. Tyson*, 41 U.S. (16 Pet.) 1 (1842).

[14] In this sense, the jurisdiction of the US Supreme Court is comparable to that of the German Federal Constitutional Court.

[15] Steven J. Burton, *An Introduction to Law and Legal Reasoning* (Walters Kluwer 2007).

[16] Frank August Schubert, *Introduction to Law and the Legal System* (Wadsworth 2023) 63.

[17] Scott Myers, *Introduction to Law* (Createspace 2011) 26.

> In order to determine the full intent of the legislature, any source that may assist in determining intent may be consulted: parliamentary or legislative debates, commission reports, and the statements of those responsible for the legislation.[18]
>
> [T]here are many aspects to a statute's history and some are more acceptably considered than others in statutory interpretation. Possible clues to meaning can be found in the social conditions that gave rise to the perceived need for the statute, how the statute changed the law, how the law had been changed earlier, and, finally, what was said in the legislature or its committees when the statute was passed.[19]
>
> At the very least, familiarity with the Act's history can inform the reader about the concerns that the legislature sought to address and the cogency and weight of the alternative constructions then being advanced.[20]
>
> The judge must 'try to think his way as best he can into the minds of the enacting legislators and imagine how they would have wanted the statute applied to the case at bar.'[21]

The last description above, which is attributed to Judge Learned Hand, echoes the process that Plowden described at the beginning of this chapter. Trying to 'imagine how [the enacting legislators] would have wanted the statute applied in the case at bar' is, indeed, a useful way to think about the mental process involved in making arguments based on history. But this mental process is not, by any means, limited to the enacting legislators. Indeed, this process of imagination is even more prominent when judges are dealing with rules from cases: in doing so, the judges are implicitly, and sometimes explicitly, asking how the precedential judges, who are occasionally still serving on the appellate court, would have wanted the rule to be applied in the case at bar.

One of the descriptions above speaks of determining the 'full intent of the legislature'. In a much-cited book,[22] William Eskridge reminds readers of what should be obvious: the intent of the legislators themselves, at least as a majority, is unknowable. The only thing we can be sure about is the text of the legislation that was enacted; and even determining the intent of the text can be troublesome, as we saw in Chapter 5. In Chapter 7 ('Purposive Argument'), we will ask whether the intent of the legislation itself (i.e. the legislative purposes) is knowable. But first, we will look at how judges employ historical arguments when applying rules directly from statutes, when applying rules indirectly from statutes(i.e. applying glosses on statutes), and when applying rules that arise from 'pure' common law.

[18] Neil Boyd, *Canadian Law: An Introduction* (Harcourt Brace 2018) 65–66.

[19] Jessie J. Horner, *Canadian Law and the Canadian Legal System* (Pearson 2007) 189.

[20] William Twining and David Miers, *How to Do Things with Rules* (Cambridge University Press 2010) 287.

[21] Archibald Cox, 'Judge Learned Hand and the Interpretation of Statutes' (1947) 60 Harv L Rev 370.

[22] William N. Eskridge, Jr, *Dynamic Statutory Interpretation* (Harvard University Press 1994) 16.

C. Historical arguments using statutes

In this section, we will look at case decisions that employ historical arguments to decide the following questions about how a statute should be applied: (1) Are minks 'farm animals'? (2) Does a specific, but limited, grant of regulatory authority to a public agency take precedence over the granting of authority for the public agency 'to do all things'? and (3) Did abolishment of a 'rebuttable presumption' also abolish the defence that a child is incapable of committing an offence?

(1) Are minks 'farm animals'?

The historical approach in Germany can be seen in a case construing a statute that requires all persons who raise vertebrates for sale to obtain a licence. To obtain a licence, the person who wishes to raise vertebrates for sale must pay a fee, supply detailed information, and agree to regular inspections to ensure compliance with any conditions that are imposed on the grant of the licence. Because the law could impose an unnecessary burden on the hundreds of thousands of farmers in Germany, the law exempts persons who raise 'farm animals' ('*landwirtschaftliche Nutztiere*'), even though farm animals are, of course, also vertebrates. Thus, those farmers who raise cows, goats, chickens, and presumably rabbits, are exempt from the licensing requirement.

A mink farmer contended that he was exempt from the licensing law because minks are 'farm animals' for the purposes of the statute. After all, minks are vertebrates, and they are kept and raised in a way similar to the way in which chickens and rabbits are kept and raised. In rejecting this contention, the Federal Administrative Court argued that the legislative history showed that the *Bundesrat* (the upper house of the German parliament), which proposed the exemption for farm animals, did not intend to exempt fur-producing animals:

> [The *Bundesrat*] considered that the breeding and raising of exotic animals, fur-producing animals, and the like often present problems. Persons who raise and breed such animals often have no, or at least insufficient, knowledge of feeding, care, housing, and breeding requirements, which sometimes leads to substantial abuses of the welfare of the animals.[23]

Why did the judges of the Federal Administrate Court employ a historical argument rather than a textual one? The answer appears to be that it would have been difficult to define 'farm animals' to exclude minks but to include other

[23] BVerwG 3 C 7.04; 9 December 2004.

small animals kept in cages, such as chickens and rabbits. Perhaps this explains why the judges did not even make a textual argument: they simply quoted the legislative record and left it at that. In any event, this case is a good illustration of the judges having made their tentative decision—not to exempt the raising of fur-producing animals—before looking for, and finding, an argument to support that decision.

(2) Does a specific but limited grant of a regulatory authority to a public agency take precedence over the grant of authority for the public agency 'to do all things'?

In 1979, the California Supreme Court was faced with two, apparently conflicting, statutory grants of authority to the California Public Utilities Commission (CPUC). The first grant of authority, which is found in §701 of the California Public Utility Code, provides:

> The [CPUC] may supervise and regulate every public utility in the State and may do all things, whether specifically designated in this part or in addition thereto, which are necessary and convenient in the exercise of such power and jurisdiction.

Section 701 grants far-reaching, general powers to the CPUC: the CPUC is empowered to 'do all things [that are] necessary and convenient'.

Many years after the initial enactment of the Public Utility Code, the California Legislature added §2782. This statute authorizes the CPUC to obligate regulated public utilities to adopt financing programmes—on terms prescribed in the statute—to help their residential customers afford home insulation. In response to §2782, the CPUC promulgated a new regulation. This new regulation mandated that public utilities implement financing programmes for home insulation on financial terms that were very unfavourable to the utilities. The largest natural gas distribution utility in California, the Southern California Gas Company, filed suit to challenge the legality of the new regulation.

In justifying the California Supreme Court's unanimous judgment that the CPUC had exceeded its authority, Justice Broussard began with a textual argument:

> The Legislature's express decision to enact a permissive program cannot reasonably be interpreted to have included an intent to allow the commission to institute mandatory programs under the general provisions of sections 701 and 702. The maxim *expressio unius est exclusio alterius* is applicable here. Clearly the express authorization of a permissive program impliedly precludes any authority to impose a mandatory program.

In order to enhance the persuasiveness of the Court's decision, Justice Broussard added a historical argument, one that invoked the legislative history:

> The Legislature gave careful consideration to the financing provisions of the Home Insulation Assistance and Financing Act ... The legislative history and specificity of the financing provisions belie the commission's assertion that the Legislature intended for the commission to be authorized to impose different financing terms.[24]

(3) Did abolishment of a 'rebuttable presumption' also abolish the defence that a child is incapable of committing an offence?

Centuries ago, common-law judges in England and Wales developed a defence, in the form of a presumption, that children lacked the capacity to know that their acts are wrong. Accordingly, children could not form criminal intent. If children did something wrong, they were being 'merely naughty or mischievous'. This presumption was conclusive for children under the age of ten, meaning that they could not be convicted of a crime. For children aged ten to thirteen, the presumption was not conclusive, meaning that the prosecution was afforded an opportunity to prove that the child knew that what he or she had done was seriously wrong.

In 1998, the UK Parliament abolished the presumption for children aged ten and older. Section 34 of the Crime and Disorder Act 1998 now states: 'The rebuttable presumption of criminal law that a child aged 10 or over is incapable of committing an offence is hereby abolished.'

In 2007, the police investigated a report that a twelve-year-old boy had been engaging in sexual activity with younger boys. The twelve-year-old boy told the investigators that he did not think what he was doing was wrong. Nevertheless, the boy was charged with violation of §13(1) of the Sexual Offences Act 2003. At the boy's trial in the Crown Court, his counsel sought to introduce evidence that the boy lacked the capacity to know that his acts were wrong. According to the boy's defence counsel, §34 had merely abolished the presumption, not the defence itself. The counsel's interpretation is, indeed, supported by a literal reading the text of the statute: 'The rebuttable presumption ... is hereby abolished.' However, the Crown Court judge refused to allow the defence to be raised, and the boy was convicted.

The conviction was unsuccessfully appealed to the Court of Appeal and to the House of Lords. The boy lost his appeals because all of the nine judges who heard his case, from the Crown Court judge to the Lord Justices on the Court of Appeal

[24] *Southern Cal. Gas Co. v Public Utilities Comm'n*, 24 Cal. 3d 653 (1979) 659–660.

to the Lords of Appeal in Ordinary, were convinced that §34 abolished not only the rebuttable presumption but also the defence itself. How did these eminent judges justify their decision?

Near the beginning of Lord Phillips's speech in support of the Law Lords' unanimous decision, Lord Phillips stated his conclusion that, '[i]n using the language of section 34 Parliament intended to abolish both the presumption and the defence'. While conceding that 'it is not possible to reach this conclusion from the language of section 34 alone', he wrote that 'it can be firmly founded once extrinsic aids to interpreting that section are taken into account'.

In this case, the 'extrinsic aids' cited by Lord Phillips were 'the mischief that the section was designed to obviate', which is a purposive argument, and, following *Pepper v. Hart*,[25] legislative history, which is a historical argument:

> Consideration of the debates discloses Ministerial statements that made the meaning of the clause quite clear, with the exception of the one statement by Lord Falconer. Furthermore, the proposed amendment was moved on the premise that the clause, as drafted, would abolish not merely the presumption but the defence of doli incapax. Parliament was in no doubt as to the meaning of the clause, in part perhaps because in the Consultation Paper and the White Paper that preceded the legislation the Home Office had made it quite clear what was meant by abolition of the presumption of doli incapax.[26]

D. Historical arguments using judicial glosses on statutes (precedents)

Historical arguments are also used when applying rules from precedents that are based on statutes; that is, the historical arguments are based on judicial glosses. Both of the examples below use glosses that are based on constitutional norms, which can rightly be understood as statutes that take precedence over other statutes. The examples below both show judges construing constitutional judicial glosses in a historical manner to help justify their answers the following questions: (1) Do the members of a church enjoy a constitutional right to enter onto the parking lot of a bank in order to solicit donations? and (2) Are self-incriminating remarks, made while driving alone in a car, admissible in a criminal case against the driver?

[25] *Pepper (Inspector of Taxes) v. Hart* [1992] UKHL 3 ruled that when judges are interpreting ambiguous statutes, they may refer to statements made in Parliament without breaching parliamentary privilege.

[26] *R v. JTB* [2009] UKHL 20. *Doli incapax* means 'incapable of evil'.

(1) Do the members of a church enjoy a constitutional right to enter onto the parking lot of a bank in order to solicit donations?

The historical approach to using precedential case decisions is widespread in California, which is also a common-law jurisdiction. The factual setting of a case might provide the historical context, which enables subsequent judges to apply the holding of the case in a manner more consistent with what they believe to have been the intentions of the judges who decided the precedential case. In other words, paraphrasing Plowden, quoted at the beginning of this chapter, the judges are 'imagining' what the judges in the precedential case 'would have done, if they had been present'.

This process can be witnessed in the justificatory reasoning, quoted below, in an opinion of the California Court of Appeal. At issue was the application of the holding, in *Robins v. Pruneyard Shopping Center*, of the California Supreme Court, which held that 'speech and petitioning, reasonably exercised', which are guaranteed in Article I, §§2 and 3 of the California Constitution, cannot be prohibited in shopping centres, even when the shopping centres are privately owned.[27] The question for the Court of Appeal was: does the holding of *Robins* extend to the parking lot of a bank that is located on a private street?

The case before the Court of Appeal involved members of a religious denomination known as the Church of Soldiers of the Cross of Christ of the State of California. These members had dressed themselves in white suits and, holding white buckets, had been standing on the private—not the public—sidewalk between the parking lot and the north entrance of a bank to solicit donations from the bank's customers as they entered and exited the bank. The bank petitioned for an injunction against the Church, which the trial court granted.

On appeal, the California Court of Appeal held that the constitutional rights to speak and to petition did not extend to the premises of a bank that was located on a city street rather than being located in a shopping centre. The Court of Appeal might have merely distinguished the *Robins* decision by stating that a city street is not a shopping centre and left it at that. That would have been a textual argument. However, the Court of Appeal employed a historical argument to distinguish *Robins*, namely that the Justices of the California Supreme Court had indicated in dicta, in *Robins*, that they did not intend to extend their holding to businesses on city streets. The Court of Appeal wrote:

> In *Robins*, the [California Supreme] court remarked: 'It bears repeated emphasis that we do not have under consideration the property or privacy rights of an individual homeowner or the proprietor of *a modest retail*

[27] *Robins v. Pruneyard Shopping Center* (1979) 23 Cal. 3d 899, holding that a shopping centre could not prevent political solicitation of signatures on the premises.

> *establishment*.' … Subsequently, the Supreme Court has never elaborated on this remark and has not revealed if it means the holding of *Robins* does not apply to modest retail establishments.[28]

In this example of using a historical argument to distinguish a precedential case, the Court of Appeal is implicitly suggesting(or 'imagining', to use Plowden's expression) that the judges in the precedential *Robins* case would agree with the Court of Appeal's decision 'if they had been present'. All judicial decisions that distinguish a potentially precedential case decision—that is, all judicial decisions that refuse to apply the *ratio* of an arguably precedential case decision—are examples of historical arguments for they explicitly state, or implicitly suggest, that the judges who decided the arguably precedential case decision would agree with the later court's decision not to apply the *ratio* of that case to the factual scenario facing by the later court.

(2) Are self-incriminating remarks, made while driving alone in a car, admissible in a criminal case against the driver?

Historical arguments based on previous judicial decisions can also be found in Germany. In the *Journal Case*, the Federal Constitutional Court let stand (due to a 4:4 split among the judges) a judgment of the Federal Supreme Court that allowed into evidence incriminating, journal-like notes that the accused had made in the course of psychotherapy before he committed a homicide and which he later voluntarily surrendered to the police who were investigating the homicide.[29]

Some years later, in another homicide investigation, the police, after obtaining a search warrant, recorded the accused making self-incriminating remarks like 'we killed her' when talking to himself while alone in his car. Were these remarks admissible? The Federal Supreme Court held that they were not. These utterances, according to the Court, belonged to the protected core of personality that is entitled to absolute protection from state intrusion.

In so holding, the Federal Supreme Court felt the need to distinguish the *Journal Case* of the Federal Constitutional Court, whose decisions are made binding by statute:[30]

> While the place in which the notes were made in [the Journal] Case was irrelevant to the question of the admissibility in a criminal proceeding of the thoughts recorded in writing, because the notes were voluntarily taken into police custody

[28] *Bank of Stockton v. Church of Soldiers*, 44 Cal. App. 4th 1623, 1629 (1996).

[29] *Tagebuchentscheidung*, BVerfGE 80, 367 (1989).

[30] Section 31 of BVerfGG(1): 'The decisions of the Federal Constitutional Court shall be binding upon federal and state constitutional organs as well as on all courts and administrative agencies.'

> with the accused's consent, in the present case the criterion of the non-public nature of the place in which the thoughts were uttered is of considerable import. While the fleetingness of the spoken word played no role in the journal decision because the person affected had written down his thoughts and in so doing had perhaps corrected them, the fleetingness of the spoken word takes on particular significance as a distinguishing feature in the present case. Furthermore, considerations of prevention were also relevant to the question of admissibility in the journal case because the journal notations in question were made before the offense was committed, and might conceivably have been of use in preventing the offense as a measure of protection of the public. In contrast, the possibility of prevention . . . plays no role in the present case.[31]

In the above passage, the Federal Supreme Court is implicitly arguing that the judges of the Federal Constitutional Court who decided the *Journal Case* would agree with the result that the Supreme Court was reaching in the case before it. This is the same type of argument that judges employ when they cite legislative history to support their conviction that the legislators who enacted a statute would agree with their interpretation of the statute.

E. Historical argumentation using 'pure' common-law precedents

The following discussion identifies rules announced in areas of law in which there is no statute that provides a rule of decision and, as a consequence, in which there is no judicial gloss on a statute that provides a rule of decision. In other words, these rules constitute 'pure' common law. After identifying these rules, the discussion will cite examples in which these rules have been applied by other courts using historical arguments.

The cases below will answer the following legal questions: (1) When does an agreement between spouses manifest an 'intent to create legal relations'? and (2) Does the *Greenman* excuse from the statutory notice requirement apply to a plaintiff who suffered only economic harm?

(1) When does an agreement between spouses manifest an 'intent to create legal relations'?

In *Balfour v. Balfour*,[32] the Court of Appeal for England and Wales refused to enforce a husband's statement, made before leaving his wife in England to take up his

[31] See *BGH*, 2 StR 509/10 of 22 December 2011; see (2012) NJW 945.
[32] *Balfour v. Balfour* [1919] 2 KB 571.

governmental duties in Ceylon (now Sri Lanka), that he would support his wife financially during their separation. The justification for refusing to do so, according to the Court, was that agreements between spouses are not ordinarily enforceable because familial financial arrangements do not manifest the intent to create legal relations. *Balfour* was decided in 1919, but this principle or rule regarding familial financial arrangements can be traced at least as far back as the case of *Weeks v. Tybald*, decided in 1605.[33] According to the short report of this 1605 case, the only report that is available, a father 'affirm'd and publish't that he would give £100 to him that should marry his daughter with his consent'.[34] According to the report of that case, the judge held that 'asseruit et publicavit doth not make words that include a promise'. The justification given by the judge in that case is reported as follows: 'It is not aver'd nor declar'd to whom the words were spoken, and it is not reason that the defendant should be bound by such general words spoken to excite suitors.'

Balfour, and by extension *Weeks v. Tybald*, were followed, in 1969, in the case of *Gould v. Gould*.[35] In *Gould*, a husband, who owned a garage business, left his wife and two children, telling his wife that he would pay her £15 a week 'so long as the business is O.K.' or 'so long as I can manage it'. The wife agreed to this arrangement. The husband made payments for over a year and then stopped. After hearing testimony from both parties, from which it could be concluded that the business was, indeed, still thriving, the judge of the County Court ruled for the wife, finding that the arrangement entered into between the parties was intended to create legal relations and to be enforceable. This brief finding constitutes a textual argument based on the holding in *Balfour*.[36]

The judgment for the wife in *Gould* was appealed to the Court of Appeal, which reversed. Two of the three judges who decided the case held that the facts as found by the County Court did not support a finding that the parties intended to create legal relations. This is also a textual argument based on the holding in *Balfour*. The third judge in the *Balfour* case, Lord Denning, dissented.[37]

[33] Discussed in Alfred William Brian Simpson, *Legal Theory and Legal History: Essays on the Common Law* (Hambledon Press 1987) 187

[34] King's Bench, 1605. Not. 11, reproduced in Arthur L. Corbin, *Cases on the Law of Contracts Selected from Decisions of English and American Courts* (West 1921).

[35] *Gould v. Gould* [1969] 3 All ER 728.

[36] It is not stated whether the County Court judge considered the case to fall under the Matrimonial Causes Act 1965. This Act was cited by the wife's counsel on appeal, but Lord Denning refused to apply the terms of the Act because the present agreement was oral. The Matrimonial Causes Act 1965, *c.* 72, §23(2)(a), reads:

> 'maintenance agreement' means any agreement in writing made, whether before or after the commencement of this Act, between the parties to a marriage for the purposes of their living separately, being—(a) an agreement containing financial arrangements, whether made during the continuance or after the dissolution or annulment of the marriage.

[37] Denning held: 'The parties probably possessed no intention one way or the other. It is not the actual intention of the parties, but the intention which the court imputes to them.'

Lord Denning returned to the topic the following year in *Merritt v. Merritt*.[38] Just as in the *Balfour Case*, the couple in *Merritt* were not on good terms. In fact, the husband had left his wife to be with another woman. Upon separation, the husband and wife made an oral agreement that he would pay her a monthly sum of money and would transfer her the full title to the house if she kept up the mortgage payments. The husband wrote out by hand and signed the following:

> In consideration of the fact that you will pay all charges in connection with the house at 133 Clayton Road, Chessington, Surrey, until such time as the mortgage repayment has been completed, when the mortgage has been completed, I will agree to transfer the property into your sole ownership.

When this dispute came to court, the husband argued that, following the *Balfour Case*, his agreement was not intended to give rise to legal relations since it was between spouses. Rejecting this argument, Lord Denning, speaking for a unanimous Court of Appeal, held:

> It is altogether different when the parties are not living in amity but are separated, or about to separate. They then bargain keenly. They do not rely on honourable understandings. They want everything cut and dried. It may safely be presumed that they intend to create legal relations.[39]

The husband's counsel had, of course, relied on the case *Gould v. Gould*, which had similar facts. Was *Gould* to be overruled? Rather than overrule *Gould*, Denning distinguished it. In doing so, he used a historical argument, and also mentioned a second ground for the decision in *Gould*:

> Counsel for the husband then relied on the recent case of *Gould v Gould*, when the parties had separated, and the husband agreed to pay the wife £12 a week 'so long as he could manage it.' The majority of the court thought that those words introduced such an element of uncertainty that the agreement was not intended to create legal relations. But for that element of uncertainty, I am sure that the majority would have held the agreement to be binding.[40]

In this example of using a historical argument to distinguish a precedential case, Lord Denning is explicitly suggesting that the judges in the precedential *Gould* case would not want the rule to be applied to the marital dispute in *Merritt*.

[38] *Merritt v. Merritt* [1970] EWCA (Civ.) 6.

[39] Ibid per Lord Denning. In his concurring opinion, Duke LJ mentions the Married Women's Property Act 1882 but holds that it is not applicable to this situation: 'I am inclined to think that the promise of the wife in respect of her separate estate could have founded an action in contract within the principles of the Married Women's Property Act, 1882.'

[40] Ibid.

(2) Does the *Greenman* excuse from the statutory notice requirement apply to a plaintiff who suffers only economic harm?

In 1963, the Supreme Court of California adopted a common-law product liability rule (not based on statute) in the case of *Greenman v. Yuba Power Products*.[41] The plaintiff in *Greenman* had suffered bodily injury while using a power tool manufactured by the defendant. The defendant in *Greenman* had raised as a defence the failure of the plaintiff to comply with the notice requirement of §2607(3)(A) of the California Commercial Code, which reads in part that a 'buyer must, within a reasonable time after he or she discovers or should have discovered any breach, notify the seller of breach or be barred from any remedy'. In refusing to apply §2607(3)(A) to a common-law claim of product liability, the Court held that the statutory notice requirement was 'not an appropriate one for the court to adopt in actions by injured consumers against manufacturers with whom they have not dealt'.[42]

Greenman was a case involving bodily injury, and the holding of the case, quoted above, speaks of 'injured consumers'. Does this mean that the holding does not apply to consumers who merely suffer economic harm? Must such consumers comply with the notice requirement of §2607(3)(A)?

That was the question presented to the trial-court judge in the case *In re Ford Motor Co. E–350 Van Products Liability Litigation (No. II)*.[43] In this case, the plaintiffs alleged that their Ford E–350 '15–passenger' van had been defectively designed, which allegedly led to an increased risk of death or injury from rollover accidents. While none of the plaintiffs had actually suffered a rollover, they all claimed that the alleged defect caused economic harm because they could not safely transport fifteen passengers in their vans.

The defendant, the Ford Motor Company, moved to dismiss the complaint on the ground that the plaintiffs had not given notice as required by §2607(3)(A) of the California Commercial Code. The case was heard in the US District Court for the District of New Jersey. However, the question was one of Californian law. Consequently, the federal judge in New Jersey had to consider how the Californian courts would interpret §2607(3)(A) in this novel situation.

41 *Greenman v. Yuba Power Products*, 377 P. 2d 897, 900 (Cal. 1963).

42 Ibid:

> As between the immediate parties to the sale [the notice requirement] is a sound commercial rule, designed to protect the seller against unduly delayed claims for damages. As applied to personal injuries, and notice to a remote seller, it becomes a booby-trap for the unwary. The injured consumer is seldom 'steeped in the business practice which justifies the rule', and at least until he has had legal advice it will not occur to him to give notice to one with whom he has had no dealings. The quotation is from William L. Prosser, 'The Assault upon the Citadel (Strict Liability to the Consumer)' (1960) 69 Yale LJ 1099, 1130.

43 *In re Ford Motor Co. E–350 Van Products Liability Litigation (No. II)* (DNJ 2008).

The federal judge denied Ford Motor Company's motion to dismiss, holding:

> *Greenman* is not directly analogous to this case [because] … the decision in *Greenman* occurred in the context of a personal injury action … Nevertheless, given the prior application of the statutory notice requirement in California cases, this Court is not persuaded that the Supreme Court of California would apply §2607(3)(A) so strictly, and necessarily foreclose the plaintiffs from pursuing [their] breach of warranty claims.

To summarize, the rule of *Greenman* refers to 'actions by injured consumers against manufacturers'. It speaks of 'consumers' plural, and it does not state that the consumers must have suffered bodily injury, merely that they have been 'injured'. It is only when one looks at the judicial history (i.e. the opinion in *Greenman*) that one has doubt about whether the rule should include consumers who have suffered economic injury. The judge in *Ford Motors* might have chosen to employ the judicial history to narrow the text of the rule by adding the word 'bodily'. Such a narrowing is referred to as a teleological reduction in this book. However, the judge chose to apply the rule to consumers generally, including those who are just injured economically.

The reader should remember that it is the justification that the judges write that is important for our purposes: 'this Court is not persuaded that the Supreme Court of California would apply §2607(3)(A) so strictly'. This is a historical argument based on the judicial history. If the rule had been a statute rather than a case-based rule, and if the legislative history had been a committee report rather than a judicial opinion, and if the committee report had discussed the proposed statute in the context of consumers who are injured bodily, making no mention of consumers who are injured economically, then the trial judge might still have concluded that the legislature did not intend to 'apply §2607(3)(A) so strictly'.

F. Summary

This chapter describes, critiques, and illustrates the use of historical arguments that are marshalled to justify the results that judges have reached in disputes about the application of legal rules to various factual scenarios. It was seen that historical arguments invoke the historical setting, or they state or insinuate that the drafters of the rules would agree with the result. Judges sometimes cite the legislative record, or *travaux préparatoires*, to bolster the persuasiveness of the results that they have in mind. A handful of judges and academics profess that only those arguments are legitimate that seek to divine the 'original intent' of the drafters. Curiously, or sophistically, this stricture only obtains for constitutional interpretation. It does not stretch to the original intent of the drafters of case decisions or even to the drafters of statutes.

After reciting various descriptions of why historical arguments should be used, the chapter proceeds to discuss three cases in which judges employed historical arguments to reach results that were arguably at odds with the texts of the statutes being interpreted but in which the judges argued that the results they reached were in consonance with the will of the legislative bodies that drafted the statutes.

Following on from the examples of historical arguments based on statutes, the discussion examined two cases in which judges in California and in Germany employed historical arguments when interpreting judicial glosses from precedential cases that had been pronounced by supreme courts in their jurisdictions. The judges in both jurisdictions suggested that the judges in the precedential cases would have agreed with their results.

Finally, two cases concerning pure common law were analysed in which the judges in England and California suggested that the judges in the precedential cases from their jurisdictions would agree with the results that they reached.

7
Purposive Argument

A. Introduction

Purposive arguments are often styled the 'teleological method' of interpretation. The word 'teleological' is derived from the ancient Greek *telos*, which means ultimate object or aim, which are other words for function or purpose. This category of argument encompasses a great many arguments that do not fall within the textual or historical categories; but all three of these arguments—textual, historical, and purposive—can be, and often are, used simultaneously in the same judgment. As seen in Chapter 5, textual arguments are flexible—some might say lithe—because of differences in how the terms of a statute or other rule can be understood and nuanced. And we have seen that the category of historical argument (Chapter 6) is quite elastic. A historical argument might be fashioned around a document or an incident that happened in the past, or it may postulate what the members of the legislature are presumed to have thought, to name just two possibilities. Textual and historical arguments concern themselves with what the terms of the rule, and what the rule's historical context, reveal about the purpose or purposes of the rule. In short, they are also purposive arguments. So why do we need a separate category of argument called purposive?

The reason for a separate category of purposive argument is that, sometimes, judges cannot find a textual or historical argument that will adequately support the result that they wish to reach. As we will see below, sometimes, the text of the rule cannot convincingly, or even reasonably, be used to justify a judgment with the result the judge desires. And the historical context may be similarly unhelpful. Indeed, the legislative record might even suggest that at least some members of the legislature or parliament would disagree with the result that the judge wishes to reach. In general, if a textual or historical argument is available, and if the judge thinks that one or the other, or both together, are conclusive, convincing, persuasive, or just merely suggestive on their own, he or she would not necessarily feel the need to design a different, or supplemental, argument in support of their preferred result. The judge might even use all three together. Or he or she might grasp for a purposive argument first, without exploring textual and historical arguments. Whether or not he or she first considers other arguments, the motivation for the use of a purposive argument is the same as the motivation for the use of the other arguments: they provide persuasive support

Universals of Legal Reasoning by Judges. Thomas Lundmark, Oxford University Press.
DOI: 10.1093/oso/9780198785675.003.0007

for the result that the judge thinks and feels to be the best possible under applicable law.

Purposive arguments are those that talk about the perceived purposes of the rule. But notice that all of the arguments discussed in this book are about purpose.[1] Every legal rule has at least one purpose, and every legal rule is the product of a balancing of interests, which means that it must contain conflicting purposes. Sometimes, a particular purpose is stated in the rule. Sometimes, the purpose appears clear from a textual application. Sometimes, the purpose can be found in the historical context of the rule's origin and later usage. And at other times, the purpose is what the judges consider to be a reasonable inference.

In the category of system-contextual argument (Chapter 8), we will be met by instances where the purpose of the rule before the court is interpreted—a better word is 'inspired'—by appeals to broad principles, to concepts of justice, and to purposes that are not closely tethered to the rule. The category of purposive argument addressed in this chapter is narrower: it requires that the judge articulate at least one function or purpose that the rule could plausibly promote, that is, a purpose that can be more or less closely tethered to the rule.

The German Federal Constitutional Court has often recognized the importance of purposive interpretation. Here is a translated quotation from the 1973 *Princess Soraya* decision of the First Senate of the Federal Constitutional Court:

> The interpretation of a legal rule cannot always adhere to the meaning attributed to it at the time of its creation. Rather, it must be asked what reasonable purpose the rule performs at the time it is applied. The rule is always to be seen in light of the social conditions and social-political views it affects; under circumstances, its contents can and must change along with it.[2]

In the *AEG Copyright Case*, discussed below, the German Supreme Court expressly held that textual interpretation must sometimes give way to purposive interpretation:

> An interpretation according to the meaning and purpose of the statute must take precedence over a linguistically clear wording if the conflict of interest that must be decided could not have been envisaged when the act was passed due to the fact that it only became obvious owing to a change after this point in time.[3]

[1] Norbert Horn, *Einführung in die Rechtswissenschaft und Rechtsphilosophie* (3rd edn, Müller C F in Hüthig Jehle Rehm 2004) mn. 183.

[2] *Entscheidungen des Bundesverfassungsgerichts* (BVerfGE) 9 June 1971, 2 BvR 544/63 (Ger.).

[3] *Entscheidungen des Bundesgerichtshofes in Zivilsachen* [BGHZ] 24 June 1955, 1ZR 88/54.

B. Descriptions of purposive argumentation

This discussion begins with a list of descriptions of purposive argumentation followed by a brief critique. These descriptions are important to the theses of this book for two reasons. First, even though the descriptions are from both legal academics and from judges and these academics and judges are from various jurisdictions, the descriptions are very similar to each other. This strongly suggests universality. Second, although all of the descriptions below refer explicitly or implicitly to statutory rules, this does not mean that the descriptions cannot apply to case-based rules. This is illustrated below:

> To achieve a sound interpretation of a legislative text, interpreters must identify and take into account the purpose of the legislation.[4]

> On a low level of abstraction, objective purpose is the hypothetical intent that a reasonable author would want to realize through the given legal text or a type of legal text. On a high level of abstraction, the objective purpose of a text is to realize the fundamental values of the legal system.[5]

> No law can tolerate a rigid limitation of its applicability to [only] such cases that correspond to the initial situation envisaged by the legislature: for it is not a dead letter, but a living, developing spirit that wants to progress with the living conditions in a meaningful manner, as long as this does not destroy the mold into which it was poured.[6]

> Purposive interpretation begins with the idea that interpretation is about pinpointing the legal meaning of a text along the spectrum of its semantic meanings. Semantic meaning sets the limits of interpretation.[7]

> In S v Zuma and Two Others, this Court dealt with the approach to be adopted in the interpretation of the fundamental rights enshrined in … the Constitution. It gave its approval to an approach which, whilst paying due regard to the language

[4] Ruth Sullivan, *Statutory Interpretation* (2nd edn, Irwin Law 2007) 194.

[5] Aharon Barak, 'A Judge on Judging: The Role of a Supreme Court in a Democracy' (2002) 116 Harv L Rev 16, 67

[6] BGHSt 10, 157, 159:

> Kein Gesetz verträft eine starre Begrenzung seiner Anwendbarkeit auf solche Fälle, die der vom Gesetzgeber ins Auge gefassten Ausgangslage entsprechen: denn es ist nicht toter Buchstabe, sondern lebendig sich entwickelnder Geist, der mit den Lebensverhältnissen fortschreiten und ihnen sinnvoll angepasst weitergelten will, solange dies nicht die Form sprengt, in die er gegossen ist.

[7] Aharon Barak, *Purposive Interpretation in Law* xiii (De Gruyter 2005).

> that has been used, is 'generous' and 'purposive' and gives expression to the underlying values of the Constitution.[8]

> To [take a purposive approach], we first have to understand, and articulate, the goals—to explain to ourselves (and to legislatures, courts, employees, and employers) the purpose of labour laws at the deepest possible level. The next step is then to reconsider our means—to ask what we need to change or improve in the laws themselves in order to better advance the goals.[9]

All of the quotations above share one thing in common: a dissatisfaction with a mechanical, textual interpretation of rules. This dissatisfaction, in turn, evidences a conviction that judges need to have more latitude to decide cases in a way that comports with their sense of justice.

C. Purposive argument with statutes

As with other arguments, purposive arguments may be employed in tandem with other arguments. However, purposive arguments are most common, and most obvious, when the judge is presented with a rule whose text seems to the judge to be too broadly, or too narrowly, written. We saw this phenomenon in previous chapters, where judges sometimes used textual and historical arguments to support so-called teleological extensions[10] and teleological reductions of the reach of a statute or case-based rule. When it comes to statutory rules, having perused dozens of publications on the topic, it appears that purposive arguments are more likely to be employed to extend the reach of a statute rather than to reduce it. When dealing with case-based rules, it is difficult to hazard a guess since it is difficult, if not impossible, to find publications on the subject.

In the following cases, we will see judges using purposive arguments to justify their application of statutory rules. The use of these arguments almost always signals either a teleological extension or a teleological reduction of the statutory language. The following cases address these issues: (1) Must reassignments of employees to a lower-paying job be in writing? (2) Is a statutory list of protected characteristics exclusive? (3) Can a woman standing in a private residence be convicted of soliciting for prostitution 'in a street or public place'? (4) Must the employees of a company being sold accept the new management? (5) Does a disease-prevention

[8] *S v. Makwanyane and another* (CCT3/94) [1995] ZACC 3; 1995 (6) BCLR 665; 1995 (3) SA 391; [1996] 2 CHRLD 164; 1995 (2) SACR 1 (6 June 1995) para 9.

[9] Guy Davidov, *A Purposive Approach to Labour Law* (Oxford University Press 2016) 4.

[10] See e.g. *Re Ford Motor Co. E-350 Van Products Liability Litigation (No. II)* (DNJ 2008), discussed in Chapter 6 and *Smith v. Hughes* [1960] 1 WLR 830, 832, discussed in Chapter 9.

act protect against being washed overboard? (6) Do credit-card customers need to provide their address and telephone number to online merchants? (7) Does photocopying articles for a company's employees constitute 'personal use'? And (8) Is a same-sex partner 'a member of the original tenant's family'?

Notice that the judges in every case below will have identified policies or principles that support the result that they want to reach, and, in doing so, they have ignored policies and principles that militate against that result.

(1) Must reassignments of employees to lower-paying jobs be in writing?

Extending the reach of a statute very often involves stretching the operative words of the statute beyond their ordinary, or even technical, meanings to encompass a situation that is related to the situation described in the text of the statute. An example of such stretching is provided by the judicial construction of §623 of the German Civil Code, which requires that, to be effective, 'termination of employment [must be by written] notice of termination or by [written] separation agreement'.[11] But what about a reassignment of an employee to a position at a lower pay scale in a company? Reassignment does not, in common parlance, amount to a termination of employment, nor is there any technical definition that equates termination with reassignment. Similarly, reassignment, linguistically speaking, does not amount to a written termination agreement. Must a reassignment of an employee within the employing company nevertheless be in writing to be effective?

By its terms, §623 would appear not to apply to reassignments. The German courts, however, have held that a reassignment to a position at a lower salary falls within the protection of §623, meaning that it, too, must be in writing to be effective.[12] According to this judicial gloss, 'termination of employment' now means 'termination of employment or reassignment' for purposes of this statute.

According to the court,

> In order to maintain the employment relationship with the plaintiff, the defendant was obliged to issue a notice of change with the contract offer dated March 21, 2002. [The defendant] was not released from this legal obligation by the plaintiff's rejection of the offer in the form submitted. Rather, it should have given the plaintiff the opportunity provided for by law to have the social justification of the changed conditions checked by giving notice of changes. As he explained in the

[11] 'Termination of employment by notice of termination or separation agreement requires written form to be effective; electronic form is excluded': §623 of the German Civil Code.

[12] *Landesarbeitsgericht Köln*, 20 November 2003, 6 Sa 645/03.

hearing before the Court of Appeal, the plaintiff would have accepted a change of notice subject to judicial review in accordance with Section 2 of the Dismissal Protection Act.

The teleological extension described here might also be described as an analogical argument: the judges have mentally equated the situation covered in the text of the statute (termination of employment) to the situation presented in the case (reassignment at a lower salary). This process of mental equivalence inherently presupposes the presence of an overriding principle (usually unarticulated) that encompasses both situations: all major changes to employment contracts to the detriment of the employee must be in writing.[13]

(2) Is a statutory list of protected characteristics exclusive?

One example of a teleological extension from California concerns a young man who was removed from the premises of a shopping centre in the 1960s, allegedly because of his long hair and his unconventional hippie dress. The young man claimed a violation of §51 of the Civil Code, the Unruh Civil Rights Act. People who feel that they have been discriminated against in violation of the Unruh Civil Rights Act can bring an action for treble damages and no less than $4,000 in statutory damages.[14] At the time, the Unruh Act read:

> All persons within the jurisdiction of this state are free and equal, and no matter what their sex, race, color, religion, ancestry, national origin, or blindness or other physical disability are entitled to the full and equal accommodations, advantages, facilities, privileges or services in all business establishments of every kind whatsoever.[15]

[13] This assessment of the difference between argument by analogy and teleological extension is controversial in legal scholarship. For an overview of the discussion, see P. Meier and F. Jocham, 'Rechtsfortbildung—Methodischer Balanceakt zwischen Gewaltenteilung und materialler Gerechtigkeit' [2016] JuS 392, 394. Compare M. Klatt, *Making the Law Explicit* (Hart 2008) 5, who states that any application of a statute beyond the scope of the possible meaning of its wording is a development of the law, which is either an analogy or a teleological reduction.

[14] Section 52(a) of the California Civil Code:

> Whoever denies, aids or incites a denial, or makes any discrimination or distinction contrary to Section 51, 51.5, or 51.6, is liable for each and every offense for the actual damages, and any amount that may be determined by a jury, or a court sitting without a jury, up to a maximum of three times the amount of actual damage but in no case less than four thousand dollars ($4,000), and any attorney's fees that may be determined by the court in addition thereto, suffered by any person denied the rights provided in Section 51, 51.5, or 51.6.

[15] The statute in its present form also covers disability, medical condition, genetic information, marital status, and sexual orientation: §51 of the Californian Civil Code.

In its defence, the shopping centre argued that any discrimination against the young man on its part had not been motivated by any of the characteristics prohibited in §51. The court rejected this defence, holding that the characteristics enumerated in §51 were illustrative rather than exclusive. The statute, according to the court, prohibits 'all arbitrary discrimination by business enterprises'.[16] This is another example of a teleological extension of the statute to include characteristics that are not articulated in the statute.

Notice also that the California Supreme Court might have ruled against the young man. In doing so, the Court could have justified its result not only by a textual argument but also by arguing that the legislative policy behind §51 was to enable businesses to refuse to do business with all people except those people having the characteristics listed in the statute. This observation should serve as a reminder that every statute (and every *ratio*) has at least two purposes or policies because legal rules reflect a balance of interests.

(3) Can a woman standing in a private residence be convicted of soliciting prostitution 'in a street or public place'?

A teleological extension can also be seen an English case concerning the Street Offences Act 1959. Two prostitutes were alleged to have been soliciting for prostitution in violation of §1(1) of that Act. Police officers had observed the women standing on a balcony, or behind ground-floor and first-floor windows, from where they would attract the attention of male passers-by and then invite them in. In itself, this activity would appear to constitute solicitation of prostitution, and the two were convicted in the Magistrates' Court. On appeal to the High Court, Queen's Bench Division, their barrister argued that the Act only prohibited soliciting 'in a street or public place', and the women were neither in a street nor a public place. Nevertheless, Lord Parker CJ held, in a judgment that the two other judges joined, that the women were guilty. His argument begins with a textual argument but then speaks only of statutory purpose:

> Observe that [§1(1)] does not say there specifically that the person who is doing the soliciting must be in the street. Equally, it does not say that it is enough if the person who receives the solicitation or to whom it is addressed is in the street. For my part, I approach the matter by considering what is the mischief aimed at by this Act. Everybody knows that this was an Act intended to clean up the streets, to enable people to walk along the streets without being molested or solicited by common prostitutes. Viewed in that way, it can matter little whether the prostitute

[16] *In re Cox*, 3 Cal. 3d 205 (1970) 216.

> is soliciting while in the street or is standing in a doorway or on a balcony, or at a window, or whether the window is shut or open or half open; in each case her solicitation is projected to and addressed to somebody walking in the street. For my part, I am content to base my decision on that ground and that ground alone.[17]

Notice that the High Court judges might readily have determined that the statutory restriction 'in a street or public place' evidenced a policy that people should feel secure in the privacy of residential dwellings.

(4) Must the employees of a company being sold accept the new management?

Just as there are teleological extensions using purposive arguments, there are also teleological reductions. These are cases in which the court concludes that the language of the statute is broader than necessary to accomplish the goals of the statute. For example, §613a of the German Civil Code provides that, in the event that a company is sold, all of the employment contracts pass to the buyer. Does this mean that all of the employees of a company being sold must accept the new management? This would likely be the conclusion based on the text alone. But why do the employees not have a right to terminate their employment contracts and, thereby, become eligible for termination benefits and unemployment compensation?

The German Federal Labour Court held that the employees have a right to terminate their contracts in this situation, in effect reducing the broad sweep of the statute:

> The court cannot presume that the legislature intended by this new regulation to deprive an employee of these protections. At least when a company is sold to a new owner, the purpose of the act, which is to ensure the survival of the employment contracts, does not compel continuation of the employment relationship over the objection of the employee.[18]

In other words, the statutory language went farther than it was meant to, according to the Court.

Notice that the German Federal Labour Court might have ruled against the employees by arguing that the purpose of the statute was to promote the marketability of companies.

[17] *Smith v. Hughes*. The mischief rule is discussed in Chapter 4.
[18] Federal Labour Court, 26 BAGE 301 (1974).

(5) Does a disease-prevention act protect against being washed overboard?

A famous example from England of a teleological reduction concerns sheep that were being transported by ship from Hamburg to Newcastle. According to the Animals Order of 1871, adopted pursuant to the Contagious Diseases (Animals) Act 1869, ships arriving from foreign ports were required to keep animals in pens not to exceed 9 feet in breadth and 15 feet in length. Further, the floors of the pens were required to be furnished with battens or foot holds. The ferry, in this case, had neither pens nor battens. As a result, according to the complaint, many of the sheep were washed overboard in a storm.

The judges of the Court of Exchequer held that, while the loss suffered by the owners of the sheep may well have been avoided had the sheep been properly penned, the loss of the sheep was not one that was covered by the Act: '[T]he damage complained of here is something totally apart from the object of the Act of Parliament, and it is in accordance with all the authorities to say that the action is not maintainable.'[19]

Notice that the Court of Exchequer might have ruled that the purpose of the Act was to force shipowners to install and employ pens on their ships, and this policy would be promoted by ruling against the shipowner in this case.

(6) Do credit-card customers need to provide their address and telephone number to online merchants?

An example from California of a teleological reduction is the judicial interpretation of §1747.08 of the Civil Code. Enacted in 1971, this provision prohibits the requesting or requiring of 'personal identification information' as a condition to accepting a credit card as payment. Violation entitles a civil plaintiff to recover statutory damages. In the present case, a consumer brought an action against Apple, Inc. for requiring him to provide his address and telephone number in order to purchase media downloads online with his credit card.

In affirming the dismissal of the consumer's action, the California Supreme Court wrote that the statute's text, structure, and purpose suggest 'that the Legislature could not have intended section 1747.08 to apply to this type of transaction.'[20]

Notice that the California Supreme Court might have ruled that the purpose of the statute was to protect the financial and personal privacy of individuals.

[19] *Gorris and another v. Scott* (1873–1874) L.R. 8 Ex. 125 at 129–130 (Kelly, C.B.).
[20] *Apple, Inc. v. Superior Court*, 56 Cal. 4th 128 (2013).

(7) Does photocopying articles for a company's employees constitute 'personal use'?

The *AEG Copyright Case* in Germany concerned the since superseded Act Concerning the Copyright on Works of Literature and Audio (*Gesetz betreffend das Urheberrecht an Werken der Literatur und der Tonkunst*), which took effect in 1902. The second sentence of §15 of that Act, in translation, read: 'A reproduction [of a work] for personal use is permitted if it does not have the purpose of generating income from the work.'

In 1953, AEG was one of the largest producers of electrical equipment in the world, with a huge number of employees. In order to keep their employees abreast of technical and scientific advances, AEG subscribed to dozens of journals. However, AEG only had two subscriptions of each journal: one for their employees in Frankfurt and the other for their employees in Berlin. Rather than circulate the journals among their employees, AEG made photocopies of relevant articles and distributed the copies to their employees. When an organization of publishers demanded that AEG pay royalties on the photocopied articles, and discontinue making photocopies in the future, AEG claimed that the copies were for the 'personal use' of the company.

At the time, §15 of the Literary Copyright Act provided that the act of copying without the consent of the party affected was permissible as long as it was 'undertaken for personal use and absent any intention to profit therefrom'. In its decision from 1955, the Federal Supreme Court explained that the legislator of §15 Literary Copyright Act could not have foreseen the rapid developments in technology in 1901:

> The present-day, photo-mechanical copying procedures have created a situation that the legislature of the year 1901 could not have contemplated, even if it had expected that the mechanical copying procedures at the time would have been further developed ... The use that the employees of a profit-making company of photocopies that are made in the interest of the company, and which the company has made precisely for that purpose, goes beyond the scope of private use that is exempted from the prohibition against reproduction by section 15 (2) of the [Act].[21]

In this passage, the Federal Supreme Court begins with a historical argument—'this case could not have been foreseen'—and then makes a purposive argument, namely that it cannot be the purpose of the exception to allow a profit-making company to circumvent the payment of royalties in this fashion.

Notice that the Federal Supreme Court might have held that the purpose of the exception was to allow copying as long as the purchaser did not profit therefrom.

[21] *Entscheidungen des Bundesgerichtshofes in Zivilsachen.*

(8) Is a same-sex partner 'a member of the original tenant's family'?

In 1999, in the case of *Fitzpatrick v. Sterling Housing Association Ltd*, the UK Law Lords were faced with an emotional, and some would say political, issue: does a same-sex partner enjoy a right to succeed to a residential tenancy under the UK Rent Act 1977 on the death of his partner. At the time, the Act accorded such a right of succession to a person who had lived with the original tenant 'as his ... wife or husband' or to a person who was 'a member of the original tenant's family'. The appellant in this case, Mr Martin Fitzpatrick, had lived in the rented dwelling with the original tenant for twenty-two years 'in a longstanding, close, loving and faithful, monogamous, homosexual relationship'. The trial-court judge felt constrained by the text of the statute. As Mr Fitzpatrick was neither wife nor husband, the judge ruled against him. The Court of Appeal expressed sympathy for Mr Fitzpatrick but felt similarly constrained, not only by the statutory language but also by their own judgment in *Harrogate Borough Council v. Simpson*, in which they ruled that the expression 'living together as husband and wife' in §50 of the Housing Act 1980 did not encompass a lesbian pair.

When Fitzpatrick's case reached the House of Lords, the majority rejected the 'spouse' alternative on textual grounds: the words of the Act are clear in assuming that spouses are of different genders. Lords Nicholls and Slynn then framed their allowance of the appeal on the second alternative—'family member'—in purposive terms. The third member of the majority, Lord Clyde, made reference in his speech to the 'purpose of the legislation' but drew heavily on 'changes in social habits' and 'updating construction' of the statutory provision. The remaining two members of the House dissented, arguing instead that it must be up to Parliament to change the Act.

The fact that these dissentients in the House of Lords, along with two of their peers in the Court of Appeal, preferred to leave the development of the law to Parliament indicates just how enormous a judicial, and political, lurch it was to apply the Act to protect a same-sex partner. And Parliament has, indeed, since amended the Act to comport with the decision in *Fitzpatrick*.

D. Purposive argument with judicial glosses on statutes (precedents)

In the two examples that follow, the rules being applied by the courts are judicial glosses from precedential judicial decisions. The first example is from the United States, the second from Germany. In both examples, the law being applied is constitutional law, specifically the US Constitution and the Basic Law of Germany, respectively. In Chapter 8 ('System-Contextual Argument'), we will see examples of judges using constitutional law to justify their decisions in cases covering a wide range of topics and areas of law. In the following examples, the areas of law are, first, criminal procedure and, second, free speech.

The cases that follow answer these questions: (1) Do the police need a warrant to search a tent at a campsite? (2) Can a call for a politically motivated boycott be enjoined? It will be seen that both of the courts will employ purposive arguments when applying the rules of the precedential cases.

(1) Do the police need a warrant to search a tent at a campsite?

An example of the purposive approach from California is provided by a criminal prosecution based on cocaine and other illicit drugs found by the police in a warrantless search of the tent-like structure that a criminal defendant had erected around his vehicle at a campsite. The legal issue was the proper application of the prohibition against unreasonable searches and seizures found in the 4th Amendment to the Constitution of the United States.

The 4th Amendment reads as follows:

> The right of the people to be secure in their persons, houses, papers, and effects, against unreasonable searches and seizures, shall not be violated, and no warrants shall issue, but upon probable cause, supported by oath or affirmation, and particularly describing the place to be searched, and the persons or things to be seized.

This Amendment, like almost all provisions of the US Constitution, has been interpreted by the US Supreme Court and other federal and state courts for over two centuries. These interpretations are glosses as that term is used in this book. According to the US Supreme Court, the purpose of the 4th Amendment is to protect an individual's reasonable expectation of privacy against unreasonable intrusion on the part of the government.[22]

Was the defendant's expectation of privacy in the present case reasonable? In other words, did the 4th Amendment require that the police obtain a judicial search warrant before entering the tent-like structure that the defendant had erected around his vehicle at a campsite? If so, then the search was unreasonable, and consequently unconstitutional, with the result that the illicit drugs found during the search could not be used in evidence against the defendant. This result follows from the judicially created exclusionary rule.[23]

[22] *Katz v. United States*, 389 U.S. 347 (1967).
[23] See *Mapp v. Ohio*, 367 U.S. 643 (1961).

In deciding that the search was unreasonable, and consequently unconstitutional, the California Court of Appeal employed a number of arguments, including a purposive one, in which it adopts the rationale (i.e. purpose) of the Supreme Court of another state, Colorado:

> As the Colorado Supreme Court reasoned in *People v. Schafer* [citation], 'Whether pitched on vacant open land or in a crowded campground, a tent screens the inhabitant therein from public view. Though it cannot be secured by a deadbolt and can be entered by those who respect not others, the thin walls of a tent nonetheless are notice of its occupant's claim to privacy unless consent to enter be asked and given. One should be free to depart the campsite for the day's adventure without fear of this expectation of privacy being violated. Whether of short or longer term duration, one's occupation of a tent is entitled to equivalent protection from unreasonable government intrusion as that afforded to homes or hotel rooms [Citation].'[24]

(2) Can a politically motivated call for a boycott be enjoined?

In 1958, the Federal Constitutional Court in Germany reviewed the constitutionality of an injunction issued against Erich Lüth.[25] Lüth, who was a local public official and President of the Hamburg Press Club, called for a boycott of a newly released film directed by Veit Harlan. Lüth called for the boycott not because the film was offensive, or even political, in any way but rather because Harlan had previously directed anti-Semitic propaganda films, such as the infamous *Jud Süß*. In fact, Harlan was considered the leading National Socialist film director. The producers of the new film, fearing lost profits, successfully petitioned for an injunction against Lüth, finding that his actions were contrary to public standards (*boni mores*). The appellate court affirmed.

But the German Federal Constitutional Court reversed, vacating the injunction. The Court's decision was based on Article 5, §(1) of the German Basic Law:

> Every person shall have the right freely to express and disseminate his opinions in speech, writing, and pictures and to inform himself without hindrance from generally accessible sources. Freedom of the press and freedom of reporting by means of broadcasts and films shall be guaranteed. There shall be no censorship.

[24] *People v. Hughston*, 168 Cal. App. 4th 1062, 1070–1071 (2008).

[25] This case is discussed at length in Donald P. Kommers and Russell A. Miller, *The Constitutional Jurisprudence of the Federal Republic of Germany* (Kindle 3rd edn, Duke University Press 2012) 442 *et seq.*

In justifying its holding, the German Federal Constitutional Court essentially employed a purposive argument that protecting the expression of an opinion must necessarily incorporate protecting the consequences of that expression:

> It is unacceptable to hold that the Constitution protects only the expression of opinion, and not its inherent or intended effect on others, for the whole point of an expression of opinion is to have 'an effect on the environment of ideas' [reference]. Thus value-judgments, which always have an intellectual aim, namely, to persuade others, are protected by Art. 5 1, 1 GG; indeed, it is the stance of the speaker as expressed in the value-judgment by which he hopes to affect others which is principally protected by this basic right. To protect the expression and not to protect its effect would be a nonsense.[26]

In a case from 2004, an appellate court in Bamberg, Germany was presented with a case in which a television programme had exposed the cruelty involved in killing animals for food. The title of the programme—'Eat Vegetarian, Forget Meat!'—was, in essence, a call for a boycott. In holding that the programme was entitled to constitutional protection, the Court employed the rationale (i.e. purpose) of the *Lüth* decision:

> The slogan 'Eat vegetarian, forget meat!' can be viewed as a call for a boycott to the disadvantage of the meat-packing industry. However, this will only violate [public standards] if it is not protected by the constitutional right of expression ... In addition to commercial interests, the appellant [television station] is undeniably being motivated by concerns for animal protection, and as such is being active in the area of social and political questions in which, according to a long line of decisions of the Federal Constitutional Court [beginning with *Lüth*], is entitled to special protection under article 5(1) of the Basic Law.

E. Purposive argument with judicial glosses on 'pure' common law (precedents)

The following examples begin with a seminal common-law case that states a rule that will be subject to a gloss in a later case. Before discussing these examples, perhaps we should remember that these and other judicial decisions are not really 'pure' common law in the sense of completely lacking statutory authority for both of the cases discussed below were heard under the procedure known as an action on the case (also called a trespass on the case), which developed under the

[26] Translated by Tony Weir, Trinity College, Cambridge.

common-law writ system.[27] The system of writs constituted, in effect, a statutory scheme of causes of action pieced together by the British Parliament over centuries. Consequently, one could describe *Wilkinson* and *Lumley v. Gye* as examples of statutory glosses.

The first case below answers the question: (1) Did the defendant's false statements constitute a 'wilfully done … act calculated to cause physical harm to the plaintiff'? The second case decides: (2) Does threatening to call a strike constitute enticing away servants?

(1) Did the defendant's false statements constitute a 'wilfully done … act calculated to cause physical harm to the plaintiff'?

In *Wilkinson v. Downton*, decided in 1897, Mrs Wilkinson had been at home one evening, waiting for her husband to return with his friends from the races, when Mr Downtown arrived and told her that her husband had sent him with an urgent message: he had been badly hurt in an accident, he had broken both his legs, he wanted her to come at once with a cab to bring him home, and she should bring two pillows. Mrs. Wilkinson had to send her friends to fetch her husband because she herself was too shocked and upset to go herself. Later that evening, Mrs Wilkinson learned that Mr Downton had been lying. It had been a joke. In fact, her husband was fine. He had not been in an accident at all. Despite this reassuring news, Mrs Wilkinson's initial nervous shock persisted and worsened. She suffered from vomiting and more serious physical consequences for weeks.

Mrs Wilkinson brought an action in the High Court of Justice, Queen's Bench Division. The judge, Mr Justice Wright, allowed the case to go to the jury. The jury found in favour of Mrs Wilkinson in the amount of £100 for the effects of her nervous shock plus railway fare for her friends, who had gone to fetch her husband. In pronouncing judgment in accordance with the verdict, Mr Justice Wright held as follows:

> I think, however, that the verdict may be supported upon another ground. The defendant has, as I assume for the moment, wilfully done an act calculated to cause physical harm to the plaintiff—that is to say, to infringe her legal right to personal safety, and has in fact thereby caused physical harm to her. That proposition without more appears to me to state a good cause of action.[28]

[27] J.H. Baker, *An Introduction to English Legal History* (5th edn, Oxford University Press 2019) 61; C.H.S. Fifoot, *History and Sources of the Common Law Tort and Contract* (Stevens and Sons1949).

[28] *Wilkinson v. Downton* [1897] 2 QB 57, 58–59.

Wilkinson v. Downton was generally followed, and approved, in 1919 by the Court of Appeal in *Janvier v. Sweeney*.[29] In that case, Miss Janvier, a Frenchwoman, had been hired as a maid servant by Mrs Rowton. Miss Janvier lived in Mrs Rowton's house along with another woman, Miss Marsh. Miss Marsh had in her possession certain letters that were of interest to a detective.

The detective knew that Miss Janvier was engaged to marry a German who had been interned on the Isle of Man for two years and that Miss Janvier corresponded with him on a regular basis. In order to induce Miss Janvier to obtain the letters for him for inspection, the private detective told Miss Janvier, 'I am a detective inspector from Scotland Yard, and represent the military authorities. You are the woman we want, as you have been corresponding with a German spy.' This was, of course, a ruse.

The ruse did not have the effect of inducing Miss Janvier to obtain the letters. Instead, it caused Miss Janvier severe shock, which, in turn, caused her to become incapacitated from working and caused neurasthenia, shingles, and other ailments.

After a trial, the jury found that the statements made by the detective were calculated to cause physical injury to Miss Javier and that they were made with knowledge that they were likely to cause such injury. The jury also found that the statements caused the illness from which Miss Javier suffered. The judge entered judgment in favour of Miss Javier, from which the detective appealed. A unanimous Court of Appeal dismissed the appeal.

The Court in *Wilkinson* ruled that the motive for the neighbour's statement—his calculation—was to cause physical, or at least severe psychological, harm. The Court in *Wilkinson* literally held that the defendant had 'wilfully done an act calculated to cause physical harm to the plaintiff'. The defendant had no other apparent motive. That contrasts with *Janvier*, where the motive was to induce Miss Janvier (through fright) into obtaining certain letters. Thus, *Janvier* cannot easily be subsumed under the rule of *Wilkinson* if the rule is interpreted textually. However, that did not stop the judges of the Court of Appeal in *Janvier* from employing historical and purposive arguments to support their decision. Duke LJ used what can be described as a historical argument, suggesting that the judge in *Wilkinson* would be even more likely to award damages in this case than in the case before him at the time:

> This is a much stronger case than *Wilkinson v. Downton*. In that case there was no intention to commit a wrongful act; the defendant merely intended to play a practical joke upon the plaintiff. In the present case there was an intention to terrify the plaintiff for the purpose of attaining an unlawful object in which both the defendants were jointly concerned.

[29] *Janvier v. Sweeney* [1919] 2 KB 316.

A.T. Lawrence J agreed, also using purposive language about a general principle not enunciated in *Wilkinson*:

> [I]t seems clear on the authority of *Wilkinson v. Downton* and on general principles that the verdict of the jury cannot be disturbed. The defendants attempted to get possession of the letters by instigating the plaintiff to commit a trespass and a breach of confidence. The means they used were false statements made to the plaintiff calculated to cause terror.

(2) Does threatening to call a strike constitute enticing away servants?

Johanna Wagner was an opera singer under contract with Benjamin Lumley to sing at Her Majesty's Theatre. Frederick Gye successfully lured Miss Wagner away from Lumley by offering her more money to sing at the Covent Garden Theatre. As a consequence, Lumley lost money. He sued Gye for damages. The Queen's Bench Division of the High Court of England and Wales in *Lumley v. Gye*[30] held, in 1853, that Gye had stated a cause of action upon which relief can be granted. Judge Crompton stated the holding as follows:

> I think that we are justified in applying the principle of the action for enticing away servants to a case where the defendant maliciously procures a party, who is under a valid contract to give her exclusive personal services to the plaintiff for a specified period, to refuse to give such services during the period for which she had so contracted, whereby the plaintiff was injured.

In 1901, the Law Lords of the United Kingdom considered a case involving Leathem & Sons, a wholesale butcher near Belfast, Northern Ireland. Leathem & Sons supplied various butcher shops with meat, one of which was owned by Andrew Munce. Munce had been buying £20–£30 pounds of meat per week from Leathem & Sons until officers of The Belfast Journeymen Butchers and Assistants' Association threatened to call a strike among Munce's employees if Munce did not stop buying meat from Leathem & Sons. Andrew Leathem brought an action against the officers of the union for lost profits. The jury found that the officers of the labour union had 'wrongfully and maliciously induced' Munce and others from dealing with Leathem & Sons, judgment was accordingly entered against the defendants, and the judgment was affirmed by the Irish Court of Appeal.

30 *Lumley v. Gye* (1853) 118 ER 749.

On appeal to the House of Lords, counsel for the union argued that the rule of *Lumley v. Gye* did not apply because Munce was not an employee of Leathem & Sons. In other words, he was arguing that the rule of *Lumley v. Gye* should be applied textually.

The House of Lords, in *Quinn v. Leathem*,[31] disagreed. According to Lord Lindley,

> [T]he principle involved in [*Lumley v. Gye*] cannot be confined to inducements to break contracts of service, nor indeed to inducements to break any contracts. The principle which underlies the decision reaches all wrongful acts done intentionally to damage a particular individual and actually damaging him.

The Law Lords in *Quinn v. Leathem* extended the holding of *Lumley* beyond the realm of employment contracts to include 'any contracts', without apparent limitation. This can be described as a teleological extension or even as an analogy.

F. Summary

Purposive arguments, which are often styled the 'teleological method', are the subject of this chapter. All of the descriptions of purposive arguments quoted at the beginning of this chapter evidence an assuredness that judges need more leeway to decide cases in accordance with the judges' sense of justice and order.

Purposive arguments are often employed alongside textual and historical arguments, but they are also put forward in cases where the judges cannot, or cannot convincingly, fashion a textual or historical argument that will credibly support the result that they wish to reach. Indeed, purposive arguments are also used to depart from what appears to be the clear wording of a statute, as illustrated in the cases discussed.

Purposive arguments employ the perceived purposes or principles embodied in a rule. All statutory and other rules, including case-based rules, are the product of a balancing of interests, which means that they all hold conflicting policies. Therefore, in employing purposive arguments, judges will cite the policies that provide support for their decisions and will eschew contradictory policies.

Because of the importance of this line of argument, this chapter outlined and critiqued eight cases in which judges invoked the perceived purposes of legislation

[31] *Quinn v. Leathem* [1901] UKHL 2. *Quinn v. Leathem* was essentially reversed by the Trade Disputes Act 1906: J. McIlroy, 'The Belfast Butchers: Quinn v Leathem after a Hundred Years' in K.D. Ewing and J. Hendy (eds), *The Right to Strike: From the Trade Disputes Act 1906 to a Trade Union Freedom Bill 2006* (IER 2007) ch 3; W.N. Hohfeld, *Fundamental Legal Conceptions as Applied in Judicial Reasoning and Other Legal Essays* (Yale University Press 1920) 42.

in support of their rulings. All of these examples involved judges who avoided the result that the text of the statute seemed to dictate.

As demonstrated in this chapter by one case from California and one from Germany, purposive arguments are also employed when construing glosses on statutes, that is, when applying the rule of a precedential case construing (i.e. concretizing or amending) a statute.

The final two case examples display judicial uses of purpose arguments to reach results that arguably violate the language of the precedential rules but not the rules' purposes or spirit, as discerned by the judges.

8
System-Contextual Argument

A. Introduction

As stated in the introductory Chapter 1, judicial decisions and legal publications often employ contextual observations and arguments, particularly concerning the textual and historical context of a rule being applied. In this book, the term 'system-contextual argument' is not employed in the sense of referring to the textual context. Nor is it employed in the sense of historical context, whether it be the historical context of the enactment or the historical context of the judicial interpretation of a statutory or constitutional provision, or even the historical context of a *ratio* announced in a judicial decision. Such historical references are subsumed in this book under the rubric 'historical argument'. Nor does the term 'system-contextual argument' or justification employed in this book refer to the purposive context, however defined. This book selects a comparatively narrow definition of 'context' when referring to contextual arguments or justifications. That being said, the category of system-contextual argument or justification employed in this book, as will be seen, still encompasses a wide assortment of arguments.

In this book, system-contextual arguments are those that invoke sources, insights, revelations, or sentiments that are felt to be superior to the mere words of the rule at hand—and often the rule's history and purposes or policies—and that are accepted as rudiments of the particular jurisdiction's legal system. In short, system-contextual arguments are those arguments that invoke perceived higher authority within the legal system. These arguments are recognized by their utilization of terms such as 'analogical', 'reasonable', 'right', 'legal', 'constitutional', 'legitimate', 'appropriate', 'proportionate', 'fair', 'just', 'equitable', 'merciful', or in accordance with '*Treu und Glauben*', 'good faith', 'the rule of law', or some other plea to justice.

Judges who invoke these higher authorities are contending, either explicitly or implicitly, that these authorities embody policies and principles that, when considered in light of the facts of the case at hand, compel a particular result, regardless of—and in some instances contrary to—the text, history, and purposes of the rule that would otherwise apply. However, even though system-contextual arguments trump[1] the text, history, and purposes of a rule, they are employed by judges in

[1] Gordley describes the historical recognition and development of a 'super-doctrine ... that could be used to trump any other doctrine ... According to this doctrine [of *abus de droit*], because every rule of law was established to serve a larger social purpose, every right and rule could be set aside when

Universals of Legal Reasoning by Judges. Thomas Lundmark, Oxford University Press. © Thomas Lundmark 2024.
DOI: 10.1093/oso/9780198785675.003.0008

the same way that judges employ arguments from texts, histories, and purposes, namely to enhance the persuasiveness and acceptance of their decisions by jurists and others in their jurisdictions.

The limitation 'in their jurisdictions' is an important one. Every jurisdiction recognizes that some arguments are acceptable, and consequently potentially persuasive, whereas others are unacceptable and consequently not persuasive. And, of course, the line between what is considered to be acceptable and what is not is blurred. And the line between the acceptable and unacceptable shifts over time.

This admonition is especially relevant to the 'legal scientific' culture of Germany and other jurisdictions in the Roman civil-law tradition. This tradition holds to the premise that law can be studied and analysed with no need for reference to any other fields such as politics, economics, psychology, religion, and other influences on everyday life.[2] In short, lawyers in the Roman tradition generally consider their legal systems to be autonomous from outside influences, particularly from politics.[3] Tony Honoré praised this Roman (as distinct from the Greek) approach: '[T]he positive values which are the basis of open arguments are system-neutral ..., that is to say that they are indifferent to the idiosyncratic features of religious, moral, philosophical or political thought systems.'[4] According to Honoré, this autonomous, legalistic approach is vastly superior to the alternative:

> In certain countries, such as the U.S.A., attempts are being made to destroy the separateness of legal discourse and to reduce legal issues to issues in which every sort of social, political and moral consideration is relevant. In my opinion this modem Hellenistic movement is to be resisted: fear the Greeks bringing gifts, even if they are disguised as devotees of the American Supreme Court.[5]

Another observer, Sir Moses Finley, with whom the author of this book agrees, notes with repugnance 'the survival of the old mystique about the law as something that stands above and outside society and its realities, with its own essence, its autonomous logic, its independent existence'.[6] A further discussion of this and other related topics is beyond the scope of this book.

this purpose was not served': James Gordley, *The Jurists: A Critical History* (Oxford University Press 2013) 292.

[2] This autonomous view of the law is explained in the context of the difficulties that this view presents to the harmonization of European law in Thomas Lundmark, 'Legal Science and European Harmonisation' (2014) 130(Jan) LQR 68, 82.

[3] This view of law is largely in accord with Kelsen's prescription for a pure theory of law: '[U]ncritically the science of law has been mixed with elements of psychology, sociology, ethics, and political theory ... The Pure Theory of Law undertakes to delimit the cognition of law against these disciplines', which Kelsen dismisses as 'alien elements'. See Hans Kelsen, *Pure Theory of Law* (University of California Press 1978).

[4] A.M. Honoré, 'Legal Reasoning in Rome and Today' (1973) 4 Cambr L Rev 58, 65.

[5] Ibid 66.

[6] M.I. Finley, *Politics in the Ancient World* (Cambridge University Press 1983) 7.

The policies and principles embodied in the terms mentioned above, and in many other terms, are not policies and principles that can be interpreted by means of any objective legal method known to mankind. For how can one interpret 'reasonable' in a textual or historical manner? How can one find a purpose in 'justice' that is not one that the interpreter already has in mind, in other words, that the interpreter is not projecting onto, or reading into, the word 'justice'? Consequently, the best way to think of these myriad system-contextual terms is as labels that are attached to judgments after the judges have reached their decisions. And if the reader should suspect that the employment by judges of such labels suggests judicial legislative activity as that term is used in this book, then the reader would be correct.

The reader might be asking why this category of argument is not called argument to higher authority or argument to principle. Let a short answer suffice. When judges argue for a reasonable, fair, or just application of a rule, we do not ordinarily think of that as a plea to some higher authority. Rather, we think of reasonableness, fairness, and justice as permeating the entire system of rules. Similarly, when judges draw an analogy to another rule, they are explicitly remaining inside the system of rules, not making a plea to a higher principle outside the legal system. Consequently, this book uses the term 'system' to denote terms (and arguments using these terms) that are accepted as appropriate in the legal culture of the jurisdiction in which they are being employed.

Because all of the arguments mentioned here involve references to other aspects of the legal system, one word that some authors use to describe these and similar arguments is 'systemic'. However, all of the arguments discussed in this book are also systemic because they refer to the text, history, or purpose of rules, all of which are components of the legal system. One needs a term which signals that the arguments being used go beyond the texts, historical settings, and purposes of the rule. The term 'system-contextual' seems to be as good as any to describe this category of argument, although there may well be others.

The use of system-contextual terms as justificatory arguments is seen, perhaps most obviously for most readers, in constitutional jurisprudence. There, statutes are sometimes construed in a way that is said to comport with a stated constitutional principle, such as liberty, or, less commonly, even ruled to be incompatible with a constitutional principle; that is, the statutes are held to be unconstitutional because they contravene the judges' understanding and belief of what the law should be. For example, the US Supreme Court has held that certain provisions of the federal Violence against Women Act of 1994 were unconstitutional because they exceeded the powers granted to the Congress,[7] and that same Court has ruled that marriage statutes in the States of Ohio, Kentucky, and Tennessee were

[7] *United States v. Morrison*, 529 U.S. 598 (2000).

unconstitutional because they prohibited marriages by same-sex couples.[8] The situation on this point in Germany is similar. According to Article 93 of Germany's Constitution, the Basic Law, the decision on whether any legislation contradicts the Basic Law lies with the Federal Constitutional Court. One German federal law that was declared invalid was a statute which required that political parties must win at least 3 per cent of the vote in order to enter the European Parliament. In a 5–3 decision, the Federal Constitutional Court decided that this 3 per cent hurdle amounted to a violation of the equality rights of small political parties.[9]

This controversial (and often inventive) use of principles is nothing unique to the constitutional arena. All of the terms mentioned above—'analogical', 'reasonable', 'right', 'legal', 'constitutional', 'legitimate', 'appropriate', 'proportionate', 'fair', 'just', 'equitable', 'merciful', '*Treu und Glauben*', 'good faith', 'the rule of law', 'justice', and many other terms—are employed in the same way. And they are employed both with statutory and constitutional law and with pure common law.

Because of the breadth of this category, this book will only treat four topics where these system-contextual arguments play an observable and readily collectible role: constitutional conformity,[10] *Drittwirkung*, *Treu und Glauben*, and analogies to principles found in other rules, both statutory and common law. And the treatment devoted to these arguments in this book will be brief as countless books and articles have been written on every one of these topics.

Before sketching these four arguments (constitutional conformity, *Drittwirkung*, *Treu und Glauben*, and analogies), it is worthwhile examining a phenomenon that lays bare the legislative nature of judicial statutory interpretation: so-called *contra legem* interpretation. The Latin expression *contra legem* means 'against the law', but here, the expression means 'against the statute'. *Contra legem* denotes the judicial 'interpretation' of a statute to mean the opposite of what the statute seems to say in clear, unequivocal wording. This phenomenon is not merely a subset of the golden rule, where statutes are construed to avoid absurdities. Rather, this phenomenon entails substituting the judges' values and beliefs for what appears, at least from the text, to be intent of the parliament. Let three examples illustrate this phenomenon, one each from England, California, and Germany.

Section 2 of the UK Limitation Act 1980 prescribes a six-year limitation period for an action founded on intentional tort. In 1993, in the case *Stubbings v. Webb*,[11] a decision upheld by the European Court of Human Rights,[12] the Law Lords unanimously ruled that an action for sexual assault including rape must be brought

[8] *Obergefell v. Hodges*, 576 U.S. 644 (2015).

[9] *Bundesverfassungsgericht* decision of 26 February 2014, 2 *Entscheidungen des Bundesverfassungsgericht* S 2/13.

[10] See generally András Jakab, Arthur Dyevre, and Giulio Itzcovich (eds), *Comparative Constitutional Reasoning* (Cambridge University Press 2017).

[11] *Stubbings v. Webb* [1993] AC 498.

[12] *Stubbings v. United Kingdom* (1995) 19 E.H.R.R. CD32.

within six years because sexual assault is an intentional tort. Consequently, the claimant could not make use of the more liberal limitation period for negligent torts found in §11. The Law Lords justified their decision not only by reference to the language of the Limitation Act but also by reference to the legislative history. A case almost identical to *Stubbings* came before the House of Lords in 2008. In that case, *A v. Hoare*,[13] the Lords overruled *Stubbings*, holding that it was, indeed, the negligence limitation period of §11 that is to be applied in cases of sexual assault and not the intentional-tort limitation period of §2, even though sexual assault is an intentional (not negligent) tort.

In 1975, the California Supreme Court adopted the doctrine of comparative negligence[14] but left open the question of contribution among joint tortfeasors. The question of contribution among joint tortfeasors was resolved three years later in *American Motorcycle Association v. Superior Court*,[15] which held that, while each tortfeasor whose negligence is a proximate cause of an indivisible injury remains individually liable for the entire loss (so-called joint and several liability), any tortfeasor who has paid damages in excess of its percentage of fault has a 'right of comparative indemnity' to recover that excess from the other tortfeasor or tortfeasors. The Supreme Court presumably chose the term 'indemnity' instead of 'contribution' in order to avoid a textual clash with §§875(a) and 876(a) of the California Code of Civil Procedure, which together read:

> Where a money judgment has been rendered jointly against two or more defendants in a tort action there shall be a right of contribution among them as hereinafter provided … The pro rata share of each tortfeasor judgment debtor shall be determined by dividing the entire judgment equally among all of them.

Incidentally (and conveniently), these statutes are not mentioned in the judges' decision in the *American Motorcycle Case*.

The 1958 *Herrenreiter*[16] (*Dressage rider*) *Case*, discussed in Chapter 5, also involves a *contra legem* interpretation of a statute. At issue in that case were advertising posters showing a photograph of a dressage rider, used without the rider's permission. The product being advertised was an over-the-counter patent medicine to alleviate male sexual impotence. The judges of the First Civil Senate might easily have ruled against the plaintiff on his claim for pain, suffering, and loss of amenity for not only is there no statute that allows for an award of damages under these circumstances, but also §253 of the German Civil Code plainly states that

[13] *A v. Hoare* [2008] UKHL 6.

[14] *Li v. Yellow Cab Co.* [1975] 13 Cal. 3d 812. The two dissenting justices wrote that 'the majority's decision deviates from settled rules of statutory construction of section 1714 of the Civil Code'.

[15] *American Motorcycle Assn v. Superior Court*, 20 Cal. 3d 578 (1975).

[16] *Entscheidungen des Bundesgerichtshofes in Zivilsachen* 26, 349 (1958). This case will be discussed in more detail in Chapter 5.

no damages shall be awarded for non-financial loss (*immaterieller Schaden*) unless expressly provided for by statute.[17] Notwithstanding §253, which the judges (conveniently) failed to cite in their decision, the judges of the First Civil Senate of the Federal Supreme Court announced a new rule: 'Damages shall be awarded for substantial injury to the right of personality of another.'[18]

The discussion below, in section B, addresses the phenomenon of interpreting statutes, if one may call it interpretation, through the lens of constitutional norms, most of which are broadly worded. It should be remembered that these and other examples of constitutional conformist 'interpretations' are merely arguments that are accepted as allowing judges to have the last word on how a statute is to be understood. Section C explains and illustrates *Drittwirkung*, which is usually translated into English as 'horizontal effect' or 'third-party effect'. *Drittwirkung*, like constitutional conformity, denotes arguments that allow judges to have the last word on how a statute is to be understood. But *Drittwirkung* has a second function, one that is jurisdictional in that it allows the constitutional courts, like the German Federal Constitutional Court, to review decisions of civil cases that are otherwise within the exclusive jurisdiction of the civil courts. *Treu und Glauben*, which is elucidated in section D, is usually translated into English as 'good faith'. Finally, section E outlines the use by judges of non-constitutional statutes as justifications for creating new causes of action.

B. Constitutional conformity

Of the four mechanisms of system-contextual argument treated in this chapter (sections B 'Constitutional conformity', C '*Drittwirkung*', D '*Treu und Glauben*', and E 'Analogies from principles found in other sources'), the mechanism of constitutional conformity seems to draw the least academic attention. Perhaps that is because the proposition that legislation must be construed to bring it into conformance with the Constitution is obvious to so many people. Whether obvious or not, the Human Rights Act of the United Kingdom makes this proposition explicit

[17] Section 253 of the German Civil Code: '(1) For an injury that is not a financial injury, damages can be claimed only in cases determined by statute. (2) If damages are awarded for bodily injury, or for injury to health, liberty, or sexual self-determination, a claim for damages can also be made for non-financial injury.'

[18] *Entscheidungen des Bundesgerichtshofes in Zivilsachen* 26, 349 (1958). Another translation: 'The Civil Code ... must also be construed to protect against injury to the "undisturbed exercise of decision-making" which constitutes the "freedom of self-determination over his personal sector of life"'; Paul M. Schwartz and Karl-Nikolaus Peifer, 'Prosser's Privacy and the German Right of Personality: Are Four Privacy Torts Better Than One Unitary Concept?' (2010) 98 Calif L Rev 1925, 1951; Basil S. Markesinis, *Comparative Law in the Courtroom: The Story of the Last Thirty-Five Years* (Hart 2003) 113. For an English translation of the decision, see Basil S. Markesinis, *A Comparative Introduction to the German Law of Tort* (Oxford University Press 1986) 195–201. For an early discussion of 'personality' rights, see Roscoe Pound, 'Interests of Personality' (1915) 28 Harv L Rev 343.

when it comes to the small-c constitutional rights embodied in the European Convention on Human Rights 1998. The UK Human Rights Act states, in section 3(1): 'So far as possible to do so, primary legislation and subordinate legislation must be read and given effect in a way which is compatible with the Convention rights.' This statutory provision essentially confers constitutional status on Convention rights.

When applying federal statutes, the US Supreme Court endeavours to avoid potential constitutional issues by adopting a 'reasonable alternative interpretation'.[19] For example, in *Bond v. United States*, Carol Bond petitioned the Supreme Court to reverse her conviction for violation of the Chemical Weapons Convention Implementation Act[20] for knowing possession or use of any 'chemical weapon', which is defined as a 'toxic chemical'. Mrs Bond had spread two mildly toxic chemicals on the car door, the mailbox, and the doorknob of the house of her husband's pregnant girlfriend. The Supreme Court reversed the conviction because Mrs Bond's activity was purely local, and local criminal law has traditionally been the exclusive responsibility of the states. No federal statute should be construed to cover purely local crimes, according to the Supreme Court, unless there is a 'clear indication' that Congress meant to do so. No such clear indication was found in this case.[21]

In Germany, the practice of construing statutes so as to conform to the judges' understanding of the meaning of the Basic Law, as in the United States, is also more common than an outright declaration of invalidity. One fairly recent example concerned a federal statute that conferred a right on newlywed spouses to adopt the previously adopted child of their new spouses (so-called successive adoptions), but that denied such a right to new same-sex partners who had entered into registered partnerships. The unequal treatment of married (different-sex) spouses, on the one hand, and registered (same-sex) partners, on the other, was held to violate the equality rights of same-sex couples and their children. Yet, rather than letting the *Bundestag* decide whether to grant both groups a right to successive adoptions or to withdraw the right from both groups, the constitutional judges, in effect, amended the existing law by ordering that the statutory right to successive adoptions be construed to apply with equal force to civil partnerships.[22] Hence,

[19] In *Gomez v. United States*, 490 U.S. 858, 864 (1989), the Supreme Court noted that, if it was to read the statute literally, it would allow federal magistrates to take on 'any assignment that is not explicitly prohibited', whereas a less controversial, and clearly constitutional, reading would be to limit the additional duties to those that are related to statutorily specified duties of the office.

[20] Section 229(a) of 18 US Code.

[21] A similar case is *Jones v. United States*, 529 U.S. 848 (2000), in which the Supreme Court reversed the conviction of a man who had thrown a Molotov cocktail into his cousin's house. The Supreme Court held that an owner-occupied residence that is not used for any commercial purpose whatever cannot be termed property 'used in' commerce or even as property affecting interstate commerce. Accordingly, arson of such a dwelling is not subject to federal prosecution under §844(i) of 18 US Code, 852–859.

[22] *Entscheidungen des Bundesverfassungsgerichts* of 19 February 2013, Neue Juristische Wochenschrift (NJW) 847; Stefan Muckel, 'Sukzessive Adoption: Ablehnung für eingetragene Lebenspartner verfassungswidrig' (2013) JA 396f.

the unconstitutionality of the statute was repaired by judicial fiat that brought the statute into conformity with the Basic Law as the judges conceived it.[23]

The judges of other courts in Germany also construe statutes in such a way as to mould them to their conception of the meaning of the Basic Law. One example is a judgment of the Federal Supreme Court concerning the National Democratic Party of Germany (NPD) in Saxony. The NPD is a right-wing party. Some people believe that the party should be banned because it allegedly does not support democratic values. Be that as it may, the NPD has not been banned. And there have been NPD members elected to the parliaments of a number of the sixteen German states.

The case before the Federal Supreme Court (not the Federal Constitutional Court) concerned a checking account that the NPD in Saxony had maintained at the *Sparkasse*, which is a form of bank that is exclusively, or primarily, owned by a public entity, such as a state government.[24] So as not to be perceived as supporting right-wing extremists, the *Sparkasse* closed the NPD's account. When the NPD failed to find a bank that would do business with it, it sued, claiming that its fundamental constitutional rights had been violated by the closing of its account. The Federal Supreme Court agreed. According to the Federal Supreme Court, unless and until the NPD is banned in accordance with proper legal procedures, it enjoys the same rights as other political parties, including the right not to be hindered by the state or by an agency of state government, like a *Sparkasse*.[25]

C. *Drittwirkung*

Drittwirkung der Grundrechte is usually translated into English as the 'third-party effect' or the 'horizontal effect' of constitutional rights. Both the German original and the English translations are misleading in that they imply that something of substance is being transmitted from the Basic Law (the German Constitution) into statute law by means of this doctrine. This is not the case. *Drittwirkung* is nothing more than an argument for interpreting or bending the law in ways that the judges who employ the doctrine see fit. And when employed by the Federal Constitutional Court, *Drittwirkung* is merely a bootstrap means (one might also provocatively call

[23] Another of many examples is the life-imprisonment case (45 *Entscheidungen des Bundesverfassungsgerichts* 187) discussed in Christian Bumke and Andreas Voßkuhle, *German Constitutional Law: Introduction, Cases, and Principles* (Oxford University Press 2019) 91–92.

[24] *Bundesgerichtshof* XI ZR 403/01, 11 March 2003.

[25] *Bundesgerichtshof* V ZR 115/11, 9 March 2012. The reader might ask why the Federal Supreme Court did not simply hold that banks are required to treat all law-abiding customers alike rather than limiting its judgment to political parties? Had the judges done so, it would have meant that private banks would also be required to accept all law-abiding customers; but this is not the case in Germany. Both before and after the *Sparkasse Case*, the Federal Supreme Court has held that private banks have the right to refuse to deal with customers whom they do not like. This also holds true for privately owned hotels.

it a ruse) for the Federal Constitutional Court to have the last word.[26] Besides the institutional, bootstrap role of *Drittwirkung*, there is another role of *Drittwirkung*, one that is identical to the use by the civil courts of the doctrine of good faith (*Treu und Glauben*) discussed in section C. This role is played out when the courts, including the civil, tax, administrative, social welfare, labour, and constitutional courts in Germany, employ the Basic Law to reach a result that the judges think is more in line with their understanding of the fundamental rights protected by the Basic Law, and, in most cases, the result is one that they felt they could not legitimately and persuasively reach by textual, historical, and purposive arguments alone. This role, which is extremely popular among academics who publish on the topic, will be discussed first.

The first case in which the German Federal Constitutional Court asserted a power to review judgments of the civil courts was the famous *Lüth decision*.[27] The *Lüth case* concerned a call by a local public official named Erich Lüth for a boycott of a newly released film that had been directed by the leading National Socialist film director Veit Harlan. Lüth called for the boycott not because the film was offensive, or even political, in any way but rather because Harlan had previously directed anti-Semitic propaganda films, such as the infamous *Jud Süß*. The producers and distributors of the new film, fearing a loss of profits, sued for an injunction against Lüth. Even though Veit Harlan was not a party to the action, the civil court considered the fact that Harlan had already been cleared of criminal wrongdoing in conjunction with the film *Jud Süß* and that the de-Nazification proceeding against him had not resulted in any restrictions on Harlan's ability to work. How could a talented director like Harlan become a contributing member of post-war society if every film he directed were to be boycotted? And what of the interests of producers, actors, and others involved in making and distributing this new film, who had no affiliation whatsoever with the National Socialist regime? All things considered, the civil court found that Lüth's actions were contrary to good morals (*gute Sitten*) and accordingly issued the prayed-for injunction. The injunction was affirmed on appeal, effectively muzzling Lüth.

Before 1957, the appeal in the civil courts would have ended the matter. Any appeal by Lüth to the Federal Constitutional Court would have failed. For then, as now, the Federal Constitutional Court could only review federal constitutional

[26] This is the 'institutional role' of *Drittwirkung*. See generally Alec Stone Sweet, 'Constitutionalism, Legal Pluralism, and International Regimes' (2009) 16 Ind J Global Legal Stud 621; Mattias Kumm, 'Who Is Afraid of the Total Constitution? Constitutional Rights as Principles and the Constitutionalization of Private Law' (2006) 7 German LJ 341, 346–351; Uwe Diederichsen, 'Das Bundesverfassungsgericht als oberstes Zivilgericht: ein Lehrstück der juristischen Methodenlehre' (1998) 198 Archiv für die civilistische Praxis 171. For an excellent discussion of *Drittwirkung* and other issues, see Stephen Gardbaum, 'The Myth and the Reality of American Constitutional Exceptionalism' (2008) 107 Mich L Rev 391.

[27] 7 *Entscheidungen des Bundesverfassungsgerichts* 189; Thilo Rensmann, *Wertordnung und Verfassung* (Nomos Verlagsgesellschaft 2007) 81f., critical: Claus-Wilhelm Canaris, *Grundrechte und Privatrecht* (C.H. Beck 1998) 27.

issues: and Lüth's case was decided exclusively on the basis of the civil law, which, by definition (at least until 1957), was considered not to touch upon constitutional issues. Nevertheless, Lüth, like others before him, filed an appeal with the Federal Constitutional Court.

Luckily for Lüth, his appeal was considered by federal constitutional judges in the First Senate, who thought that he should have won in the civil courts. This presented a quandary for the constitutional judges. They could not reverse as a matter of course, on the basis of statute law alone, as then they would have had no jurisdiction to hear the case in the first place for the case was purely of a civil nature and consequently beyond the purview of the constitutional judges. So the constitutional judges made use of a bootstrap argument that had been proposed by a law professor in an article published the year before.[28]

This argument, first put to use in the *Lüth Case*, is known in German as *Drittwirkung der Grundrechte*. As stated above, when employed by the Federal Constitutional Court, *Drittwirkung* is simply a means for the Federal Constitutional Court to have the last word. In the *Lüth Case*, the federal constitutional judges had the last word because they announced that Lüth's call for a boycott was protected by freedom of speech, which is protected by the Basic Law. By virtue of this announcement, the constitutional judges conferred jurisdiction upon themselves. Armed with jurisdiction over the subject matter of the action, they proceeded to reverse the grant of the injunction on the ground that the injunction unconstitutionally impinged upon Lüth's freedom of speech.

It is crucial to a proper understanding of *Drittwirkung* to realize that the federal constitutional judges need not have decided the case the way they did. They might, for example, have refused to hear the appeal on the basis that it did not raise a constitutional issue. They might have granted review on the basis of freedom of speech but affirmed the issuance of the injunction. Indeed, if the civil courts had refused to grant an injunction against Lüth, the constitutional judges might well have decided that (1) the refusal to grant an injunction violated Harlan's constitutional artistic freedom, which is guaranteed by Article 5 of the Basic Law; (2) the refusal to grant an injunction violated Harlan's constitutional right to practice his profession, which is guaranteed by Article 12; or (3) the refusal to grant an injunction violated the business interests of the producers and distributors, whose rights are arguably protected by Article 14.[29] The doctrine of *Drittwirkung* does not in any way dictate the result that must be reached in any particular case, including in the *Lüth Case*. In other words, the bootstrap use of constitutional rights merely had the effect of conferring jurisdiction on the Federal Constitutional Court, nothing more.

[28] Günter Dürig, 'Grundrechte und Privatrechtsprechung' in Theodor Maunz (ed.), *Festschrift für H. Nawiasky* (Duncker & Humblot 1956) 157 *et seq.*

[29] See generally Canaris, *Grundrechte und Privatrecht*, 27ff.

Another illustration of *Drittwirkung* is provided by a judicial challenge to a long-standing practice of many, if not most, banks of requiring spouses, close friends, or even children of would-be borrowers to guarantee repayment of business loans. These are loans for which the spouse, close friends, and children would not otherwise be liable in the absence of a guaranty. The banks defended their practice as a prudent, even necessary device to deter debtors from sheltering assets with close family members and friends in the event of default on their obligations under the promissory note. According to banks' argument, upon the default of the debtor, the banks should not be required to prove that assets were, in fact, transferred to the guarantor to evade the banks' collection efforts since that avenue would be available to the banks even without the guaranty. Rather, to achieve the desired deterrence effect, the guarantor's obligation must be automatically enforceable against these potential recipients of the debtor's assets.

One problem with this line of argument is that it no longer (assuming it ever did) reflects the actual collection practices of banks. Indeed, in years past, it seemed that more and more cases were reaching the courts in which banks were mercilessly pursuing collection from gratuitous guarantors who had never received assets from the promissory note's promisor and who had no prospect whatsoever of ever having the financial wherewithal to make good on their guaranties. Because bankruptcy was not available to them until recently, these well-meaning friends and family members were saddled with debt they could never hope to pay off.

The German Federal Constitutional Court finally stepped into the fray in 1993 in a case in which a twenty-one-year-old unskilled factory worker with no assets of her own had guaranteed a loan of 100,000 Deutschmarks (almost €50,000) to her real-estate broker father. When her father defaulted on the promissory note, judgment in the civil courts was entered on the guaranty against the woman, who was earning just 1,150 Deutschmarks monthly, despite her offer of proof that she had been told by an officer of the bank that she would not be incurring any serious financial obligation by signing the guaranty.[30]

Previous challenges to familial guaranties had been rejected by the courts by reference to notions of freedom of contract.[31] But this time was different. The Federal Constitutional Court granted the petition of the real-estate broker's daughter and reversed on constitutional grounds.

The Federal Constitutional Court based its holding on Article 2 of the German Constitution. Article 2, which literally protects the amorphous free unfolding of one's personality (*freie Entfaltung der Persönlichkeit*), has been construed to protect freedom of contract. According to the Federal Constitutional Court, freedom of

[30] Discussed in Reinhard Zimmermann and Mathias Habersack, 'Legal Change in a Codified System: Recent Developments in Germany Suretyship Law' (1999) Edin L Rev 273.

[31] See generally B.G.B. Staudinger, Norbert Horn, and Heinz-Peter Mansel (eds) (14th edn, De Gruyter 2012) §765 no. 162 *et seq*.

contract presupposes relative equality of bargaining position. Absent such equality, the 'structurally weaker' party to a contract is not acting freely. Accordingly, it would violate Article 2 of the German Constitution if courts were to sanction the imposition of excessive financial burdens upon people in 'structurally weak' bargaining positions.

The Federal Constitutional Court ordered that the civil judges in the future inject Article 2 indirectly into their deliberations about familial guaranties by construing the general clauses of the German Civil Code in accordance with constitutional rights.[32] Specifically, the Constitutional Court decreed, in this case, that the terms 'good morals' (*gute Sitten*) in §138 and 'good faith' (*Treu und Glauben*) in §242 of the German Civil Code must be construed in the context of familial guaranties to protect 'structurally weak' relatives and loved ones from exploitation by lending institutions.[33] Of course, this only means that the civil judges were directed to reverse their decision based on statute, not on constitutional, law for their decision is based solely on statute law.[34]

Although one can find a great deal of literature on the topic of German *Drittwirkung*, even in English,[35] particularly about the use of *Drittwirkung* by the courts of the European Union,[36] in fact, there are relatively few instances in which

32 89 *Entscheidungen des Bundesverfassungsgerichts* 214, 237.

33 See generally Reinhard Zimmermann, *Introduction to German Law* (Werner Ebke and Matthew W. Finkin eds, 1st edn, C.H. Beck 1996) 17.

34 Jan M. Smits, *Private Law and Fundamental Rights: A Sceptical View* (Intersentia 2006–08) 9.

35 See e.g. Daniel Friedmann and Daphne Barak-Erez (eds), *Human Rights in Private Law* (Oxford University Press 2001); Christian Starck, 'Human Rights and Private Law in German Constitutional Development and in the Jurisdiction of the Federal Constitutional Court' in Friedmann and Barak-Erez, *Human Rights in Private Law*, 98; Björg Thorarensen, *The Drittwirkung of the European Convention on Human Rights and Positive Obligations of States Deriving from the Convention* (University of Edinburgh Press 1993); Johan van der Wal, The Horizontal Effect Revolution and the Question of Sovereignty (De Gruyter 2014).

36 On the methodology of the CJEU, see generally, e.g. Jochen Anweiler, *Auslegungsmethoden des Gerichthofs der Europäischen Gemeinschaften* (Peter Lang 1997); Christian Baldus and Friederike Vogel, *Gedanken zu einer europäischen Auslegungslehre: Grammatikalisches und historisches Element in Fiat iustitia, Recht als Aufgabe der Vernunft* (Ducker & Humblot 2006) 237–252; Albert Bleckmann, 'Zu den Auslegungsmethoden des Europäischen Gerichtshofs' (1982) NJW 1177; Carsten Buck, *Über die Auslegungsmethoden des Gerichtshofs der Europäischen Gemeinschaft* (Lang 1998); Wolfgang Buerstedde, *Juristische Methodik des Europäischen Gemeinschaftsrechts* (Nomos 2006); Ninon Colneric, *Auslegung des Gemeinschaftsrechts und gemeinschaftsrechtskonforme Auslegung in Zeitschrift für Europäisches Privatrecht* (ZeuP 2005) 225ff; Hans-Wolfram Daig, 'Auslegung und Anwendung von Art. 177 EWG-Vertrag durch den Gerichtshof der Europäischen Gemeinschaften' in Wilhelm G. Grewe, Hans Rupp, and Hans Schneider (eds), *Festschrift Kutscher* (Nomos 1981) 281; Ulrich Everling, *Zur Begründung der Urteile des Gerichtshofs der Europäischen Gemeinschaften in Zeitschrift Europarecht* (EuR 1994) 127ff; Franzen Martin, 'Auslegung und Fortbildung von privatrechtsangleichenden Richtlinien' in Thomas Ackermann (ed.), *Jahrbuch junger Zivilrechtswissenschaftler 1997* (Nomos 1997); Thomas Henninger, *Europäisches Privatrecht und Methode* (Mohr Siebeck 2009); Bruno Heusinger, *Rechtsfindung und Rechtsfortbildung im Spiegel richterlicher Erfahrung* (Carl Heymanns 1975); Matthias Herdegen, *Europarecht* (15th edn, C.H. Beck 2013); Hans Kutscher, *Über den Gerichtshof der Europäischen Gemeinschaft, Zeitschrift Europarecht* (EuR 1994) 392ff; Katja Langenhuber, 'Vorüberlegungen zu einer Europarechtlichen Methodenlehre' in Thomas Ackermann (ed.), *Jahrbuch junger Zivilrechtswissenschaftler 1999* (Nomos 1999); Michael Potacs, Effet utile als Auslegungsgrundsatz (EuR 2009) 465; Karl Riesenhuber (ed.), *Europäische Methodenlehre: Handbuch für Ausbildung und Praxis* (2nd edn, De Gruyter Berlin 2012); Christopher Schmidt, 'Desintegration

the federal constitutional judges in Germany have reversed the civil courts in this way. One fairly recent example concerns an injunction against a tenant to remove a satellite dish that the tenant had erected without the approval of the landlord, as was required under the tenant's lease. In holding that the injunction must be reversed, the constitutional judges ruled that a person's fundamental constitutional right to inform herself, which is guaranteed by Article 5(1) of the Basic Law, encompasses a right by foreigners to inform themselves on political developments in their home countries; and if this information is not available by means of the cable television access provided by the landlord, then the foreign tenant generally has a right to erect a satellite dish on the rental premises over the landlord's objection.[37]

The doctrine of *Drittwirkung* has not been limited to reversing the grant of injunctions by the civil courts in cases where free speech is at risk,[38] to setting aside sharp familial guaranties, or to obliging landlords to allow unsightly satellite dishes on their apartment buildings. The doctrine has been employed in a number of subject-matter areas. There are cases, for example, involving dissolution of marriage[39] and antitrust law.[40] These infusions of constitutional considerations into traditional areas of private (i.e. civil) law is often described as the constitutionalization of private law.[41] Many, if not most, of the German cases and all of the cases of the courts of the European Union have been discussed in English elsewhere. But few authors in English have pointed out that *Drittwirkung* is much more dangerous to separation of powers than the use of general clauses, such as *Treu und Glauben* discussed in section C below. The reason is this: if the non-constitutional judges use general clauses in their judgments to refine and rewrite

und Neuordnungsperspektiven im europäischen Privatrecht: Plädoyer für ein europäisches Rechtsinstitut und für "Restatements" im europäischen Recht' in Thomas Ackermann (ed.), *Jahrbuch junger Zivilrechtswissenschaftler 1999* (Nomos 1999); Stefan Vogenauer, *Eine gemeineuropäische Methodenlehre des Rechts—Plädoyer und Programm, Zeitschrift für Europäisches Privatrecht* (Zeitschrift für europäisches Privatrecht 2005) 234ff.

[37] 90 *Entscheidungen des Bundesverfassungsgerichts* 21; Werner Niedenführ, Johanna Schmidt-Räntsch, and Nicole Vandenhouten, *WEG: Kommentar und Handbuch zum Wohnungseigentumsrecht* (9th edn, Deutscher Anwaltverlag 2010) 344; Matthias Ruffert, *Vorrang der Verfassung und Eigenständigkeit des Privatrechts* (Mohr Siebeck 2001) 545f.

[38] Another example of a conflict with free speech is the *'Eat Vegetarian, Forget Meat!' Case* discussed in Chapter 7.

[39] 103 *Entscheidungen des Bundesverfassungsgerichts* 89; Matthias Cornils, *Die Ausgestaltung der Grundrechte: Untersuchungen zur Grundrechtsbindung des Ausgestaltungsgesetzgebers* (Mohr Siebeck 2005) 364f.

[40] Stefan Storr, *Der Staat als Unternehmer: Öffentliche Unternehmen in der Freiheits- und Gleichheitsdogmatik des nationalen Rechts und des Gemeinschaftsrechts* (Mohr Siebeck 2001) 525f; Andreas Neef, *Kartellrecht* (C.F. Müller 2008) 128; Christian Alexander, *Schadensersatz und Abschöpfung im Lauterkeits- und Kartellrecht: Privatrechtliche Sanktionsinstrumente zum Schutz individueller und überindividueller Interessen im Wettbewerb* (Mohr Siebeck 2010) 98. See also the Fraport decision, 128 *Entscheidungen des Bundesverfassungsgerichts* 226 and the Beer Can Flash Mob decision, *Entscheidungen des Bundesverfassungsgerichts* of 18 July 2015, 1 BvQ 25/15 (2015) NJW 2485.

[41] Hans Micklitz (ed.), *Constitutionalization of European Private Law* (Oxford University Press 2014) XXII(2); Olha O. Cherednychenko and Norbert Reich, 'The Constitutionalization of European Private Law: Gateways, Constraints, and Challenges' (2015) 23 ERPL 797.

statutes, it is always possible for the legislature to amend the statutes, even if the judges base their judgments in part on constitutional grounds, which gives the legislature the last word. This is not the case if the federal constitutional judges hold that certain outcomes are mandated for the protection of constitutional rights. Such holdings can only be overruled by the Federal Constitutional Court for, according to the text of the 'eternity clause' (*Ewigkeitsklausel*) of Article 79 of the Basic Law, the principles of the fundamental rights that are found in the Basic Law cannot be changed, even by amending the Basic Law.

D. *Treu und Glauben*

The German Civil Code contains a number of so-called general clauses (*Generalklauseln*).[42] The most commonly employed statement of the principle of good faith can be found in §242 of the German Civil Code. According to §242, 'an obligor is obliged to fulfil the obligation as required by good faith [*Treu und Glauben*], giving consideration to customary practice'. Although §242, by its terms, only applies to obligors, the courts have resorted to §242 in cases involving employment law,[43] public law, and even the law of civil procedure. Indeed, today it is recognized as a comprehensive legal principle that applies to any person who exerts legal rights or fulfils legal duties.[44]

As shown by examples below, §242 of the German Civil Code can be used by German judges as a trump card to enable them to reach decisions that they consider to be correct but which cannot be justified by citation to explicit statutory authority, or sometimes apparently in opposition to that authority.

(1) Can notice of termination of a lease be effective even if not actually received?

Section 130(1) of the German Civil Code states: 'A declaration of intent that is to be made to another becomes effective, if made in his absence, at the point of time

[42] Other general clauses include §§138, 157, 242, 314, 626, and 826 of the German Civil Code and §1 of the Unfair Competition Act: Basil S. Markesinis, Hannes Unberath, and Angus C. Johnston, *The German Law of Contract: A Comparative Treatise* (2nd edn, Hart 2006) 23 *et seq*. See generally Hannes Unberath and Astrid Stadler, *Comparative Law in the German Courts, in Courts and Comparative Law* (Mads Andenas and Duncan Fairgrieve eds, Oxford University Press 2015) 581, 588.

[43] Bernd Waas, 'Good Faith and Fair Dealing in the Individual Employment Relationship' (2011) 32 Comp Lab L & Pol'y J 603.

[44] Reiner Schulze, '§242 Leistung nach Treu und Glauben' in Reiner Schulze (ed.), *Bürgerliches Gesetzbuch* (C.H. Beck 2016); 85 *Entscheidungen des Bundesgerichtshofes in Zivilsachen* 48 (1958); *Bundesarbeitsgericht* (2005) NJW 775; *Bundesgerichtshof* (2009) NJW 1882; Lennart Matzke, *Münchener Kommentar zum Bürgerlichen Gesetzbuch* (6th edn, C.H. Beck 2012) §242, para. 165.

when this declaration reaches him.' In a case from 1976, the City of Munich posted notice of termination of a lease to the plaintiff at the plaintiff's home, with proof of receipt requested. The plaintiff was not home when the letter was to be delivered, so the postman left a chit at the plaintiff's house, informing the plaintiff that the letter awaited him at the post office.

The court held that a declaration of intention reaches the addressee for purposes of §130 of the German Civil Code 'as soon as it comes within his area of control such that in normal circumstances he could be expected to learn of it'. While this holding might readily be described as a purposive argument based on §130, the Federal Supreme Court, for good measure, also cited §242: 'But in some cases para. 242 BGB permits one to treat a declaration of intention as having arrived in due time although it did not reach the reception area of the person to whom it was directed [case citations omitted].'[45] However, the reader should notice that the facts of this case bear little resemblance to the text of §242, which speaks of an 'obligor' fulfilling an 'obligation' in good faith. In this case, it is the court, and not the statute, that is imposing an obligation on the plaintiff to 'reach for' the notice by fetching it from the post office rather than, as stated in §130(1), to have the notice 'reach him'.

(2) Does delivery to the insured's sister constitute valid delivery under §130(1)?

In a case that preceded the case just discussed, an insurance company sent a registered letter with a notice of failure to pay life insurance premiums to the home of the insured, identified as AZ Jr. The envelope was addressed to the decedent's father, AZ, even though the insurance policy was in the name of AZ Jr. There were four family members living at the address at the time, including the decedent's sister, who signed for the letter. AZ Jr was killed in a motorcycle accident. When his father, the beneficiary under the policy of life insurance, made a claim, the insurance company refused payment because his son was in default on his payments at the time of his death.

The trial and appellate courts ruled that the notice of failure to pay the premiums had 'reached' the son for purposes of §130(1) of the Civil Code. The Imperial

[45] In one of the earlier cases considering this issue, a posted notice of termination of a lease was held to be timely where the landlord had moved and the forwarding instructions that the landlord had provided to the post office had expired: *Entscheidungen des Reichsgerichts in Zivilsachen* (RGZ) 144, 289 (3 May 1934), reported in translation by Tony Weir in Markesinis *et al.*, *The German Law of Contract*, 533. According to case decisions and opinions of scholars, the time of receipt will depend upon when it would be expected that the addressee would have knowledge of the declaration under the circumstance and business practice: Ulrich Burgard, 'Das Wirksamwerden empfangsbedürftiger Willenserklärungen im Zeitalter moderner Telekommunikation' (1995) 195 Archiv für die civilistische Praxis 74, 108.

Court (*Reichsgericht*), disagreed. Citing §242 of the Civil Code, the Imperial Court wrote: '[S]o long as it was uncertain which of the two Messrs. AZ, father and son, the letter was for, it did not "reach" either of them.'[46]

(3) Can one football (soccer) club recover a transfer fee paid to another club for a player involved in bribery?

The infamous Bundesliga Scandal of 1971 resulted in a number of players being barred from playing in the German Football League. In June of that year, one of the players who was later implicated in that scandal was transferred to another team for a substantial transfer fee. After he had played only three games for his new team, the player confessed to having taken a bribe and was promptly fired and barred from play. Neither the selling team nor the acquiring team was aware of the player's involvement in the bribery scandal.

The new team demanded the return of the transfer fee. In the litigation that resulted, the trial court and the appellate court both gave judgment for the team that had acquired the player. The selling team appealed, unsuccessfully. In dismissing the appeal, the Federal Supreme Court relied on §242 and its own previous decisions, and those of its predecessor, the Imperial Court (*Reichsgericht*) for, at the time, there was no statute that would allow recovery.[47] However, the Civil Code was amended in 2002 to include §313, which was intended to codify case law.[48] Section 313(1) reads:

> Each party may terminate a contract for the performance of a continuing obligation for a compelling reason without a notice period. There is a compelling reason if the terminating party, taking into account all the circumstances of the specific case and weighing the interests of both parties, cannot reasonably be expected to continue the contractual relationship until the agreed end or until the expiry of a notice period.

The reader should notice that the facts of this case bear little resemblance to the text of §242, which speaks of an 'obligor' fulfilling an 'obligation' in good faith. In this case, it is the court, and not any statute in existence at the time the case was decided, that is imposing an obligation on the second football club.

[46] Markesinis *et al.*, *The German Law of Contract*, 557, translating *Reichsgericht* (Seventh Civil Senate) 15 June 1929, 125 *Entscheidungen des Reichsgerichts in Zivilsachen* (RGZ) 68.

[47] *Bundesgerichtshof* I ZR 191/87, judgment of 30 November 1989, reported in English translation at <https://law.utexas.edu> accessed 23 November 2023.

[48] Hans Brox and Wolf-Dietrich Walker, *Allgemeines Schuldrecht* (35th edn, C.H. Beck 2012) §27.

(4) Can an insurance company that has refused to conduct an autopsy later claim that the death was not accidental?

In another case involving a death and an accidental death insurance policy, the insurance company refused the family's offer to have the body of the deceased autopsied but then also refused to pay out the benefit on the basis that the deceased had not died as a result of an accident. The trial court made short shrift of the insurance company's argument, holding that §242 of the Civil Code embodied the maxim *venire contra factum proprium*. Consequently, the insurance company was estopped by its previous conduct.[49]

Lest the reader be enamoured of the general clauses like §§138 and 242 of the Civil Code, one should remember that judges in the 1930s and 1940s in National Socialist Germany employed them to deprive Jews of contractual rights.[50]

E. Statutory analogy

As discussed in Chapter 4, most usages of the term 'analogy' in legal discourse are as a synonym for 'comparison'. Rupert Cross seems to use the word 'analogy' in this sense in his book *Statutory Interpretation* when he writes that the phrase 'the intention of Parliament', when used by judges, 'is meaningless unless it is recognized for what it is, an expression used by analogy'.[51] Other academics employ 'analogy' to describe case-by-case development. Arthur Lenhoff does so when he describes legal analogy as the 'force which created the bulk' of the 'unwritten law' of 'the Anglo-American legal system'.[52]

By contrast, the term 'statutory analogy' in this section refers to the technique of legal argument in which judges borrow policies, usually called 'principles', from other statutes to justify a decision that cannot readily be justified by textual, historical, or purposeful arguments emanating from the statute that they purport to

[49] *Landgericht Bautzen* 3 O 392/94, judgment of 20 October 1994.

[50] On the abuse of general clauses, see the seminal work Bernd Rüthers, *Die unbegrenzte Auslegung: Zum Wandel der Privatrechtsordnung im Nationalsozialismus* (8th edn, Mohr Siebeck 2017); also Vivian Grosswald Curran, 'Fear of Formalism: Indications from the Fascist Period in Germany of Judicial Methodology's Impact on Substantive Law' (2001) 35 Cornell Int'l LJ 101, 102ff; Arthur Kaufmann, 'National Socialism and German Jurisprudence from 1933–1945' (1988) 9 Cardozo L Rev 1629.

[51] Rupert Cross, *Statutory Interpretation* (Butterworths 1995) 34. See generally Martin P. Golding, *Legal Reasoning* (Routledge & Kegan Paul 1984) 103; Scott Brewer, 'Exemplary Reasoning: Semantics, Pragmatics, and the Rational Force of Legal Argument by Analogy' (1996) 109 HLR 923, 944; William Twining and David Miers, *How to Do Things with Rules* (Cambridge University Press 2010) 262; Cass Sunstein, 'On Analogical Reasoning' (1993) 106 HLR 741, 743; John H. Farrar, 'Reasoning by Analogy in the Law' (1997) 9 Bond L Rev [i]; Hans W. Baade, 'The Casus Omissus: A Pre-History of Statutory Analogy' (1994) 20 Syracuse J Int'l L & Com 45.

[52] Arthur Lenhoff, *Comments Cases and Other Materials on Legislation* 945 (Dennis & Co. 1949).

be applying. This technique of argument can be thought of as a legal transplant,[53] where the policy of a donor statute is grafted onto the beneficiary statute. This technique of argument is similar to the arguments using constitutional conformity and *Drittwirkung*, both of which are discussed above in this chapter. But the usage of the technique of statutory analogy in Germany precedes passage of the German Basic Law. And sometimes, these two techniques—constitutional arguments and arguments using statutory analogies—are employed simultaneously, as juristic 'belts and suspenders (braces)', as in the case below (1) of the humiliated dressage rider, which is also discussed in Chapter 5. Statutory analogical arguments are also used similarly to the use of general clauses, such as *Treu und Glauben*, which is discussed earlier in this chapter. However, unlike *Treu und Glauben*, judges in Germany can use statutory analogies to create new causes of action, as is seen below (2) in the case of the careless viola player.

Statutory analogy also differs from constitutional conformity and *Drittwirkung* in that the judges who employ statutory analogies, unlike those who employ constitutional arguments, expound a fiction that there is a gap, or lacuna, in existing statute law. This fictional gap, which can only be perceived by the judges and by the party who would otherwise lose, is shorthand for the judges' conclusion that a certain party should prevail at court, but the party cannot prevail unless the statute that the judges are applying is amended.[54] In reaching their conclusion to amend the beneficiary statute, the judges will ask themselves whether the legislature would likely agree with the amendment for they will not ordinarily bother to consider a statutory analogy if they believe that the legislature would disagree with them.[55] However, (3) in the case of the disadvantaged Thai importers of cassava,

[53] On legal transplants between jurisdictions, see generally W.A.J. Watson, *Legal Transplants: An Approach to Comparative Law* (Edinburgh University Press 1974).

[54] Accordingly, this technique is an extreme example of putting a gloss on a statute. Hans Kelsen explained gap-filling as follows:

> The so-called 'gap', then, is nothing but the difference between the positive law and a system held to be better, more just, more nearly right. Only by placing this 'better' system alongside the system of positive law and thereby ascertaining the latter's shortcomings, only thus can one claim something like a 'gap'. The fact that it cannot be filled by way of interpretation is obvious as soon as one recognises its nature. Interpretation here does not serve to bring about application of the interpreted norm; on the contrary, interpretation here serves to eliminate the interpreted norm and to replace it with a norm that is better, more just, more nearly right—in short, the norm desired by the official applying it. Under the pretext that the original norm is being supplemented to make up for its deficiencies, it is overturned in the course of being applied and is replaced by a new norm. Hans Kelsen, 'On the Theory of Interpretation' (BL Paulson and SL Paulson trans. 1990) 10 Legal Studies 133. See Sergey Drobyshevskiy and Evgeny Tikhonravov, *Способы восполнения пробелов в праве* (*Methods of Filling Gaps in the Law*) (Norma Publishing House 2014), reviewed by Thomas Lundmark, 'Sergey Drobyshevskiy and Evgeny Tikhonravov, Methods of Filling Gaps in the Law (Способы восполнения пробелов в праве)' (2015) 46 Rechtstheorie 421.

[55] This would open the judges up to the charge that they are usurping legislative power. It might also prompt the legislature to enact a law to 'overrule' the statutory analogy. This would prove embarrassing to German judges, who maintain that they are merely acting on behalf of the legislature when they employ statutory analogies. On the use of statutory analogies in National Socialist Germany, see Carolyn

the European Court of Justice did, indeed, disagree with the legislative body, the European Commission. Sometimes, the party to a lawsuit who would otherwise lose the case will unsuccessfully plead with the judges to amend the relevant statute by means of a statutory analogy. An example of such an unsuccessful plea can be seen below (4) in the case of the jilted bridegroom's father.

(1) The case of the humiliated dressage rider

In 1958, the First Civil Senate of the German Federal Supreme Court decided the famous *Herrenreiter* (*Dressage rider*) *Case*, which centred on advertising posters showing a photograph of a dressage rider astride his jumping horse. The product being advertised was an over-the-counter patent medicine to alleviate male sexual impotence. The horseman in the photograph was the plaintiff in the trial court. The photograph, which had been taken by a press photographer at an equestrian competition, had been used without the plaintiff's permission. While the poster caused no measurable financial detriment to the plaintiff or to his brewery, it was insulting in that it implied that the plaintiff suffered from impotence. This exposed the plaintiff to public ridicule among the members of his social sphere. Further, an award to the plaintiff of a licensing fee, which might be permitted under existing law, would not compensate the plaintiff for his pain, suffering, and loss of amenity (*Schmerzensgeld*).[56]

The judges of the First Civil Senate might easily have ruled against the plaintiff on his claim for pain, suffering, and loss of amenity for there is no statute in the German Civil Code that provides for an award of damages under these circumstances; and §253 of the German Civil Code states that no damages shall be awarded for non-financial loss (*immaterieller Schaden*) unless expressly provided for by statute.[57] Notwithstanding §253, which the judges (conveniently) failed even to cite in their decision,[58] the judges of the First Civil Senate of the Federal Supreme

Benson and Julian Fink, 'Legal Oughts, Normative Transmission, and the Nazi Use of Analogy' (2012) 3 Jurisprudence 445.

[56] P.R. Handford, 'Moral Damage in Germany' (1978) 27 Int'l & Comp LQ 849.

[57] Section 253 of the German Civil Code reads: '(1) For an injury that is not a financial injury, damages can be claimed only in cases determined by statute. (2) If damages are awarded for bodily injury, or for injury to health, liberty, or sexual self-determination, a claim for damages can also be made for non-financial injury.'

[58] The judges justified their ruling by citing Articles 1 and 2 of the German Basic Law, the Constitution, and by employing an analogy to §847, which has since been repealed: Huw Beverley-Smith, Ansgar Ohly, and Agnes Lucas-Schloetter, *Privacy, Property and Personality: Civil Law Perspectives on Commercial Appropriation* (Cambridge University Press 2006) 101. At the time, §847 read: (1) In a case of bodily injury or injury to health, as well as in a case of deprivation of liberty, the injured person can also claim damages for non-financial injury. (2) The same claim may be made by a female person against whom a felony or a crime against morals was committed, or who has been forced to co-habit through deceit, threat, or abuse of a relationship of dependence.

Court announced a new rule: 'Damages shall be awarded for substantial injury to the right of personality of another.'[59]

The judges justified their holding both by referring to the Basic Law and by drawing an analogy to §847(1) of the German Civil Code, which read, at the time, as follows: 'In a case of bodily injury or injury to health, as well as in a case of deprivation of liberty, the injured person can also claim damages for non-financial injury.' Here is how they justified the creation of a new cause of action:

> Articles I and 2 of the Constitution protect—and indeed must be applied by the courts in the administration of justice—what is called the concept of human personality; they recognise in it one of the supra-legal basic values of the law. Thereby they are directly concerned with the protection of the inner realm of the personality which, in principle, only affords a basis for the free and responsible self-determination of the individual and an infringement of which produces primarily so called immaterial damage, damage expressed in a degradation of the personality. To respect this inner realm and to refrain from invading it without authorisation is a legal command issuing from the Basic Law itself. And it follows from the Constitution that in cases of invasion of this sphere, protection must be given against damage characteristic of such an invasion.
>
> ...
>
> Once the violation of the right to one's picture is seen as affecting one's personality it is possible to seek an answer to the question how to compensate immaterial damage in §847 BGB ... Now that the Constitution guarantees a comprehensive protection to the personality and recognizes human dignity and the right to free development of the personality as a fundamental value, it has done away with the dogma held by the original draftsmen of the BGB that there can be no civil law protection of general personality right; and since a protection of 'inner freedom' without a right to compensation for immaterial damage would be in great part illusory, it would be intolerable to refuse compensation for that immaterial damage. Moreover, there is no obvious reason why §847 BGB should not be extended by analogy to such attacks as injure the right to free exercise of the will, especially where that deprivation of intellectual liberty, just like deprivation of bodily freedom, renders natural restitution impossible. Where such blameworthy depreciations of the personality right are in question, the effective legal protection offered by the Constitution can, in the absence of any special legal provision, be attained only through its inclusion in the injuries mentioned in §847 BGB, since their injurious consequences are of necessity primarily immaterial.[60]

[59] 26 *Entscheidungen des Bundesgerichtshofes in Zivilsachen* 349 (1958).

[60] Markesinis, *A Comparative Introduction to the German Law of Tort*, 195–201.

(2) The case of the careless viola player

In a case from 2000, a violist broke his bow while practicing for a concert in a practice room at his employer's concert house. Unfortunately for the violist, regardless of how extensively the statutes are interpreted, there is no statute in Germany that makes employers liable for the damage caused to an employee's property by the employee himself. However, beginning with a case in 1961, the German courts have been allowing recovery on the basis of a statute that, even if construed purposively, cannot be stretched to cover a viola bow broken by an employee. In other words, the courts have been applying the statute by analogy; that is, they have been judicially amending the statute. In doing so, they have created a new cause of action.

The statute in question, §670 of the Civil Code, is routinely used by the German courts for this purpose. Yet, it applies, by its terms, only to unpaid agents, not paid employees:

> If the mandatary [an unpaid agent], for the purpose of performing the mandate, incurs expenses that he may consider to be necessary in the circumstances, then the mandator is obliged to make reimbursement.

Neither the text nor the legislative history suggests that this statute was meant to benefit employees. Indeed, there are separate statutory provisions for employees, and these provisions contain no corollary to §670. And it is not even superficially plausible to give §670 a purposive interpretation that extends its application to employees for doing so would do violence to the express terms of the statute. Consequently, if the judges merely followed existing statute law, the violist's employer would have no obligation to reimburse its employee for his loss because German statute law confers no right of compensation upon employees who damage their own property within the course and scope of their employment. This is, in fact, what the German courts held from 1900, the year in which the Civil Code went into effect, until the Federal Labour Court reversed itself in 1961 and ruled for the employee. In order to rule in favour of the employee, the court resorted to applying a statute by analogy.

This is the justification, lightly redacted, that the Federal Labour Court furnished when it applied §670 to the employee/employer relationship for the first time:

> Section 670 applies to agency agreements. One sees the same general idea of activity on behalf of another person. But even if one follows the weight of authority and refuses to classify an employment contract as an agency agreement, and only sees it as an independent activity of an economic nature within the sphere of influence of another's economic activity, the result cannot be otherwise. For the principle [of reimbursement] behind Civil Code section 670 is so obvious and

> in the nature of things so necessary that it is to be applied even without express legislation.[61]

By declaring that 'the result cannot be otherwise', the Court is intimating that it would be incorrect not to apply §670 analogically to employment contracts, in other words, that the application of §670 is somehow logically necessary. If this were so, then the Court below, whose judgment was reversed, and all previous courts during the preceding sixty years, was wrong in failing to apply §670 analogically to employment contracts. Obviously, this is an untenable position, particularly when one considers that the academic literature by and large supported the earlier judicial construction. It should therefore be obvious that the result is not dictated by logic. Indeed, if one were merely employing formal logic, one could more easily make an *argumentum e contrario*: the fact that the legislature stipulated that only agents, and not employees, be entitled to reimbursement means that employees are not entitled to reimbursement.

What is happening, of course, is that the judges are merely stating in their judgment why they chose to apply §670 and not some other statutory provision by analogy. They are not stating the policy reasons for their decision to allow employees to recover for their losses. They are not enunciating the values and the political, social, economic, and other considerations that motivated them to break with traditional employment law and with 'the weight of authority'. If not for these policy reasons, the judges would never have concluded that there was a gap in the law. If not for these policy reasons, they would never have considered applying §670 or any other statute by analogy. These policy reasons might include the poor position of employees in the business world, the weakened role of unions, the economic argument that employee losses are a cost of business that should be internalized, or even the argument that it is more efficient for employers to take out insurance and, in that way, to spread the risk of loss. To summarize, German judges decided that employees should be entitled to reimbursement for their losses, so they looked for a device—an artifice or fiction—to allow employees to recover from their employers. They found that device in the so-called application of §670 by analogy. The judges justified the application of a statute by analogy by saying that doing so was 'so obvious and in the nature of things so necessary' because both employment contracts and unpaid agency contracts involve economic activity on behalf of another. Yet, this is but a mere statement of what the two situations have in common. It is not the reason for their decision to create a cause of action in favour of employees.

[61] 12 *Entscheidungen des Bundesarbeitsgerichts* 15 (1962).

(3) The case of the disadvantaged Thai cassava importers

Justifications that are styled 'applying statutes by analogy' are also found in the judgments of the Court of Justice of the European Union (CJEU), previously styled the European Court of Justice (ECJ). In a case from 1984, the judges in the Third Chamber of the ECJ felt that importers of cassava (manioc) from Thailand, who operated under their own Regulation of the European Commission, should be entitled to the same favourable treatment accorded to importers from Brazil and Indonesia, who operated under a separate Regulation of their own.[62] The judges noted, 'Both regulations sought to protect the same Community interest and concerned importers whose interests were identical.'

Dismissing the Commission's contentions that 'the situation in regard to Thailand was completely different' and that the less favourable treatment of Thailand was intentional, the Third Chamber went on to hold that the Commission's disadvantageous treatment of importers from Thailand was 'contrary to the principle in Community law of equal treatment of traders in comparable situations'. Continuing, the judges argued, 'The concern to take account of legitimate expectations [of the importers] ... should therefore also have provided a justification for similar measures in favour of importers of manioc from Thailand.' Consequently, according to the judgment of the Third Chamber, the Regulation applying to Thailand 'contains a lacuna which is to be filled by applying by analogy' to the more favourable provision of the other Regulation. In effect, these European judges, under the guise of analogical reasoning, judicially amended the Regulation that applied to Thailand by inserting a provision from the other, more favourable Regulation. The justifications for the ruling are typically short and declaratory, with no mention of the real motivations underlying the judges' decision.

Notice that, in this case, the ECJ expressly disagrees with the European Commission, which is the legislative body in this context. In effect, the ECJ is using an analogical argument as an argument of constitutional conformity, meaning that the European Commission is prohibited from changing the law.[63]

(4) The case of the jilted bridegroom's father

To illustrate, in another way, that application of statutes by analogy is a choice made by judges and not a dictate of logic, consider the following case in which the

[62] *J.F. Krohn GmbH & Co KG v. Bundesanstalt für Landwirtschaftliche Marktordnung* [1985] European Court Reports 1985–03997.

[63] See generally Sandor Vida, 'Analogies in the Case Law of the Court of Justice EU' (2013) 54 Acta Jurid Hung 286.

German courts declined to apply a statute by analogy. Section 1301 of the German Civil Code reads:

> If the marriage does not take place, each engaged person may require the other to return what the former gave as a present or as a sign of the engagement.

Considering the ease by which the court above concluded that it was 'so obvious and in the nature of things so necessary' to employ §670 by analogy, would it not be obvious and necessary for them to apply §1301 to a gift by the bridegroom's father to his future daughter-in-law? Do not the interests of the father of the bridegroom closely coincide with those of the bridegroom under these circumstances? Or what about applying §1301 to gifts given by couples who pool their finances by opening a joint bank account with the intention of cohabiting but who do not plan, at least at present, to marry? Do not the interests of the couple who plan to cohabit but who do not have definite marriage plans substantially overlap with the interests of a couple who have definite plans to marry at some point? Yet, despite the fact that lawyers have urged the courts to apply §1301 by analogy to these situations, and despite the fact that there is support in the academic literature for doing this,[64] the courts have adamantly refused to do so.[65] This is the justification, lightly redacted, for refusing to apply §1301 to a couple who intended to cohabit without marrying:

> At the outset it appears doubtful whether the statutes regarding engagements are to be applied here at all, for it is usual to assume that gifts in the course of a non-marital relationship are given solely for the purpose of supporting the partner, with the result that Civil Code section 1301 is not applicable even in the case of a contemporary engagement. Even larger contributions which are considered to fall within the customary give and take of a non-marital living arrangement are not considered gifts for purposes of Civil Code section 1301.[66]

Missing, of course, is any mention of the fact that the legislature, when faced with a similar situation in another context, weighed up the conflicting interests

[64] Peter Schlechtriem, *Restitution und Bereicherungsausgleich in Europa: Eine rechtsvergleichende Darstellung*, vol. 1 (Mohr Siebeck 2000) 831 n. 532; Günter H. Roth, in *Münchener Kommentar*, vol. 7, §1301 BGB, para 7.

[65] *Bundesgerichtshof Zeitschrift für das gesamte Familienrecht* (FamRZ) 2010, 985; *Bundesgerichtshof Zeitschrift für das gesamte Familienrecht* (FamRZ) 2010, 1626. The parents might be able to recover under §530(1) of the German Civil Code: 'A donation may be revoked if the donee is guilty of gross ingratitude by doing serious wrong to the donor or a close relative of the donor.' The parents also might be able to recover under §812(1) of the German Civil Code:

> A person who obtains something as a result of the performance of another person or otherwise at his expense without legal grounds for doing so is under a duty to make restitution to him. This duty also exists if the legal grounds later lapse or if the result intended to be achieved by those efforts in accordance with the contents of the legal transaction does not occur.

[66] *Oberlandesgericht Köln*, 3 U 74/94, 10 March 1995.

and came to a conclusion which would imply that the legislature might agree if the courts were to draw an analogy in the present situation. A discussion of the similarity of interests is missing because the judges refused to find a lacuna. As explained above, this must mean one of two things: either the judges think that couples who give gifts in contemplation of non-marital cohabitation should not recover their gifts, or they think that the legislature would disagree with the outcome. If they think that the legislature would disagree, they will not apply a statute by analogy for fear of their action being seen as a political usurpation of the legislative prerogative.

F. Summary

The subject of this chapter—system-contextual argument—is extremely broad. It encompasses pleas to reason, fairness, justice, legality, legitimacy, appropriateness, proportionality, equity, mercy, and countless other concepts, principles, and doctrines, including Shariah law, if that is a component of the particular legal system. What these concepts share in common is that they are understood to permeate the legal system and, thus, can be employed like trump cards in almost any legal situation.

This chapter treats only four system-contextual arguments: constitutional conformity, *Drittwirkung*, *Treu und Glauben*, and analogies. These have been chosen because of their importance in civil-law jurisdictions like Germany and because three of them—*Drittwirkung*, *Treu und Glauben*, and analogies—are poorly understood in the English-speaking legal world.

Arguments to constitutional conformity have a dimension that is often overlooked outside Germany. In Germany, for example, the Federal Constitutional Court, in most cases, only has jurisdiction over controversies involving constitutional issues, such as constitutional rights. As demonstrated in the *Herrenreiter Case*, if the Federal Constitutional Court discerns a constitutional issue in a controversy otherwise outside its jurisdiction, the Court can substitute itself as the last appellate instance in place of, for example, the Federal Supreme Court.

Drittwirkung is usually translated into English as the 'third-party effect' or the 'horizontal effect' of constitutional rights. In practice, *Drittwirkung* is merely an argument for bending the law in the direction that the judges see fit. This is illustrated by the examples in the *Lüth* case and the familial guaranties case.

The use of *Treu und Glauben* ('good faith') in Germany has a longer history than constitutional conformity, but it works in a similar way except that it does not confer jurisdiction on the Federal Constitutional Court. This is illustrated by the cases that are discussed in this chapter.

Section E of this chapter addressed statutory analogies as that term is understood in the civil-law world: the technique of legal argument in which judges borrow policies from other statutes to justify a decision that cannot readily be justified by textual, historical, or purposeful arguments. Statutory analogies are hidden behind fictional gaps in the statutory scheme, fictional in the sense of legal fictions. Unlike arguments to *Treu und Glauben*, the doctrine of statutory analogies can be employed to create new causes of action.

9

A Plea for Transparency and Candour

A. Introduction

This final chapter begins in section B with a short summary of the preceding eight chapters. Thereafter, in section C, the author will comment upon and criticize the examples of judicial reasoning in the case decisions that were reported in Chapters 5 ('Textual Argument'), 6 ('Historical Argument'), 7 ('Purposive Argument'), and 8 ('System-Contextual Argument'). Section C concludes with final remarks on the importance of transparency and candour in legal reasoning to enhance the persuasiveness and efficacy of judicial precedents, to foster democratic legitimacy, and to permit political accountability.

B. Summary of the chapters

The introductory chapter of this book (Chapter 1) defined the most important legal terms that are found frequently in these pages. Perhaps the most important term of all is 'rule', which includes broader 'principles'; for rules also serve as the ties that bind together those who make, find, apply, and justify the use of rules in legal systems.

Statutory rules are routinely interpreted by judges. In doing so, the judges are, in effect, defining, amending, or supplementing the statutory rule. These definitions, amendments, and supplements, which can usefully be thought of as subsidiary legislation, are referred to in this book as 'glosses'.

Just as statutory rules can be the subject of glosses, so, too, can case-based rules. And, as is illustrated by numerous examples, the case-based rules that are the subject of glosses can have their source in both judicially created rules in the absence of statute, so-called 'pure' common law (*Richterrecht* in German), and in judicially created glosses on rules from statutes, that is, glosses on glosses.

While most authors of treatises and articles employ the word 'method' to refer to the various categories of judicial justificatory reasons, this book primarily employs the nomenclature 'arguments' or 'justifications'. One reason for choosing the word 'argument' is that there are vast differences in how these authors define and treat contextual interpretation and also analogical reasoning and interpretation. Also, some of these authors are prone to making fine, and untenable, distinctions among the methods that are generally accepted—the textual, historical,

Universals of Legal Reasoning by Judges. Thomas Lundmark, Oxford University Press. © Thomas Lundmark 2024.
DOI: 10.1093/oso/9780198785675.003.0009

and purposive—and by asserting that one method is inherently, or constitutionally, superior to another method.

Another reason for avoiding the term 'method' is that statutory interpretation is often misunderstood to imply that there is only one particular procedure for approaching the interpretive task at hand: one need only select the correct method to reach the right decision. This common misunderstanding puts the cart before the horse: the method does not dictate the decision; it is merely the justification for the decision.

And, perhaps obviously, another reason for avoiding the word 'method' for the interpretation of rules is that the word has been pre-empted by statutory interpretation. The word 'method' is seldom employed when discussing how one applies or uses judicial decisions for the assumption is that, while statutes can be 'methodically' applied to factual scenarios, judicial decisions can only be analogically or suggestively applied to factual scenarios. As this book proves, statutory and case-based rules are, in fact, used in the same way.

The first chapter also introduced the four categories of argument or justification that are addressed in this book. These are the textual, historical, purposive, and system-contextual categories. Finally, this first chapter made clear that, while the author chronicles criticisms levelled at these categories of arguments, he deliberately avoids making any claims as to the innate superiority of any particular argument over another.

Chapter 2 also began with definitions. Specifically, the categories of law for purposes of this book were defined as (1) statute law (including subsidiary legislation, such as regulations); (2) law that is announced by judges when concretizing (amending) statutes (i.e. statutory glosses); and (3) judge-made law in the absence of a statute, called *Richterrecht* in German, and here referred to as 'pure' common law.

The process of enacting statutes involves legal reasoning in a broader sense. In proposing statutes, the legislative body must consider legal issues such as the purpose of the proposed legislation, the appropriateness of the means chosen to serve those purposes, the authority to enact the chosen means, and the existence of other laws, including constitutional law, which might be in conflict with the proposed legislation.

These issues should also be considered by judges when they are applying statutory law and pronouncing rules of 'pure' common law. As explained in this second chapter, judges also make law, as that term is used in this book, when they construe statutes and when they pronounce law in the absence of a statute. When making this law, judges have less access to relevant information than legislative bodies, and they enjoy less democratic legitimacy as they are not, in general, elected. However, judges should still consider the same legal issues as the legislative bodies. In addition, judges must also consider the issue of separation of powers. The consideration of separation of powers means that judges will sometimes decline to decide, preferring to defer to the legislative body. As was shown, this practice of deferral also results in pronouncing law.

As was illustrated in this chapter, finding the law also involves legal reasoning. The process of finding both statute law and case law entails the recognition of rules and of insights drawn from the factual scenarios (i.e. the stories) enshrined in the rules that might conceivably be applied.

The discussion of applying the law began with the legal syllogism. This sometimes misleads people into believing that applying the law is a more or less mechanical, deductive process. As the examples in this chapter illustrated, even if rules are applied using a deductive format, reaching a result often involves a great deal of discretion. Judges employ intuition or 'hunches' to arrive at the result that they consider to be correct and just. They then attempt to subsume the result under the rule. This sometimes requires art, or sometimes even artifice, in addition to a great deal of effort. This process is described here as the heavy lifting of legal reasoning.

After the judge has reached a result, she or he must explain or justify it. Justifying the result is an act of artistic expression. It calls upon the judge's training, experience, and ingenuity to tell a story—or spin a yarn—which convinces others that the result is rooted in law. According to Savigny, these stories—he referred to them as 'elements'—fit into four groups. Savigny did not develop his elements in any detail, and he described them somewhat differently from how they are employed in this book. That being said, the categories into which justificatory arguments are organized in this book substantially correspond to Savigny's elements.

So-called political judging, the topic of Chapter 3, is widely criticized in the press. But what is meant by political judging? If one considers all value-laden judicial activity to be political, then all judicial glosses and statements of common law rules are political because they are value-laden. Also, judicial intuition, here referred to as 'hunching',[1] although generally unconscious, is also value-laden and therefore political. Fact-finding is also influenced by value-laden factors.

The practice of judicial overruling of previous decisions brings the political-ness of judging into clearer focus. Some overruling is due to a perceived need to correct a precedent or to renovate the law in cases where the precedent was decided against a legal or factual background that no longer exits. However, some instances of overruling can only be explained by the ascension of new judges to the court, resulting in political (value-laden) overruling. But this is not a bad thing for why should the values of the first judges who decide an issue be allowed to preordain the future?

Finally, Chapter 3 discussed the issue of ideological judging. It was seen that a judge's ideology, whether conscious or unconscious, can have a major influence on the judge's decision-making. Critically, this influence, and the influence of other

[1] The 'lurches' that were discussed in this chapter are more obvious examples of value-laden judging because the changes that they make in the law are major.

factors discussed, is seldom revealed in the rationalization of the judge's decisions, that is, in the arguments or so-called reasoning of the court. In short, politics, by any definition, has at least the potential to influence almost all judicial activity.

After reviewing the academic literature on the subject, it was concluded, at the outset of Chapter 4, that there is no comprehensive methodology on the use of *ratios* from statutory glosses and 'pure' common law (*Richterrecht*). Employing the Savigny canons of textual, historical, and purposive interpretation to justify different solutions to a simple, hypothetical, factual scenario, it was shown in that chapter that it makes no difference whether the rule being applied is statutory or judge-made. Chapter 4 then quoted a number of rules from German statutory and case law to illustrate that judicial *ratios* are generally indistinguishable from statutory rules.

Chapter 4 then explained and illustrated what is meant in the civilian world, and in these pages, by statutory analogies. Statutory analogies are those justificatory arguments that identify, and ostensibly apply, a rule from a statute that cannot be applied to the fact pattern before the court in a textual, historical, or purposive manner. In so doing, the judges expressly or impliedly discern a principle that is common to both the statute and the fact pattern before the court.

Finally, Chapter 4 discussed case-law analogies and the importance of facts in judicial decisions, noting that the term 'analogy' is commonly used in legal writing to mean any comparison whatsoever. If analogical reasoning is understood in this way, then even the process of the *Normsuche* is analogical because the process of the *Normsuche* consists of comparing the facts before the court to various rules in order to select the most comparable rule or rules.

The facts of a precedential case can play a role in the ascertainment of the *ratio*. Generally, the *ratio* of a case is the rule announced by the judges in the decision itself. However, one can expand or contract the *ratio* of a case depending on whether one chooses to use the result of the judicial decision (i.e. the fact-based holding) or some other principle, one that is narrower or broader than the rule announced by the judges.

Chapter 5 adopted an elastic interpretation of textual argument as an argument that focuses, either sharply or fuzzily, on one or more words of the rule that is sought to be employed, regardless of whether the rule is statutory or case-based. While academics routinely contend that the text of a statute must be followed when the text is clear, they do not extend their contention to case-based rules. Nor do such academics seem to realize that the text itself must always be understood in its historical and cultural context.

Chapter 6 described, critiqued, and illustrated the use of historical arguments that are used to justify the result that has been reached in a legal dispute. Historical arguments were defined as those arguments that invoke the historical setting or that insinuate that the drafter of the rule would agree with the result. Courts sometimes cite the legislative record or *travaux préparatoires* to reinforce the strength of the results that they had selected. While a handful of judges and academics profess that only those arguments are legitimate that seek to divine the 'original intent' of the drafters of a constitution, this profession does not extend to the original intent of the drafters of case decisions or even the drafters of statutes. In other words, only the intent of the drafters of a constitution is entitled to eternal respect according to these judges and academics.

After reciting various descriptions of why historical arguments should be used, section A of Chapter 6 discussed three cases in which judges employed historical arguments to reach results that were arguably at odds with the texts of the statutes being interpreted but that were argued to be in consonance with the will of the legislative bodies. These cases are examples of what is sometimes called *contra legem* interpretation.

Then, two cases were examined in which courts in California and Germany employed similar historical arguments when interpreting judicial glosses that had been pronounced by supreme courts when construing their respective constitutions. The opinions in both of these cases suggest that the judges in the precedential cases would agree with the result. Finally, two cases were analysed in which the courts in England and California also suggested that the judges in the precedential cases would agree with the results that they reached. These are all examples of historical arguments.

Section B of Chapter 6 provided examples of historical argument based directly on the wording of statutory rules. Section C did the same for historical argument based on judicial glosses on statutes. Put another way, these are arguments based upon precedents that construed specific statutes. Section D of Chapter 6 considered historical arguments based on precedents that articulate rules of 'pure' common law, that is, where there is no statute or statutory gloss that provides the rule of decision.

Chapter 7 elucidated purposive arguments. These arguments are often styled the 'teleological method'. Purposive arguments are often employed alongside textual and historical arguments, but they are also put forward in cases where the judges cannot (conveniently) fashion a textual or historical argument that will convincingly support the result that they wish to reach. Indeed, purposive arguments are also used to depart from what appears to be the clear wording of a statute, as illustrated in cases discussed in this chapter.

Purposive arguments talk about the perceived purposes or principles embodied in a rule. All of the descriptions of purposive arguments quoted in this chapter evidenced an assuredness by judges that they needed more leeway to decide cases in accordance with their sense of justice and order.

Because of the importance of this line of argument to contemporary legal debate, this chapter outlined and critiqued eight cases in which judges invoked the perceived purposes of legislation in support of their rulings. All of these examples involved judges who avoided the result that the text of the statute seemed to dictate.

As demonstrated in this chapter by one case from California and one from Germany, purposive arguments are also employed when construing glosses on statutes, that is, when applying the rule of a precedential case construing (i.e. concretizing or amending) a statute.

The final two case examples in Chapter 7 displayed the judicial use of purposive arguments to reach results that arguably violate the language of the precedential rules but not the rules' purposes or spirit as discerned by the judges.

The subject of Chapter 8 was system-contextual argument. This category is extremely broad. It encompasses pleas to reason, fairness, justice, legality, legitimacy, appropriateness, proportionality, equity, mercy, and countless other concepts, principles, and doctrines, including Shariah law if that is a component of the particular legal system. What these concepts share in common is that they are understood to permeate the legal system and, thus, can be employed like trump cards in almost any legal situation.

In light of the broadness of the category of system-contextual argument, Chapter 8 treated only four examples of system-contextual arguments: constitutional conformity, *Drittwirkung*, *Treu und Glauben*, and analogies. These were chosen because of their importance in civil-law jurisdictions like Germany and because three of them—*Drittwirkung*, *Treu und Glauben*, and analogies—are poorly understood in the English-speaking legal world.

Arguments to constitutional conformity have a dimension that is often overlooked outside Germany. In Germany, for example, the Federal Constitutional Court, in most cases, only has jurisdiction over controversies involving constitutional issues, such as constitutional rights. As demonstrated in the *Herrenreiter Case*, if the Federal Constitutional Court discerns a constitutional issue in a controversy otherwise outside its jurisdiction, the Constitutional Court can substitute itself as the last appellate instance in place of the other federal courts, which are the highest courts in (almost) all non-constitutional cases.

Drittwirkung is usually translated into English as the 'third-party effect' or the 'horizontal effect' of constitutional rights. In practice, *Drittwirkung* is merely an argument for bending the law in the direction that the judges see fit. This was illustrated in Chapter 8 by the examples in the *Lüth* case and the familial guaranties case.

The use of *Treu und Glauben* ('good faith') in Germany has a longer history than constitutional conformity, but it works in a similar way, except that it does not confer jurisdiction on the Federal Constitutional Court. This was illustrated by the cases that were discussed in Chapter 8.

The final part of Chapter 8 addressed statutory analogies as that term is understood in the civil-law world: the technique of legal argument in which judges borrow policies from other statutes to justify a decision that cannot readily be justified by textual, historical, or purposeful arguments. Statutory analogies are hidden behind fictional gaps in the statutory scheme, fictional in the sense of legal fictions.

Unlike arguments to *Treu und Glauben*, the doctrine of statutory analogies can be employed to create new causes of action.

C. Comments on, and criticisms of, the judicial reasoning in the exemplar case decisions

In this section, the author comments upon, and criticizes, the examples of judicial reasoning (in the sense of reason-giving) in the case decisions that were reported in Chapters 5 ('Textual Argument'), 6 ('Historical Argument'), 7 ('Purposive Argument'), and 8 ('System-Contextual Argument'). These examples will demonstrate that judges shy away from revealing the thoughts, motivations, value judgements, and even policy considerations that underlie their decisions. Instead, they employ various formulaic, legalistic arguments to justify the decisions that they have reached on the basis of their thoughts, motivations, value judgments, and policy considerations. This pervasive judicial practice obscures the value-laden nature of the judges' calling and, consequently, both diminishes the persuasiveness and the efficacy of judicial precedents, on the one hand, and hampers political accountability, on the other, thus compromising democratic legitimacy.[2]

(1) Chapter 5 ('Textual Argument') comments and criticism

Chapter 5 collected and examined instances of the use of textual arguments to justify judicial decisions that were founded directly on statute law, on judicial glosses on statutes (statutory precedents), and on 'pure' common-law precedents. It was revealed that the style of argument is identical regardless of the source of the rule.

It was also revealed in Chapter 5 that, in every case, the judges could have decided differently, had they wanted to. The judges of the German Federal Supreme Court might well have concluded that electricity is a 'movable thing' and that translucent, but not transparent, glass blocks are not 'windows'.[3] The judges of the German Federal Supreme Court need not have overruled the precedential case holding that acid was not a 'dangerous instrument' (*gefährliches Werkzeug*),[4] and they might have agreed with the trial court that in vitro fertilization does not constitute 'palliative treatment for an illness'.[5] And, in the 'milked-out goat' case, the

[2] For an argument to the contrary, at least for present-day Russia, see Sergey Drobyshevskiy and Evgeny Tikhonravov, *Способы восполнения пробелов в праве* (*Methods of Filling Gaps in the Law*) (Moscow: Norma Publishing House 2014), reviewed by Thomas Lundmark, 'Sergey Drobyshevskiy and Evgeny Tikhonravov, Methods of Filling Gaps in the Law (Способы восполнения пробелов в праве)' (2015) 46 Rechtstheorie 421.

[3] *Bundesgerichtshof*, judgment of 13 July 960—V ZR 90/59.

[4] *Bundesgerichtshof für Strafsachen* 1, judgment of 20 November 1950.

[5] *Bundesgerichtshof*, decision of 17 December 1986—IVa ZR 78/85; BGHZ 99, 228 (1986).

First Civil Senate of the German Federal Supreme Court might have referred the case for decision to the Grand Senate for Civil Matters.[6]

Similarly, the judges of the California Court of Appeal might have concluded that the would-be bride must make restitution to the parents of the bridegroom for the expensive wristwatch given to her as a gift;[7] and they could have held that 'tubing' is not 'an active sport'.[8] And the judges of the California Court of Appeal might have employed a purposive argument to hold that the defendant in *Fisher v. Morrison Homes, Inc.* can be liable for a defective pedestrian pathway.[9]

Turning to the United Kingdom, if just one of the three Law Lords in the majority of the decision in *Berriman v. London & North Eastern Railway Co.*[10] had wanted Berriman's widow to prevail on her claim, the case would have been decided the other way. In effect, the Lords would have concluded that oiling and cleaning also constituted 'repairing'. Continuing to other examples, the trial judge in *Zarvos v. Pradhan*[11] could have ruled that Zarvos had a 'reasonable prospect' of being able to occupy the premises 'for the purposes of a business carried on by him'. And the Law Lords might have upheld the judgment of the trial-court judge in *Read v. Lyons*,[12] who held that the defendants were liable because they were carrying out an ultra-hazardous activity.

In summary, the judges who decided these cases were not forced by the rule that they were applying—whether that rule was statutory or case-based—to decide the cases in the way that they did. Yet, they all employed seemingly mechanical reasoning to justify their decisions, as if their decisions were somehow, perhaps grammatically or even logically, necessary. In these and other cases, the use of textual argumentation is undoubtedly deliberate: judges can conceal their real considerations and motivations behind terminological arguments that appear, at first glance at least, to be objective and almost scientific.

What were the real considerations and motivations of the judges in these cases? For one thing, all appellate court judges in the jurisdictions discussed here are well aware that their decisions have consequences beyond the disputes that they are

[6] The appellate court correctly assumed that, in the present case, the stated prerequisites for the claim for payment of satisfaction are met. It rightly pointed out that the infringement of rights for which the defendants are responsible is particularly serious in view of the nature of the defamation and the considerable encroachment on the private sphere, with the widespread dissemination of the newspaper being particularly significant. [*Das Berufungsgereicht hat zutreffend angenommen, dass im vorliegenden Fall die dargelegten Voraussetzungen für den Anspruch auf Zahlung einer Genugtuung gegeben sind. Es hat mit Recht darauf hingewiesen, dass die von den Beklagten zu vertretende Rechtsverletzung angesichts der Art der Ehrkränkung und der erheblichen Eingriffe in die private Sphäre besonders schwerwiegend ist, wobei die weite Verbreitung der Zeitschrift besonders ins Gewicht fällt.*]

[7] *Simonian v. Donoian*, 96 Cal. App. 2d 259, 262 (1950).

[8] *Record v. Reason*, 73 Cal. App. 4th 472 (1999).

[9] *Fisher v. Morrison Homes, Inc.*, 109 Cal. App. 3d 131 (1980).

[10] *Berriman v. London & North Eastern Railway Co.* [1946] AC 278.

[11] *Zarvos v. Pradhan* [2003] EWCA (Civ.) 208. See Michael Haley, 'Section 30(1)(g) of the Landlord and Tenant Act of 1954: The Unjust Relegation of Renewal Rights' (2012) 71 Cambridge LJ 118, 146.

[12] *Read v. Lyons* [1947] AC 156.

deciding. Their decisions will have repercussions. The foreseeable consequences of the German in vitro fertilization case,[13] for example, is that, in the future, a congenitally malformed fallopian tube or similar congenital malformation that prevents pregnancy will be classified as an insured illness so that the treatment of in vitro fertilization, and perhaps other treatments, will be covered by health insurance. In response to a shrinking population, the German government has adopted numerous policies to encourage families to have children. Making in vitro fertilization available to more women would align with these policies. And, because the group of women with such illnesses who seek such treatment would likely be relatively small, the additional medical costs, which would also likely be relatively small, would be spread by higher insurance premiums. If this is what the judges were thinking, they should have said so explicitly, in the interests of candour and transparency. Candidness about the motivational thoughts and policies of the judges would not only help lawyers and judges in applying the rule announced in the case but also enable a debate about these motivations in an open and democratic fashion. The judges in this case, and other cases here discussed, presumably did not reveal their considerations because of concern that they would be criticized for acting politically. Thus, they preferred to hide behind a textualist veil.

Reading the long-winded textual judgments of the three Law Lords in the majority in the case of *Berriman v. London & North Eastern Railway Co.*,[14] one might be left with the impression that public policies and consequences had no bearing whatsoever on their decisions to deny compensation to the widows of Berriman and Rowe. On the contrary: one is left with the impression that the matter was purely one of construing the word 'repairing'. This impression is dispelled by one single sentence penned by Lord Macmillan, who was one of the judges in the majority:

> If the word 'repairing' were to be extended to include the simple and routine matter of oiling and cleaning, the railway companies would require [*sic.*] to provide persons or apparatus for the purpose of maintaining a good look-out or for giving warning of an approaching train or engine every time one of their servants oiled a single bearing.

This sentence reveals what we already know: that appellate judges are well aware that their decisions have consequences beyond the disputes that they are deciding. Lord Wright, in dissent, countered Macmillan's argument: '[T]he construction which I adopt ... would impose some additional burden on the railway company. That drawback must yield to the purpose of saving life, which must outweigh some

[13] *Bundesgerichtshof*, decision of 17 December 1986—IVa ZR 78/85; BGHZ 99, 228 (1986).
[14] *Berriman v. London & North Eastern Railway Co.*

small extra expense or trouble to the company.'[15] Which judges are acting politically? Those in the majority or the minority?

We do not know how onerous the burden would have been on railway companies if they had been required to provide a look-out for men who were 'merely' cleaning and oiling, rather than repairing, the metal connections and other mechanical devices; and there is no further mention of this matter in the judgments of the Law Lords or of the Lord Justices of the Court of Appeal.[16] But, considering the fact that cleaning and oiling were usually done on a weekly basis, the burden would probably have been quite burdensome and the extra costs would have been passed on to customers by the Big Four railway companies in Britain at the time, assuming that the companies could even find additional personnel to hire. One should not forget that this case arose in 1943 during Second World War. The judges in the majority were certainly thinking about these and other matters in making their decision. But, aside from the one sentence by Lord Macmillan, they did not say so. If the judges had been more candid, the decision would have been more comprehensible to railway workers and the general public and would have enabled a discussion of the underlying issues in Parliament or another public forum.

It will be recalled that, in the case of *Fisher v. Morrison Homes, Inc.*,[17] the California Court of Appeal did, in fact, allow that case to proceed to trial on a claim of negligence but not on a claim of strict liability. Indeed, the Court of Appeal made short shrift of the claim of strict liability, disposing of the claim in a two-sentence footnote following the clause in the decision that 'a developer performs a service'. Here is the footnote, which makes a textual argument:

> [P]athways ... are not 'products' placed in the stream of commerce for profit, but are more akin to a service. Strict liability principles are therefore inapposite.[18]

But why are pathways services and not products? They are, in fact, designed and constructed (i.e. produced) by the developer just as a toaster might be produced. Is it because defective pathways—because the claimant must prove that the claimant's injury was caused by a defect in the product—are less dangerous that defective toasters? Is it because the pathways, although privately designed and constructed, are eventually passed to the ownership of a public authority, such as a municipality? If so, would a toaster that is purchased by a municipality stop being a 'product' the

15 Ibid 301.

16 See *Berriman v. London and North Eastern Railway Company* [1945] KB 462.

17 *Fisher v. Morrison Homes, Inc.*

18 Ibid n. 2. According to the federal Ninth Circuit Court of Appeals, whose decisions are not binding on the California courts: '[T]he doctrine of products liability does not apply as between parties who: (1) deal in a commercial setting; (2) from positions of relatively equal economic strength; (3) bargain the specifications of the product; and (4) negotiate concerning the risk of loss from defects in it': *Southwest Forest Indus. v. Westinghouse Elec. Corp.* (9th Cir. 1970), 422 F. 2d 1013, cert. denied 400 U.S. 902.

instant it was acquired by the municipality? This textual distinction is just not very convincing.

What, then, motivated the justices of the California Court of Appeal in ruling that the plaintiff in *Fisher v. Morrison Homes, Inc.*[19] could not proceed to trial on a claim of product liability? One can only speculate, but since appellate judges are well aware that their decisions have consequences beyond the disputes facing the judges, to classify pedestrian pathways as 'products' for the purpose of product liability law would make such a claim available for accidents allegedly caused by defective roads, streets, bridges, and buildings. It might 'open the floodgates' to claims. Furthermore, there is already a statutory claim that can be made for injuries caused by a dangerous condition of public property.[20] A product liability claim is arguably unnecessary.

(i) Can someone in a private residence be convicted of soliciting prostitution 'in a street or public place'?

A teleological extension can also be seen an English case, *Smith v. Hughes*,[21] concerning the Street Offences Act 1959. Several prostitutes were alleged to have been soliciting for prostitution in violation of §1(1) of that Act. Police officers had observed the women standing on a balcony, or behind ground-floor windows, from where they would attract the attention of male passers-by and then invite them in. In itself, this activity would appear to constitute solicitation of prostitution, and the two were convicted in the Magistrates' Court. On appeal to the High Court, Queen's Bench Division, their barrister argued that the Act only prohibited soliciting 'in a street or public place', and the women were in neither a street nor a public place. Nevertheless, Lord Parker CJ held, in a judgment that the two other judges joined, that the women were guilty. His argument begins with a textual argument but then speaks only of statutory purpose:

> Observe that [§1(1)] does not say there specifically that the person who is doing the soliciting must be in the street. Equally, it does not say that it is enough if the

[19] *Fisher v. Morrison Homes, Inc.*

[20] See §835 of the California Government Code:

> Except as provided by statute, a public entity is liable for injury caused by a dangerous condition of its property if the plaintiff establishes that the property was in a dangerous condition at the time of the injury, that the injury was proximately caused by the dangerous condition, that the dangerous condition created a reasonably foreseeable risk of the kind of injury which was incurred, and that either:
>
> (a) A negligent or wrongful act or omission of an employee of the public entity within the scope of his employment created the dangerous condition; or
>
> (b) The public entity had actual or constructive notice of the dangerous condition under Section 835.2 a sufficient time prior to the injury to have taken measures to protect against the dangerous condition.

[21] *Smith v. Hughes* [1960] 1 WLR 830, 832.

person who receives the solicitation or to whom it is addressed is in the street. For my part, I approach the matter by considering what is the mischief aimed at by this Act. Everybody knows that this was an Act intended to clean up the streets, to enable people to walk along the streets without being molested or solicited by common prostitutes. Viewed in that way, it can matter little whether the prostitute is soliciting while in the street or is standing in a doorway or on a balcony, or at a window, or whether the window is shut or open or half open; in each case her solicitation is projected to and addressed to somebody walking in the street. For my part, I am content to base my decision on that ground and that ground alone.[22]

(2) Chapter 6 ('Historical Argument') comments and criticism

Chapter 6 collected and examined instances of the use of historical arguments to justify judicial decisions that were founded directly on statute law, on judicial glosses on statutes (statutory precedents), and on 'pure' common-law precedents. It was revealed that the style of argument is identical regardless of the source of the rule.

It was also revealed that, in every case, the judges could have decided differently had they wanted to. For example, the judges of the Federal Administrative Court in Germany ruled that minks were not 'farm animals' even though they are raised in cages on farms like rabbits: and rabbits are considered farm animals. In other words, it would be difficult to craft a persuasive textual argument that minks are not 'farm animals'.

However, in the course of their deliberations, the judges had decided that mink farmers should be treated differently from rabbit farmers. To buttress their decision, they turned to the legislative history, where they found that the *Bundesrat*, which is the upper house of the German Parliament, 'considered ... that the breeding and raising of ... fur-producing animals ... often present problems'.

How serious were these concerns to the members of the *Bundesrat*? If a majority of the members really had serious concerns about the raising of fur-producing animals, they could easily have required that the legislation clarify that such animals were not to be considered 'farm animals' for the purposes of this legislation. But they did not do so. Cannot this failure to act be understood as evidence that the members did, indeed, want minks to be considered 'farm animals'? Yet, the judges of the Federal Administrative Court cite this language from the legislative record in support of the exact opposite: that the members of the *Bundesrat* did not want minks to be considered 'farm animals'. From our standpoint, one conclusion

[22] Ibid. The mischief rule is discussed in Chapter 4.

is inescapable: the judges of the Federal Administrative Court first decided that they did not think mink farming should be exempt from the licensing requirement; then, because textual arguments were not very persuasive, they found some evidence in the legislative record that seemed to support their decision. This example neatly illustrates that the judges first decide, and only then do they provide the justification.

The *doli incapax* decision of the Law Lords in *R v. JTB*[23] is another example of judges turning to the legislative record when textual arguments were insufficient to support their predetermined decision. According to the *doli incapax* defence, children under the age of ten could not be convicted of a crime, and children aged ten to thirteen were presumed to lack the capacity to know that their acts were wrong. Because this was merely a presumption, the prosecution was afforded an opportunity to prove that the child did, indeed, know that what he or she had done was seriously wrong.

In 1998, the doctrine of *doli incapax* was amended by Parliament but only as to children aged ten and older: 'The rebuttable presumption of criminal law that a child aged 10 or over is incapable of committing an offence is hereby abolished.'[24]

This statute seems clear on its face: only the presumption is abolished but not the defence itself. For if Parliament had intended to abolish the defence as well as the presumption, it could well have said so. Also, if there were any doubt about this, according to the age-old doctrine of lenity, if a statute is 'capable of two meanings, however unreasonable one of those meanings might be, it [must be] applied if favourable to the accused'.[25] According to this doctrine, it would have been possible for the judges who decided *R v. JTB* to allow the accused twelve-year-old boy in that case to introduce evidence that he lacked the capacity to know that his acts were seriously wrong.

Despite the fact that, as Lord Phillips ingenuously conceded, 'it is not possible to reach this conclusion from the language of section 34 alone', all of the judges who heard the boy's case refused to allow the boy to raise the defence of *doli incapax*. To support their refusal, they resorted to the legislative record, which, they wrote, 'made it quite clear what was meant by abolition of the presumption of doli incapax'.[26]

Turning to the United States and the case of the allegedly defective fifteen-passenger Ford van, it will be recalled that the plaintiffs had failed to give notice to the sellers as required by the express terms of §2607(3)(A) of the California Commercial Code, which states that the buyer must 'notify the seller of breach or

[23] *R v. JTB* [2009] UKHL 20. *Doli incapax* means 'incapable of evil'.

[24] Section 34 of the UK Crime and Disorder Act 1998.

[25] Rupert Cross, John Bell, and Sir George Engle, *Cross on Statutory Interpretation* (3rd edn, Butterworths 1995) 134; discussed in Adam Perry, 'Strained Interpretations' (2019) 39(2) OJLS 316–343.

[26] *R v. JTB*.

be barred from any remedy'.[27] This language could not be clearer. However, in a precedential case, the California Supreme Court had held that this statutory notice requirement was 'not an appropriate one for the court to adopt in actions by injured consumers against manufacturers with whom they have not dealt'.[28] But that was a case of bodily injury, and the case of the fifteen-passenger Ford van was a case of merely economic injury. Consequently, if the judge in the case of the fifteen-passenger Ford van had wanted to, he could have ruled that the failure to give notice was fatal to the plaintiffs' case. However, the judge employed a historical argument to support his ruling that the statutory notice provision did not apply: '[T]his Court is not persuaded that the Supreme Court of California would apply §2607(3)(A) so strictly.'

In summary, the judges who decided these cases were not forced by the rule that they were applying—whether that rule was statutory or case-based—to decide the cases in the way that they did. Indeed, in each of these cases, the text of the rule dictated a contrary result. In order to justify their departures from the text of the rule, the judges resorted to historical arguments to suggest, but in no way prove, that the people who pronounced the rule—the legislators in Germany, the United Kingdom, and California (as 'glossed' by the California Supreme Court)—would agree with their result.

Why did all of these judges seemingly ignore what appeared to be the clear language of the rules that they were applying? It was previously noted that all judges in cases such as these are well aware that their decisions will have consequences beyond the disputes that they are deciding. In the case of the mink farmers, the expected consequences would presumably be fairly small—and obviously desirable to the judges who decided the case: mink farmers and other farmers of fur-producing animals must apply for a licence, must pay a fee, must supply detailed information, and must agree to regular inspections to ensure compliance with any conditions that are imposed on the grant of their licence. One would not expect the licensing burden to be onerous. And the costs would be passed on to the purchasers of the furs.

In the *doli incapax* case, children aged ten to thirteen will no longer be able to argue that they lacked the capacity to understand that what they were doing was

[27] Section 2607(3)(A) of the California Commercial Code: '[A] buyer must, within a reasonable time after he or she discovers or should have discovered any breach, notify the seller of breach or be barred from any remedy.'

[28] *Greenman v. Yuba Power Products*, 377 P. 2d 897, 900 (Cal. 1963):

> As between the immediate parties to the sale [the notice requirement] is a sound commercial rule, designed to protect the seller against unduly delayed claims for damages. As applied to personal injuries, and notice to a remote seller, it becomes a booby-trap for the unwary. The injured consumer is seldom 'steeped in the business practice which justifies the rule', and at least until he has had legal advice it will not occur to him to give notice to one with whom he has had no dealings. The quotation is from William L. Prosser, 'The Assault upon the Citadel (Strict Liability to the Consumer)' 69 Yale LJ 1099, 1130 (1960).

seriously wrong. The ruling of the Law Lords will presumably result in more confessions and convictions.[29]

The effect of the decision not to apply §2607(3)(A) of the California Commercial Code to product liability cases is difficult to predict because it will only apply if it is followed by the Californian courts and only in cases in which Californian law applies.[30]

Examining these three examples, two conclusions suggest themselves. The first conclusion is that the judges who decided these cases genuinely believed that the people who announced the rules, the rule-makers, would agree with their decisions for, by being so blatant about their disregard of the text of the rules and by invoking the will of the law-makers, they can be seen as beseeching the rule-makers to amend the rules if they disagree with how the judges have interpreted them.

From a democratic perspective, a perspective that respects the separation of judicial and legislative powers,[31] one might welcome the use of historical arguments because they seem to accord subservience to parliamentary and legislative supremacy. But this subservience masks the second conclusion that can be reached from the actions of the judges in the cases discussed here: that the judges who decided these cases disagreed with what appears to be the textual meaning of the rules. This conclusion can be reached by the simple observation that, if they had, indeed, agreed with the textual meanings of the rules, they would not have resorted to historical arguments. A healthy respect for democracy, separation of powers, and transparency demands that judges who find themselves in this situation explicitly admit that they agree with the rule-makers.

(3) Chapter 7 ('Purposive Argument') comments and criticism

Chapter 7 collected and examined instances of the use of purposive arguments to justify judicial decisions that were founded directly on statute law, on judicial glosses on statutes (statutory precedents), and on 'pure' common-law precedents. It was revealed that the style of argument is identical regardless of the source of the rule.

[29] On the expected consequences, see Sue Bandalli, 'Abolition of the Presumption of *Doli Incapax* and the Criminalisation of Children' (1998) 37 Howard J Crime Justice 112.

[30] On these and other issues, see Elizabeth Chamblee Burch and Margaret S. Williams, 'Judicial Adjuncts in Multidistrict Litigation' (2020) 120 Colum L Rev 2129.

[31] See generally Alec Stone Sweet, *Governing with Judges: Constitutional Politics in Europe* (Oxford University Press 2000) ch. 5; Vicki C. Jackson and Mark Tushnet, *Comparative Constitutional Law* (Foundation Press 1999) ch. VI; Erhard Blankenburg, 'Changes in Political Regimes and Continuity of the Rule of Law in Germany' in Herbert Jacob, Erhard Blankenburg, Herbert M. Kritzer, Doris Marie Provine, and Joseph Sanders (eds), *Courts, Law, and Politics in Comparative Perspective* (Sage Publications 1996) 249 *et seq*; John Bell, 'Judiciaries within Europe' in Jeffrey Goldsworthy (ed.), *Interpreting Constitutions: A Comparative Study* (Cambridge University Press 2006) ch. 7; Elaine Mak, *Judicial Decision-Making in a Globalised World: A Comparative Analysis of the Changing Practices of Western Highest Courts* (Routledge 2013) ch. 4.

It was also revealed that, in every case discussed here, the judges could have decided differently had they wanted to. For example, in the German case concerning reassignments of employees to lower-paying positions, the judges ruled that such reassignments were ineffective unless they were in writing. The rule that they were purporting to apply to support this ruling does not mention reassignments: it only speaks of 'termination of employment'.[32] If the judges had wanted the employer defendant to win, they would simply have employed the statutory language to deny the claim by the employee.

Similarly, the long-haired young man with unconventional hippie dress in the California case was not, in the words of §51 of the California Civil Code, denied access to a shopping centre because of his 'sex, race, color, religion, ancestry, national origin, or blindness or other physical disability'. Despite this fact, the California Supreme Court held that the young man enjoyed the protection of that statute which, according to the Court, prohibits 'all arbitrary discrimination by business enterprises'.[33] If the judges of the California Supreme Court had wanted the young man to lose, they would simply have stressed the apparent exclusivity of the statutory list, which does not mention what clothes people wear or how they wear their hair.

Returning to the United Kingdom and the case *Smith v. Hughes*,[34] which concerned the solicitation for prostitution by various women from the balcony or windows of a private residence,[35] this case could readily have been resolved in the women's favour by employing a literal reading of the statute, which only proscribed solicitation 'in a street or public place'.[36] Neither a private balcony nor a private room is normally considered to be a street, nor are they normally considered to be a public place.

Indeed, the case in the women's favour was much stronger than the judges of the Queen's Bench Division acknowledged. The Street Offences Act 1959 might have prohibited soliciting within view of a street or public place or within, say, 50 feet of a street or public place, but it did not: it only prohibited solicitation 'in' a street or public place. And the Street Offences Act 1959, in §1(4), actually furnishes a definition of what Parliament meant by 'in a street or public place' in quite a graphic description of outdoor venues. Notice that the meaning of the term 'street' is limited to 'the doorways and entrances of premises abutting the street':

> For the purposes of this section, 'street' includes any bridge, road, lane, footway, subway, square, court, alley or passage, whether a thoroughfare or not, which is for the time being open to the public; and the doorways and entrances of premises

32 Section 623 of the German Civil Code.
33 *In re Cox*, 3 Cal. 3d 205 (1970) 216.
34 *Smith v. Hughes* [1960] 1 WLR 830. Discussed at n. 21.
35 Ibid 832.
36 Section 1(1) of the UK Street Offences Act 1959.

> abutting on a street (as hereinbefore defined), and any ground adjoining and open to a street, shall be treated as forming part of the street.[37]

To illustrate one of the theses of this book namely, that judges, after hearing a case, first get a feeling for what they think the result should be and only then search for arguments that will allow them to reach that result, it is instructive to examine the argument employed in a case later that same year: *Fisher v. Bell*. The leading judgments in both *Smith v. Hughes* and *Fisher v. Bell* were both penned by Lord Parker CJ. The judgment in *Smith v. Hughes* was announced in June of 1960. In November of the same year, Lord Parker and two other judges decided the case of *Fisher v. Bell*, which, like *Smith v. Hughes*, also involved the interpretation of a criminal statute.[38]

The statute that was interpreted in *Fisher v. Bell* was the Restriction of Offensive Weapons Act 1959, which, in §1(1), provided: 'Any person who ... sells or hires or offers for sale or hire ... any knife which has a blade which opens automatically by hand pressure applied to a button, ... sometimes known as a 'flick knife' ... shall be guilty of an offence.'

According to what appears to be the clear language of the statute, any person who offers a flick knife for sale is guilty of an offence. Presumably, then, if a shopkeeper were to display a flick knife in his shop window with a price on it, the shopkeeper would be guilty of an offence. But Lord Parker and his brethren ruled that a shopkeeper who did, indeed, display a flick knife in his shop window with a price on it was not guilty of an offence. In effect, the judges wrote the words 'offers for sale' out of the statute. Why? While admitting that 'The Act ... is aimed at preventing people from getting possession of flick knives', Lord Parker stated the following:

> It is perfectly clear that according to the ordinary law of contract the display of an article with a price on it in a shop window is merely an invitation to treat. It is in no sense an offer for sale the acceptance of which constitutes a contract. That is clearly the general law of the country ... Approaching this matter apart from authority, I find it quite impossible to say that an exhibition of goods in a shop window is itself an offer for sale.[39]

To summarize what was done in these two cases from a methodological standpoint, in the first case, *Smith v. Hughes*, the Queen's Bench Division extended[40] the reach of the criminal statute, but in the second case, *Fisher v. Bell*, the Queen's Bench Division, including one judge who had sat in the case of *Smith v. Hughes*, reduced the reach of the statutory language of a criminal statute.[41] Why the difference?

[37] Ibid §1(4). Perhaps unsurprisingly, the judgment of the judges does not mention the definition.
[38] *Fisher v. Bell* [1960] 3 WLR 919.
[39] Ibid.
[40] One could say teleologically extended.
[41] One could say teleologically reduced.

Remembering, as judges well know, that judges' decisions affect future decisions, one would expect that, following publication of the holding in the *Smith Case*, prostitutes would avoid soliciting from windows and balconies that can be seen from streets and public places. This extension of the statute might cause them to seek other means of solicitation, such as the displaying a card on a noticeboard, which is not punishable.[42] Furthermore, this broad interpretation of the statute would be unlikely to catch anyone unawares because the statutory prohibition against solicitation only applies to 'common' (which means 'known') prostitutes. In short, the expected burden on prostitutes and their clients would likely be small. While these and other considerations were probably on the judges' minds, none are referred to in the decision.

What of the prohibition against offering flick knives for sale? Advertising flick knives in shop windows might continue; and it would be practically impossible to catch a shopkeeper in the act of selling a flick knife to a customer. Yet, in all probability, shopkeepers and, more importantly, their suppliers, would be unlikely to continue the practice of displaying such knives for sale, much less selling such knives, knowing the potential negative consequences. Flick knives are not high-priced merchandise. Further, flick knives are seldom sold in shops as they can be readily bought on the street. Accordingly, one would not expect that the judges' reduction in the reach of the statute would seriously hamper the efforts of the police to reduce the number of flick knives in circulation. None of these considerations are mentioned in the decision.

Let us return to the German decision that extended the language of §623 of the German Civil Code—which only speaks of termination of employment—to reassignments of employees to lower-paying positions. This decision means that future reassignments at lower wages will trigger the protections afforded to terminated employees under German law. Importantly, this decision will enable those who are effectively demoted to demand a written statement of the reasons for the reassignment and then to attack those reasons in court on factual grounds and, further, to allege that the demotion was motivated by discrimination against protected actions and characteristics such as whistle-blowing, national origin, or was otherwise 'socially unjustifiable' (*sozial ungerechtfertigt*) in the words of the statute.[43]

This decision is unlikely to have major repercussions because the number of demotions is quite small. Consequently, the judges would have little concern that, in ruling as they did, they would effect a major change in the law. This consideration is not mentioned in the decision.

[42] Displaying a card on a noticeboard outside a tobacconists' shop does not constitute solicitation: *Weisz v. Monahan* [1962] 1 WLR 262. On the issue of solicitation, see Kathy Laster, *Law as Culture* (2nd edn, Toronto University Press 2001).

[43] *Kündigungsschutzgesetz*, §1.

To enable the long-haired man in California to make use of the Unruh Civil Rights Act, the California Supreme Court essentially stretched the statute, both by the result that the court reached and by the rule that was announced. The result of the case (i.e. the fact-based holding) is that business may not discriminate against people on the basis of what they wear, or how they look, or at least how they wear their hair. The rule articulated by the California Court is much broader: the Act prohibits 'all arbitrary discrimination by business enterprises'.[44]

This last case provides a good illustration of the legislative, or some might say quasi-legislative, role of the courts. Whereas the California Supreme Court has broadly declared that 'all arbitrary discrimination' violates the Unruh Act, the California legislation has stuck to the practice of specifying the characteristics that are protected by the Act.[45] Section 51 of the California Civil Code now reads:

> All persons within the jurisdiction of this state are free and equal, and no matter what their sex, race, color, religion, ancestry, national origin, disability, medical condition, genetic information, marital status, sexual orientation, citizenship, primary language, or immigration status are entitled to the full and equal accommodations, advantages, facilities, privileges, or services in all business establishments of every kind whatsoever.

From a democratic perspective, one perspective that respects the separation of judicial and legislative powers, one might welcome the use of purposive arguments because they purport to serve the goals that the legislature purposed. But notice that the purposive arguments, like other arguments, seek to justify decisions that the judges have already reached; for the goals that the judges articulate are ones that they themselves choose to articulate. For example, in the German case concerning reassignments of employees, the judges could just as well have stated that the goal of the statute, which, by its terms, is limited to termination of employment, was to accord employers flexibility by not requiring that they give written reasons for mere reassignments of employees, even reassignments at lower wages. In the case of the long-haired California hippie, the judges might well have stated that the goal of the Unruh Civil Rights Act was only to limit discrimination on the basis of the listed characteristics, so as not to burden businesses unnecessarily. In the solicitation case from the United Kingdom, the judges might readily have determined that the Street Offences Act was not intended to intrude upon the privacy of people in residential dwellings.

44 *In re Cox.*

45 On the effectiveness of the Unruh Civil Rights Act, see Timothy B. Liebaert, 'The Death of the Unruh Civil Rights Act: An Examination of the Act after Harris v. Capital Growth Investors XIV and an Argument in Favor of Liberalizing the Act' (2001) 29 W St U L Rev 1; Steven B. Arbuss, 'The Unruh Civil Rights Act: An Uncertain Guarantee' (1983) 31 UCLA L Rev 443.

Notice that, in all of these cases, the judges have departed from the text of the rules because the texts could not support the decisions they wished to reach. Following the text, the reassigned employee in Germany would have lost, the long-haired hippie in California would have lost, and the prosecution in the solicitation case in the United Kingdom would have lost. In all of these cases, the judges extended the reach of the statute beyond its text so that the reassigned employee in Germany and the long-haired hippie in California would win and the prostitutes in England would lose.[46]

Rather than purporting to divine the intrinsic purpose of the statute, it would be preferable if the judges in these and other cases would acknowledge and embrace their role as cooperative legislators. They should articulate what they believe to be the opposing policies and then candidly spell out, for a legal and wider audience, why they personally think that the statute should, in effect, be amended.[47]

(4) Chapter 8 ('System-Contextual Argument') comments and criticism

Chapter 8 collected and examined instances of the use of system-contextual arguments to justify judicial decisions. Because of the extremely broad nature of this arena of judicial activity, the discussion had to be limited to constitutional conformity, as practiced in the United States and Germany, and to three styles of argument that are characteristic of the German judicial tradition: *Drittwirkung*, *Treu und Glauben*, and analogies. The examples in this chapter could have been multiplied by the addition of arguments to reason, fairness, justice, legality, legitimacy, appropriateness, proportionality, equity, mercy, and countless other concepts, principles, and doctrines, including Shariah law.

As was true of the arguments in the preceding chapters (textual, historical, and purposive), it was also revealed that, in every case discussed here, the judges could have decided differently had they wanted to. For example, the US Supreme Court might have ruled that the federal Violence against Women Act was constitutional in all respects and that the marriage statutes in Ohio, Kentucky, and Tennessee were constitutional despite the fact that they prohibited marriage by same-sex couples. The US Supreme Court might also have upheld the conviction of Mrs Bond for violation of the Chemical Weapons Convention Implementation Act.

46 This is sometimes referred to as a teleological extension.

47 The author has argued elsewhere that, particularly when they are interpreting European Union law, judges should openly state the real reasons for their rulings because this would significantly aid comprehension of the judgments, whilst also allowing the opportunity for proper and necessary assessment and critique: Thomas Lundmark, '"Soft" *Stare Decisis:* The Common Law Doctrine Retooled for Europe' in Reiner Schulze and Ulrike Seif (eds), *Richterrecht und Rechtsfortbildung in der Europäischen Rechtsgemeinschaft* (Mohr Siebeck 2003) 161.

By the same token, the German Federal Constitutional Court might have upheld the statute that denied the right of successive adoptions to same-sex partners. That court might also have ruled that the 3-per cent vote requirement for parties to enter the European Parliament was constitutional. In the German *Lüth Case*, which concerned a call for a boycott, the Federal Constitutional Court might have decided that the case did not raise constitutional issues, or it might even have accepted jurisdiction of the case and then decided against Lüth, who was calling for the boycott. And the German Federal Supreme Court might have decided that the *Sparkasse* could legally refuse to allow the right-wing National Democratic Part of Germany to open a bank account. In addition, the German Federal Constitutional Court might have allowed the judgment against the daughter who had guaranteed a loan for her father to stand. And the German Imperial Court could have affirmed the judgment against the father, denying the father recovery under a life insurance policy on his son.

In the German case involving notice of termination of a lease, where the notice did not, in fact, physically reach the plaintiff, the Federal Supreme Court might well have decided in the plaintiff's favour. That court might also have decided against the humiliated dressage rider in the *Herrenreiter Case* by holding that there was no statute that accorded the dressage rider a remedy. Similarly, the Federal Labour Court in Germany might have denied recovery to the careless viola player for the same reason: there was no statute that accorded the violist a remedy. The jilted bridegroom's father could also have been left without a remedy, if the judges so chose. What these and other cases illustrate is that the statutory rule did not dictate the result: the result was determined by the judges who decided the case.

Rather than purporting to divine the intrinsic purpose of the statute, whether that be found in the text, history, or purpose of a statutory or case-based rule, the judges in these and other cases should acknowledge and embrace their role as co-operative legislators. They should articulate what they believe to be the opposing interests and policies and then candidly spell out, for a legal and wider audience, why they personally think that the statute or case-based rule should effectively be amended in the way that the judges have chosen.

From start to finish, this book is itself one argument: an argument for judicial transparency. Judicial transparency requires that judges reveal their thoughts and motivations—their ultimate reasons. This is necessary to enhance the persuasiveness and efficacy of judicial precedents, to foster democratic legitimacy, and to permit political accountability.

D. Transparency and candour in legal reasoning

Transparency and candour in legal reasoning—both in the sense of drawing inferences and conclusions and in the sense of providing reasons for one's inferences and conclusions—enhance the persuasiveness and efficacy of judicial precedents, foster democratic legitimacy, and permit political accountability. Accordingly, the author disagrees with Professor Tony Honoré on this point:

> In certain countries, such as the USA, attempts are being made to destroy the separateness of legal discourse and to reduce legal issues to issues in which every sort of social, political and moral consideration is relevant. In my opinion this modem Hellenistic movement is to be resisted: fear the Greeks bringing gifts, even if they are disguised as devotees of the American Supreme Court.[48]

That being said, the author wholeheartedly agrees with Lord Browne-Wilkinson:

> When I was first made a judge, a wily old judge advised me—'just remember Nick, dirty dogs don't win.' That is a principle which lies at the heart of the common law. It is the basis on which the overwhelming majority of cases are decided. The judge looks for what are called 'the merits' and having found them seeks to reach a result, consistent with legal reasoning, whereby the deserving win and the undeserving lose.
>
> Unfortunately, this judicial method is seldom reflected in judicial behaviour or in the reasons given by judges for their decisions . . . When we get to the judgment, we very seldom find any reference to 'the merits'. The articulated reasoning purports to be based on a process of compelling legal argument leading inexorably to the result achieved . . .
>
> In the case of statutory interpretation, the courts have acted in much the same way.[49]

[48] A.M. Honoré, 'Legal Reasoning in Rome and Today' (1973) 4 Cambr Law Rev 58, 66. See also Mitchel De S.-O.-L'E. Lasser, *Judicial Deliberations: A Comparative Analysis of Judicial Transparency and Legitimacy* (Oxford University Press 2009) vii: 'Unlike the American system, which grounds the legitimacy of its judgments in their (public) argumentation, the French system grounds it in the expertise and quality of its judicial institutions.' Reviewed and criticized by Jan Komárek, 'Questioning Judicial Deliberations' (2009) 29(4) OJLS 805.

[49] Stephen Bate, *Resolving Business Disputes: How to Get Better Outcomes from Commercial Conflicts* (Spiramus Press 2020) 74.

APPENDIX

Theses and Conclusions

A. Legal reasoning and argument in general

'Reasoning' in legal parlance usually means—and in this book almost always means—providing reasons or justifications in support of inferences and conclusions that have already been drawn and decided. Legal reasoning in this sense means legal reason-giving to justify these inferences and conclusions.

All legal reasoning in the sense of providing justifications described is rule-based.

Principles are also rules.

The so-called methods or rules of statutory interpretation are categories of argument that justify results.

All such arguments are value-laden and goal-orientated; that is, they are directed towards justifying the result that has already been reached.

The categories of argument are limited in number.

The most descriptive and convenient number of categories is four: textual, historical, purposive, and system-contextual.

The textual, historical, and purposive categories are recognized generally, although there are nuances in how they are defined.

The system-contextual category encompasses every kind of legal justificatory argument that does not fit into the categories textual, historical, and purposive but which is considered to be appropriate in the jurisdiction.

Very often, more than one kind of argument is employed to justify a result.

While these arguments may influence and even suggest a particular result, they do not dictate a particular result.

'Reasoning' in legal parlance can also refer to the process of using one's ability to draw inferences and reach conclusions.

The reasoning process of reaching conclusions is an intuitive, value-laden process that is shaped and coloured by feelings, conscious and unconscious biases and associations, and a sense of order, legitimacy, and justice. This process is sometimes described as 'hunching'.

All statutory and case-based rules are factual in nature; they are hypothetical judgments.

Reasoning with statutes and reasoning with judicial case decisions involve the same intellectual processes.

None of the arguments is intrinsically superior.

Judges' decisions affect future decisions.

Judges make law as that term is employed in this book.

Judges make law when they grant relief.

Judges make law when they deny relief, even if, in doing so, they defer to the legislature.

The law made by judges when construing statutes is referred to as statutory 'glosses' in this book.

Statutory glosses concretize or amend the statutes.

'Pure' common law, called *Richterrecht* ('judges' law') in German, consists of judicial pronouncements that appear not to be based on statute.

When making law, judges are at a disadvantage when compared with members of the legislature, who have more access to information, including access to the general opinion of the public.

Both judges and legislators employ the same thought processes in making law.

The thought processes involved in finding the law (*Normsuche*) are identical, regardless of the source of the rule.

While the process of applying a legal rule to a factual scenario can indeed be described as deduction, the process is only deductive after the judge has interpreted (massaged and judged) the facts of the scenario to look like a minor premise that can be subsumed under the major premise (the rule).

The process of massaging and judging the facts involves thinking and feeling by analogy, induction, abduction, and even emotional, intuitive thinking.

Judicial decision-making is a complex, personal, and poorly understood subject.

Judges sometimes announce major changes to the existing legal order, a phenomenon referred to in this book as 'lurches'.

If one defines political judging as decision-making that is value-laden, then all judicial decision-making is political.

If one defines political judging as decision-making that could have been undertaken by legislative bodies in the first instance, then all judicial pronouncements of pure common law (*Richterrecht*) and statutory glosses are political.

B. The application of rules to factual scenarios

This book offers the first comprehensive methodology on the use of *ratios* from statutory glosses and from pure common law (*Richterrecht*).

Judicial *ratios* are indistinguishable from statutory rules.

When applying a *ratio* from a precedential case, one may, according to Lewis A. Kornhauser, expand or contract the *ratio* depending on whether one chooses to use the fact-based holding (the result), the *ratio* itself as stated by the judges, or some broader principle.

All judicial decisions that distinguish a potentially precedential case decision—that is, all judicial decisions that refuse to apply the *ratio* of an arguably precedential case decision—are examples of historical arguments for they explicitly state, or implicitly suggest, that the judges who decided the arguably precedential case decision would agree with the later court's decision not to apply the *ratio* of that case to the factual scenario faced by the later court.

Textual arguments are those that focus, either sharply or fuzzily, on one or more words of the rule that is sought to be employed, regardless of whether the rule is statutory or case-based.

Historical arguments are those that invoke the historical setting or that insinuate that the drafter of the rule, whether the legislature or the judiciary, would agree with the result.

Purposive arguments talk about the perceived purposes or principles embodied in a rule.

All rules are the product of a balancing of interests and therefore possess opposing policies and principles.

It is the judges themselves who pick which of the opposing policies or principles to emphasize.

System-contextual arguments are pleas to a perceived higher authority that is understood to permeate the particular legal system.

Statutory analogies are those justificatory arguments that identify, and ostensibly apply, a rule from a statute that cannot be applied to the fact pattern before the court in a textual, historical, or purposive manner.

Statutory analogies are hidden behind fictional gaps in the statutory scheme that are in the value-laden eye of the beholder.

All appellate judicial decisions might have been decided the opposite way.

Judges should reveal their thoughts and motivations—their ultimate reasons—to enhance the persuasiveness and efficacy of their precedents, to foster democratic legitimacy, and to permit political accountability.

Index

For the benefit of digital users, indexed terms that span two pages (e.g., 52–53) may, on occasion, appear on only one of those pages.